The Union

Contents

Introduction. 7

Castlereagh and the Making of the Union. 9
Patrick Geoghegan

The Law, the Constitution and the Act of Union. 21
Norman SJ Baxter

From Rebels to Unionists: The Political
Transformation of Ulster's Presbyterians. 34
Finlay Holmes

Home Rule, Partition
and the Northern Nationalists, 1870–1930. 48
Eamon Phoenix

A Question of Degree?
The Union, Unionism and the Belfast Agreement 60
Arthur Aughey

Unionism Among the Paramilitaries. 72
Steve Bruce

The Union: A Republican Perspective. 86
Danny Morrison

In Limbo: Europe, Britain and the Unionist
Community. 97
Antony Alcock

Identity, Security, and Self-Determination:
The Long Road towards an Agreed Ireland. 111
Martin Mansergh

Orangeism and the Union:
A Special Relationship?. 124
Clifford Smyth

Ulster Protestants and the Union:. 138
Susan McKay

Shaping the New Political Landscape:
An Engagement Strategy for Thinking
Unionism. 151
Dave Christopher

Down the Aisle or Down the Isles?
Norman Davies' Prophecy of the Break-up of
the United Kingdom. 168
Esmond Birnie

Index. 176

Introduction

The Union of Great Britain and Ireland (now Northern Ireland) has been a subject of debate, discussion and argument since it came into being, on 1 January 1801. Two hundred years later, that debate and argument continues.

In *The Dawning of Democracy* (Dublin, 1987), Donal Macartney has noted:

> . . . Irish history, at least down to 1922, has been a history of Ireland under the union. Every nationalist movement, whether constitutional and parliamentary or republican and physical force, has aimed at the abolition of the union. Every unionist movement has aimed at its maintenance. The first principle for every political leader in Irish history since 1800 has been his attitude to the union.

The Union: Essays on Ireland and the British Connection provides both a historical evaluation of the birth and development of the Union, an analysis of its current status and a projection of its future. This is not just a book about history and politics – it is also a study of society, economics and culture, and therefore offers the reader a panoramic overview of the whole subject.

In its issue of 5 October 2000, the Enniskillen-based *Impartial Reporter* commented on the two hundredth anniversary of the Union:

> An Act of Parliament would seem to lack the ingredients necessary to stir up popular interest and the bicentenary has gone singularly unnoticed in comparison to commemorations regarding the United Irishmen or the Great Famine. This does not diminish the significance of the event which was one of the most controversial and contested in modern history.

With contributions from noted academics, politicians, writers and commentators, *The Union* therefore makes a valuable contribution to informed debate on what has been and continues to be one of the great questions of modern times.

Ronnie Hanna
Editor
Newtownards
January 2001

The Union

Castlereagh and the Making of the Union

Patrick M Geoghegan

The passing of the Irish Act of Union (1800) made Castlereagh's reputation in Britain, but destroyed it in Ireland. Five years later, when he stood for re-election in Co Down, having received another cabinet portfolio, he suffered an embarrassing defeat. Neither his status as President of the Board of Control and Secretary of State for War and the Colonies, nor his high-profile service in Ireland offered any protection. In a vitriolic campaign he was mercilessly abused in poems, songs, and pamphlets, much to the enjoyment of his enemies. For the deviousness he had displayed during the Union negotiations he was denigrated as "Bobby", the "boy with two strings to his bow and the father of hypocrites truly."[1] His private life did not escape comment either. Eleven years of marriage had not produced any children and Castlereagh was taken to task for his negligence. Explanations were not slow in coming forward: "He does not sweep the chimney." Castlereagh's defeat in Down was cheered throughout the country. In Dublin, only the veto of the mayor prevented a large public celebration in response to the news. Castlereagh soon found a safe seat at Westminster, but his tainted Irish past was never allowed to rest. Defending his reputation, years later, during a debate in the House of Commons, he summed up his position in one sentence: "With respect to Ireland I know I shall never be forgiven."[2] Nevertheless, Castlereagh's Irish career is more complex than the caricature of popular legend. For him, the country was "the most valuable and interesting portion of the Empire", and with the Union he left an enduring political legacy that should not be forgotten.

The 1798 Rebellion was the event that both thrust Castlereagh into national prominence and made a legislative union inevitable. Still only 28 years old when it broke out in May, Castlereagh had been appointed acting Chief Secretary for Ireland just two months previously, at the instigation of his step-uncle, the Lord Lieutenant, Earl Camden. Thus, in the summer of 1798, Castlereagh found himself occupying one of the most sensitive offices in the Irish administration at one of the most difficult times in its entire history. During the rebellion he showed great ability, but won few friends. His cold and aloof manner alienated many, and his ruthlessness in extracting information and suppressing dissent made him a hate-figure for contemporary liberals. However, he did manage to impress the new

The Union

Viceroy, Lord Cornwallis, and this ensured that he remained as Chief Secretary even though his benefactor had been replaced. Cornwallis held the dual positions of Lord Lieutenant and Commander-in-Chief of the army, and had been sent to Ireland with a double mission: to quell the rebellion and as quickly as possible, and then follow it with a legislative Union. In Castlereagh he found a confident and willing deputy who was capable of playing a major role in achieving both.

Although born in Dublin, Castlereagh (or Robert Stewart as he was known until 1796) came from a distinguished and wealthy Co Down family, and his father had represented the constituency in the Irish House of Commons. He spent much of his childhood on the family estate of Mount Stewart and was educated at the Royal School Armagh, and by the Rev William Sturrock at Portaferry. Following in his father's footsteps, Castlereagh was elected for Co Down in the 1790 general election, but quickly discarded the elements of the Whig platform that had assisted his rise. His father's advances in the peerage meant that on 8 August 1796 he received the courtesy title of Viscount Castlereagh, and it is by this name that he is remembered in history, even though it was one he held for less than half his life. The grandson of a Lord Lieutenant for Ireland, in 1794 he married Emily Hobart, the daughter of another Lord Lieutenant. The following year his step-uncle Camden became Viceroy and this third connection to an Irish chief governor propelled his rapid ascent along the political ladder. His genuine ability maintained his lofty position.

As Chief Secretary, it was Castlereagh's responsibility to present the Union before the House of Commons and guide the measure through Parliament. It was also his job to lead the government in debates, while all the time working privately to build and maintain a majority in favour of the question. He was helped in this work by the wily and experienced Under Secretary for the Civil Department, Edward Cooke, who had calculated that the Union must be "drunk-up, sung-up, and bribed-up".[3] The triumvirate of Cornwallis, Castlereagh and Cooke devised and directed the government's strategy on the Union, but the impetus for everything they did came from Whitehall. It was the Prime Minister, William Pitt, who had decided to press for a Union for security reasons, to resolve the ambiguities in the Anglo-Irish relationship, and to create a new political matrix. For Pitt, only a Union would allow the means for resolving the problems between the two islands, including the thorny issue of Catholic emancipation. Cabinet and Castle were obliged to liaise closely on the Union, and much of this responsibility fell to Castlereagh. Indeed an important part of his work involved using all his skills to smooth over various personality conflicts. For example, Cornwallis and the Home

Secretary, the Duke of Portland, were not on good terms and communications were usually terse and strained; very often there were no communications at all. Nor did Cornwallis and Cooke get on much better, but as Castlereagh retained the trust of all sides any destabilising clashes were avoided.

The opening of the Irish Parliament on 22 January 1799 witnessed a combined assault on the principle of Union and the personality of Castlereagh. Union was only hinted at in the King's address, but the opposition was determined to seize the initiative and strike first. The attacks on Castlereagh were vicious, direct, and highly effective. The debate proper began with a speech from George Ponsonby, the opposition MP, who declared that a usurper was sitting illegally in the chamber. It was an attack on an unexpected flank and succeeded in confusing the government benches. This confusion quickly turned to embarrassment when it was revealed that the member in question was Castlereagh himself. In a tactical masterstroke, Ponsonby turned the recent amendment to the Place Act against the Chief Secretary, arguing that under its terms Castlereagh should have vacated his seat to seek re-election. Two hours of debate followed that did nothing for morale on the government benches, but everything for the spirits of the opposition. The dispute was only resolved when the Attorney General, John Toler, intervened and claimed, spuriously, that Castlereagh had not been required to vacate his seat. First blood had been drawn, and the opposition scented that more was likely. In a nineteen hour debate on the Union Castlereagh was called an "unspotted veteran", an "unassuming stripling" and "a green and sapless twig"[4] (the last another snide reference to his apparent inability to produce children). With his wife watching from the gallery as these charges hit home, Castlereagh delivered one of the finest speeches of his life. It was not enough. The government was shipping water all over, and Castlereagh watched helplessly as the Union sunk to defeat. In an embarrassing rejection of the measure, the paragraph suggesting a Union was deleted from the King's address. Bonfires were lit in Dublin to celebrate the news and Castlereagh retreated from his first political failure, his credibility shaken and his confidence broken. As one observer commented, the government had "very many rats".

The Union strategy changed significantly after this defeat in Parliament. The principle of borough compensation was quickly conceded, to appease the powerful country proprietors, at a cost of over £1 million. The government's original intention had been to keep the questions of Catholic emancipation and the Union separate, and resolve the matter in the united Parliament. This had been a vain attempt to secure popular support without alienating Protestant opinion. After the shambles in the Irish Parliament in January 1799 Pitt accepted, reluctantly, that some gesture would have to be made to enlist the support of the Catholics. It was a belief that had long been held by Cornwallis, and was also one that Castlereagh had come to share. He was to become the link man in the increasingly complex negotiations between Whitehall and Dublin Castle over the fate of the Catholic question.

In the autumn of 1799 Castlereagh visited England to discuss the Union with the government. He found that the cabinet was beset with the twin problems of war and scarcity, and had little time for Irish concerns. It was only in mid-November that he was finally able to seek clarification about how far the government was prepared to go for victory in Ireland. Insisting that the Union would not succeed unless the support of the Catholics was enlisted, or at least their hostility neutralised, Castlereagh left the cabinet in no doubt that a decision could not be postponed indefinitely. And so, Catholic emancipation became part of the Union package. The Chief Secretary returned home with permission to call "forth the Catholic support in whatever degree he found it practicable to obtain it".[5] But no direct promise was to be given to the Catholics unless such a pledge became unavoidable. As it turned out, no direct promise was necessary although Castlereagh made it implicitly clear to the Catholic hierarchy that emancipation would follow after the Union. This was enough to ensure the acquiescence of the Catholics, and their benign neutrality prevented any popular reaction against the measure.

As the Castle waited for the beginning of 1800 before attempting the Union a second time, it fell to Castlereagh to secure a majority in the Commons and keep it. Theoretically the Union could be attempted annually until it succeeded; in reality the government had just one more chance. Repeated defeats would only encourage resistance, and give credence to the claims that the government was determined to pass the Union over the wishes of the people and the Parliament. The responsibility was great, but Castlereagh did not shirk from the challenge. He was determined to do whatever was necessary for victory, whatever the cost. One of Castlereagh's favourite sayings was "Patience, and all will be well." He would find his equable temperament sorely tested in the final months of the Irish Parliament.

Much of the abuse that fell on Castlereagh in the years ahead resulted from his conduct during the passing of the Union. Daniel O'Connell called him "the assassin of his country", while Jonah Barrington referred to him as "one of the most mischievous statesmen and unfortunate ministers that ever appeared in modern Europe". In nationalist propaganda the Union soon came to be seen as a corrupt bargain that had been passed against the wishes of the country after the government had purchased the Commons. A late nineteenth century poem epitomised the allegations against Castlereagh:

How did they pass the Union?
By perjury and fraud;
By slaves who sold their land for gold,
As Judas sold his God.

And thus they passed the Union
By Pitt and Castlereagh:
Could Satan send for such an end
More worthy tools than they?[6]

The charges of corruption levelled at Castlereagh for his role during the Union represent the most serious taint on his character. For the most part they are true. To ensure success, the Dublin Castle administration was prepared to do whatever was necessary for victory: this included the establishment of a covert secret service slush fund to aid the campaign. As Castlereagh himself stated, the objective was nothing less than "buying out and securing to the crown for ever the fee-simple of Irish corruption".[7] The amount of money spent in this illegal fund exceeded £63,000. Of this total, £30,850 came through the Alien Office, the shadowy sub-section of the Home Office which directed British intelligence. A further £18,000 was tapped from a saving on the Irish Civil List Act and diverted into the fighting fund. It was the false accounting for this sum that almost resulted in the exposure of the entire Union dealings in 1801. An additional £14,800 was spent on various Union promises, and replaced in the years ahead by mortgaging the patronage of the country. For Castlereagh this money was "the means by which so much depends",[8] and he was ruthless in ensuring its effectiveness.

With the threat of Catholic unrest neutralised, and the twin engines of bribery and patronage at work, Castlereagh had every reason to be enthusiastic in January 1800. The smugness of the previous year had been replaced by a cold concentration and a ruthless determination to make sure that no mistakes were made. Although the Chief Secretary warned Whitehall that the government was "in great distress", its adversaries were in a far worse state. The anti-Union factions, naturally separated by temperament and ideology, were further divided about how far to go in their opposition. Some wanted to match the government's bribery and began a subscription to purchase as many seats as possible. Another group wanted to fight a public campaign to mobilise national opposition against the measure, but this was seen as coming too late to rouse the country from its apathetic slumber. Perpetually unable to agree on the Catholic question, the opposition became increasingly desperate as they saw the full resources of the government arrayed against them. One impetuous scheme did not get far. Some brash young men suggested setting up a duelling club to challenge the leading members of the Castle, thereby making the battle a literal one. Had it not been rejected, the proposal could well have given rise to quarrels in the club over who would get to fight Castlereagh. His duelling skills were not highly rated and he was seen as "rather cold to be a warrior".[9] Even writing years after the event, Henry Grattan's son was not inclined to show any kindness to the Chief Secretary, insisting that for his role in the Union he deserved to die: it "would have been a national as well as a noble sentence. Some weak old women might have cried out murder".[10]

The opening of Parliament on 15 January was marked by a repeat performance of the previous year, with simultaneous attacks on both the principle of Union and the person of Castlereagh. This time the Chief Secretary was completely prepared for the taunts, and his composure never wavered, much to his opponents' disappointment. In a speech dripping with sarcasm George Ponsonby declaimed his conviction "that the noble lord has not made undue use of the prerogatives of the crown".[11] The personal abuse was left to William Plunket, who sneered at the Chief Secretary's "puny sophistry".[12] Once more Lady Castlereagh watched proceedings from the gallery, and in an impressive display of endurance remained for the entire debate. As one observer noted facetiously, "She must be at least as retentive as her husband."[13] The debate is famous for witnessing the theatrical return of Henry Grattan from his self-imposed parliamentary exile. Having purchased his seat at midnight, he made a dramatic entrance and speech the following morning, the debate having continued throughout the night. Over the following months he would add considerable flair and debating firepower to the opposition benches, but little else. His reappearance disturbed the anti-Catholic opponents of the Union, who almost uniformly despised him, and his rhetoric was useless against the committed phalanx of government supporters.

The first real test of the government's strength came when the Union was presented before the House on 5 February. Delayed for two days because of Castlereagh's influenza, the resumption of hostilities began as soon as the still shaky minister outlined the eight foundation articles of the measure. Standing his ground, the Chief Secretary answered the opposition charges point by point in a rousing speech that offered great encouragement to the government benches. His imperious manner, however, was reflected in some of his more aristocratic statements, such as "Everyone knows the ignorance of the lower classes in this kingdom and how easily they may be misled by the most shallow and pitiful misrepresentations."[14] Constantly shifting the attack to the opposition, he accused them of running vicious smear campaigns to discredit the Catholic clergy. Refusing to admit that there was any change in the status of the emancipation question, he skilfully disengaged the government from further attacks on that flank. Only the charge of corruption remained, and Castlereagh defused this in a brazen, point-blank denial. Solemnly and with a straight face he declared that "There are bribes I am not prepared to offer."[15] He differentiated these bribes – hard cash – from borough compensation, which was "consonant to the principles of private justice". His speech provoked more heated debate. Once again Grattan accused him of packing the Parliament and overturning the liberties of the people. Troops monitored the proceedings, prepared for any violence, and Castlereagh was obliged to make a threat that the debate would be moved to Cork if the House did not calm down. An uneasy quiet prevailed, allowing a division to be called which the government won by 43 votes. It was 17 fewer than the Chief Secretary had predicted, but it was convincing enough.

With a majority behind the Union in the Commons, it was now up to Castlereagh to maintain it. This proved difficult, as MPs competed to have their interests satisfied, and the Chief Secretary was forced to request further secret service funds from the Alien Office. These were not to be used on opposition members: the opponents of the Union were now fully committed and Castlereagh conceded that it would be impossible to convert anyone further. The money was to be used to stiffen the resolve of the government's numbers, and Castlereagh warned that it was imperative "to fulfil the expectations which it was impossible to avoid creating at the moment of difficulty". Giving reassurances that the previous sums had not been misspent, he claimed instead that "we have rather erred on the side of moderation".[16]

The debate of 14 March was particularly bruising for Castlereagh. Having made a rash attack on the speaker, John Foster, the Chief Secretary was subjected to sustained and damaging retaliation, first from Foster himself and then from Grattan. Castlereagh's membership of the Northern Whig Club was used against him, as Grattan quoted from papers to show what ideals he had previously espoused and, with a jeering and partisan House, Castlereagh was made to look "very foolish".[17] Nevertheless, the Union articles continued their inexorable passage through the House, and in May the first reading of the bill took place. Sensing victory, the Castle authorities became complacent for the only time that year and were surprised by the ambush at the second reading on 26 May. Grattan was defeated twice on motions against the Union and faced off to Castlereagh in one of the most charged confrontations of the session. In one of his most powerful rhetorical declamations Grattan declared that under the Union Ireland would be in a "state of slavery", and announced that he, unlike the "courtier", would remain "faithful to her freedom, faithful to her fall".[18] Furious, Castlereagh lost his famous control over his temper and delivered an embittered attack on the old patriot. Implicating Grattan in "prophetic treason", he accused him of "inviting future rebellion by cloaking it with the idea of liberty".[19] There was immediate uproar in the House, and the opposition benches demanded an apology; none was forthcoming. For once Castlereagh's icy reserve had been pierced, and Edward Cooke, the Under Secretary, reported that his reputation was all the better for it. But neither the Chief Secretary nor Grattan were prepared to leave it at that. It seems both men considered issuing a challenge, but Castlereagh was persuaded out of it by his friends, and Grattan only backed down when he discovered that the Chief Secretary had prevented his arraignment on a charge of being implicated in the 1798 conspiracy.

Emotions were running high in the first week of June as the Irish Parliament waited for the final reading of the bill that would end its existence. His composure restored, Castlereagh waited calmly for the final victory of the Union. The opposition were now thoroughly demoralised, and many were unable to come to terms with their defeat. On 7 June every effort, no matter how unlikely, was made to defeat the Union. Aware that they were making their final speeches, the leading anti-unionists soon returned to their favourite themes. William Plunket rose slowly to his feet for one last attack on Castlereagh's unscrupulous and illegal methods. These charges had lost their power, however, and, with every option exhausted, two-thirds of the anti-Union MPs walked out of the House, "with safe consciences but with breaking hearts".[20] The Union was carried without a division. Whatever Castlereagh was feeling, he did not show it, and he remained expressionless at the moment of his greatest triumph. For Henry Grattan junior, this epitomised the Chief Secretary's "cold-blooded" arrogance. When the enemies of Castlereagh would look back on his life they would see this exact moment as the defining one of his life and character, for in the younger Grattan's words, "At that moment he had no country, no God but his ambition."[21]

Although the Union was set to come into effect on 1 January 1801, much work remained to be done. The most pressing concern for Castlereagh in the summer of 1800 was to ensure that all the Union promises were honoured. This would be his great challenge over the next twelve months, as the British government developed a dangerous reluctance to validate the methods that had been used to secure victory in Ireland. The first hint that his actions and character could be repudiated by Whitehall came when the Castle submitted their list of Irish peers who would sit in the new, united House of Lords. Castlereagh's father, Lord Londonderry, was included among the names, but it was soon revealed that both King and cabinet were unwilling to approve all of the nominations. Furious, Castlereagh and Cornwallis both threatened resignation, and the Chief Secretary was particularly disgusted by the treatment which was little more than "disgracing the Irish government".[22] Not only that, if the Union pledges were not honoured, Castlereagh realised that people would talk, and the government risked exposure of the illegal and unethical methods that had been used. In a letter that Castlereagh knew would be shown to the cabinet, he made this explicitly clear: " . . . it will be no secret what has been promised, and by what means the Union was achieved. Disappointment will encourage, not prevent disclosure".[23] Faced with the risk that the entire Union project would be contaminated by the taint of corruption, the cabinet had no choice but to cave in to the threats. Most of the pledges were honoured reluctantly, although Castlereagh was persuaded to postpone his father's peerage, on the understanding that it would be there for the asking on any future date. This was to reduce the numbers of new peers that the King would have to create, but the request was presented to Castlereagh in a deliberately ingratiating way. He was told that the cabinet considered him so valuable that they were afraid to risk losing his services in the Commons, if in the future he had to succeed his father in the Lords. It was flattering, but insincere, and although Castlereagh conceded the point, he remained bitterly disappointed about his treatment at the hands of the ministers.

If there had been trouble over issues of patronage, then Castlereagh was under no illusions that the question of Catholic emancipation would prove much more stormy. Sent to London in August, he discovered over the following months that there was no longer cabinet consensus on the issue; indeed, it threatened to destabilise the entire ministry. Returning to Ireland, he prepared a paper on the Catholic question that attempted to answer the fears that had been expressed in England. This was circulated among key figures in both countries and eventually even found its way to King George III, who was decidedly unimpressed. In December Castlereagh set out once more for London, determined to prevent the cabal of anti-Catholic conspirators from leaving the Union incomplete. On

The Union

1 January 1801 the United Kingdom of Great Britain and Ireland came into existence, and with it a new flag for the Empire, the Union Jack. That same day Castlereagh wrote a decisive letter to Pitt, giving a complete history of the shifts in policy on the Catholic question, and a full account of what had been agreed in the November 1799 cabinets. It was a brave attempt to stiffen Pitt's resolve and prevent any wavering on the subject. In January 1801, however, everything went wrong. The mind of the King was secretly influenced by a group of intriguers who were determined to replace Pitt and prevent emancipation, and the cabinet split permanently on the Catholic question. Everything became public on 28 January when, at a royal levée, George III exploded into a bitter attack against emancipation. Marching up to Henry Dundas, one of the pro-Catholic ministers, the King delivered an astonishing rebuke, with the figure of Castlereagh at the centre of his accusations. The crisis was now out in the open. Faced with a defiant king and a divided cabinet, Pitt was in no position to manoeuvre. With an ultimatum from George III on the Catholic question, he felt he had no option but to tender his resignation. Cornwallis and Castlereagh soon followed him, and this was not just an automatic response but a genuine signalling of their frustration that the one measure that would make the Union complete had been prevented by royal intransigence. The King had a similarly low opinion of Castlereagh and repeatedly criticised him for having stubbornly pursued the Catholic question.[24]

Careers were not the only casualties of the turmoil. The King had a reoccurrence of the mental illness that had afflicted him in 1788–89, and the formation of a new ministry was put on hold until he recovered. This only added to the political instability, and Castlereagh made a delicate effort to persuade Pitt to remain in office. In a carefully argued paper on the subject in March he made a case for postponing the Catholic question until a later date, as the interests of the Empire were more important than any one issue. It fell on deaf ears, as Pitt had no intention of returning as long as his authority was in doubt, but the attempt gives an important indication of Castlereagh's priorities. His career as an Irish politician was over, and he was now thinking on an imperial, not a local, scale. And if this meant sacrificing the Catholic question for larger concerns, then so be it.

A far more disturbing aspect of the King's illness was that it threatened exposure of the Union dealings. George III had to approve a fictitious set of accounts to cover up some of the illegal funds that had been used, but when he recovered he had no recollection of ever having sanctioned these transactions. Indeed, he suspected the Home Secretary, the Duke of

Portland, of having embezzled the missing money. Having ruined his reputation among the anti-Unionists in Ireland by masterminding the enactment of the Union, Castlereagh now risked having his career destroyed in Britain by the accusations of an enfeebled monarch. The strain was too much, and in April Castlereagh's own mental stability gave way. Suffering from a dangerous temperature, his life was threatened by a "brain fever", and Cornwallis admitted that he was "and indeed am still, very uneasy about Lord Castlereagh".[25] A partial recovery in May was only temporary, and as his fever returned there were more fears about his survival. It seems that the crisis only passed when he received guarantees that the covert secret service funds would be replaced and that the threat of exposure would be removed. As Henry Hobhouse wrote years later, the Chief Secretary recovered when the new Prime Minister, Henry Addington, intervened and promised to honour all Union commitments: " . . . this relief operated so powerfully on Lord Castlereagh's mind that he has never ceased to be on the most cordial terms of intimacy with Lord Sidmouth [Henry Addington]".[26] His nerve restored, Castlereagh's health slowly recovered. Resting at Harrowgate, his good spirits returned, and he joked that he had forgotten politics and had "grown very fat".[27]

Years later the mental instability that had afflicted Castlereagh in 1801 would return with fatal consequences: he committed suicide in 1822. Buried at Westminster Abbey, his tombstone was inscribed with an elegiac commentary on his life: "History will record the success and splendour of his public career, during a period of unexampled difficulty in the annals of Europe in which he successively filled the highest offices under the crown." The final line was rich with unintended irony: "And Ireland will never forget the statesman of the legislative union." During the passing of the Union Castlereagh employed methods that were often ruthless, and sometimes illegal, but which he believed were necessary for the future of Ireland and the Empire. For his work as Chief Secretary he is sometimes credited with being the architect of the Union. This is not true. It was the Prime Minister, William Pitt, who was the inspiration behind the measure, and who should really be seen as the architect of the Union project. But if Pitt devised the legislation then it was Castlereagh who dragged it through the Irish Parliament, and made it a reality. He executed the government's plan for Union; and with it, the Irish Parliament.

Notes

1 *County of Down Election, 1805: the Patriotic Miscellany, or Mirror of Wit, Genius and Truth*, London, 1805, p 15.
2 *Hansard I*, xxxvi, 11 July 1817, col 1406.
3 Cooke to Auckland, 27 October 1798, PRONI, T/3229/2/37.

4 JC Hoey (ed), *Speeches at the Bar and in the Senate by the Rt Hon. William Conyngham*, Dublin, 1873, pp 45–6.
5 Castlereagh to Pitt (memorandum of events), 1 January 1801, Cambridge University Library, Add MS 6958, f 2827.
6 James McGuire, 'The Act of Union' in Liam de Paor (ed), *Milestones in Irish History*, Cork, 1986, pp 72–3. The poem is attributed to John O'Hagan.
7 Castlereagh to Camden, 24 July 1799, PRONI, T/2627/4/114.
8 Castlereagh to John King, 2 January 1800 in Charles Ross (ed), *The Correspondence of Charles, First Marquis Cornwallis*, 3 vols, London, 1859, iii, p 156.
9 Henry Grattan Jnr (ed), *Memoirs of the Life and Times of the Rt Hon. Henry Grattan*, 5 vols, London, 1839–46, v, p 74.
10 Ibid, p 68.
11 *A Report of the Debate in the House of Commons of Ireland on 15th January 1800*, Dublin, 1800, p 35.
12 Ibid, p 90.
13 William Drennan to Martha McTier, 16 January 1800 in Jean Agnew (ed), *The Drennan–McTier Letters*, 3 vols, Dublin, 1998–9, ii, p 565.
14 *A Report of the Debate in the House of Commons of Ireland on 5th and 6th February 1800*, Dublin, 1800, p 7.
15 Ibid, p 37.
16 Castlereagh to John King, 27 February 1800 in Ross (ed), *Cornwallis Correspondence*, iii, p 201.
17 Beresford to Auckland, 19 March 1800, PRONI, T/3229/2/60.
18 Grattan (ed), *Memoirs*, v, 176.
19 Cornwallis to Portland, 27 May 1800, PRO, HO 100/96, f 293.
20 Jonah Barrington, *Historic Memoirs of Ireland*, 2 vols, London, 1833, ii, p 368
21 Grattan (ed), *Memoirs*, v, 178.
22 Castlereagh to Cooke, 21 June 1800 in *Castlereagh Correspondence*, iii, pp 330–1.
23 Ibid, p 331.
24 For a full account see Patrick M Geoghegan, *The Irish Act of Union*, Dublin, 1999, chapters 6–7.
25 Cornwallis to Ross, 7 May 1801 in Ross (ed), *Cornwallis Correspondence*, iii, p 359.
26 A Aspinall (ed), *The Diary of Henry Hobhouse*, London, 1947, p 93.
27 Ibid, p 166.

Dr Patrick M Geoghegan is a historian with the Royal Irish Academy's *Dictionary of Irish Biography* and teaches in Trinity College Dublin. His first book, *The Irish Act of Union*, was published in 1999 and he is also the author of a short biography of Lord Castlereagh (2000).

The Law, the Constitution and the Act of Union of 1801

Norman SJ Baxter

There have been very few legislative instruments created within the British parliamentary democracy which have had far-reaching legal and constitutional significance extending over two centuries. The Act of Union 1801[1] was such an instrument. This legislation was the result of the passage of two separate Acts of Parliament, one passed in Westminster and the second by the Irish Parliament in Dublin.[2] Unfortunately, there has been some confusion regarding the constitutional significance of the 1801 Act.

British sovereignty in Ireland since 1801 has not been dependent on this Act, nor upon the Government of Ireland Act 1920, which amended part of the original legislation. The claim of Crown sovereignty in Ireland dates back to 1155, when Pope Adrian IV issued a bull that granted and donated Ireland to Henry II, to be held by him and his successors.[3] Henry II arrived in Ireland to accept his gift in 1171, thus giving effect to Crown sovereignty over the Irish kingdom.[4]

There is a clear legal distinction between the sovereignty of the Crown (sovereignty of the state), as represented by the monarchy, and that of parliamentary sovereignty. The Act of Union 1801 addressed the issue of parliamentary sovereignty, with the Irish Parliament assenting to being prorogued and using its sovereign status to translate that selfsame sovereignty to a newly constituted sovereign Parliament for the United Kingdom of Great Britain and Ireland.[5] In a similar manner, the sovereign Parliament of Great Britain, which existed since 1707,[6] assented to pass its sovereignty to the new Parliament.[7]

Parliament, which comprises the Lords and Commons, is subservient to the Crown. The sovereignty of the Crown is enshrined in the constitutional doctrine that the monarch is the embodiment of the state; such authority being vested by Royal proclamation during the coronation ceremony, when the representatives of Church and state confer authority and proffer allegiance.[8] The authority for the sovereign prerogative of the monarch is rooted in ancient legal practice. In the era of Edward I, the Statute of Winchester included the direction from the king that every person between the ages of 15 and 40 should have arms in his house for the preservation of the king's peace, with constables having the power to inspect them.[9] This enactment clearly demonstrated that the making of laws for the maintenance of the peace resided solely in the Crown, with the Parliament simply enacting the directions into law.[10]

The doctrine of the Crown permeated throughout all the institutions of the state. The authority of the king extended from that of lawmaker and governor to judge. As society developed, and the functions of civil administration expanded, many of the duties performed personally by the monarch were delegated initially to individuals and then to Crown bodies.[11] For example, members of the executive (cabinet) are ministers of the Crown, holding their office under Royal seal;[12] judges are appointed by the sovereign to administer justice on behalf of the Crown;[13] and constables have an original jurisdiction vested in the Crown to uphold the peace.[14]

Parliament, although sovereign in respect of the will of its members, is subject to the Crown.[15] In the Prince's Case (1606), it was held that an Act of Parliament could not be regarded as such unless signed by the monarch and assented to by both the House of Lords and the House of Commons.[16] Parliamentary sovereignty is therefore not simply the decisions of the House of Commons and the House of Lords, but of the monarch and both Houses of Parliament acting collectively in their legislative capacity. In view of this unique constitutional arrangement, it has been suggested[17] that if the United Kingdom had a constitution, then it could be summarised in one sentence stating that "parliament can make or repeal any law whatsoever".[18]

The acquiescence of the Irish Commons and Lords in passing the Act for the Union of Great Britain and Ireland (Ireland) 1800 was vital in maintaining this constitutional model.[19] The failure to obtain initial consent in 1799 for such an Act could have been overridden by King George using his constitutional position of being the sovereign, whose sovereignty is vested in the proclamation made at his coronation which declared that he was "King of Great Britain and Ireland".[20] Instead of enforcing the wishes of the Crown on a dissenting Irish Parliament, the king and his British ministers decided to continue to strive to achieve their policy through parliamentary and other less scrupulous, but nonetheless legal methods.

In order to persuade some leading anti-Union MPs and peers, the government embarked on a policy of patronage, granting new peerages, elevating existing peers, and granting military commissions. For example,[21] Viscount Bandon (Cork) was elevated to the Earl of Bandon (6 August 1800); Viscount Alexander and Baron of Caledon was elevated to the Earl of Caledon (29 December 1800); Lord Dunally (Tipperary) was created Baron Kilboy (30 July 1800); Lord Moore (Kildare) was created Baron (17

January 1801); and Lord Loftus (Fermanagh) was created Baron (19 January 1801).

There had been continuous conflict between the two sovereign Parliaments of Great Britain and Ireland during the eighteenth century. Disputes arose over the raising of revenues required to maintain the army and navy, necessary to pursue Britain's foreign wars. These wars arose as a consequence of the foreign policy of the Parliament of Great Britain, and as a consequence resistance arose in Ireland in respect of the taxation and revenues set by the British exchequer. Matters came to a head in 1782, when a general meeting of the Volunteers of the province of Ulster resolved that:

> The claim of any body of men, other than the king, lords and commons of Ireland to make laws to bind that kingdom, is unconstitutional, illegal and a grievance; that the powers exercised by the privy councils of both kingdoms, under the colour of Poyning's [sic] law, are unconstitutional; and that all restraints imposed upon the trade of Ireland, except by the parliament of that kingdom, are likewise unconstitutional.[22]

The debate moved to the Irish House of Commons on 8 April 1782, and Grattan moved an address to His Majesty clearly stating the legal and constitutional position regarding the Crown and Parliament of Ireland. This address was unanimously passed, and declared that:

> Ireland was a distinct kingdom, the crown of Ireland an imperial crown; and that no authority except the king, lords and commons of Ireland could make laws to bind that nation. The powers assumed by the councils of both kingdoms of altering bills was unconstitutional and insisted a Mutiny bill limited in duration as essential to the liberty of the nation.[23]

The Parliament then proceeded to repeal Acts of Parliament emanating from England, which they viewed as unconstitutional, thus establishing the legislative sovereignty of the Irish Parliament. The right of the Parliament of Great Britain to influence the laws of Ireland was overturned. In return for the establishment of this constitutional right, the Irish Parliament voted £100,000 to raise 20,000 seamen for public service.[24]

The constitutional settlement of 1782 created new problems for George III. An independent Parliament in Ireland was difficult to control and posed a threat to the security of Great Britain, when war with France developed following the French Revolution in 1789. Britain's conflict with the French, and the 1798 Rebellion in Ireland by the United Irishmen, had brought about a realisation that Ireland was vulnerable to foreign influence. The negotiations between the leadership of the United Irishmen and the French had resulted in the promise of France to aid the rebellion. Although only a small military force did in fact arrive in Ireland, the mere threat of a French invasion caused the King and his ministers in London to fear a future intervention.

Constitutionally the Irish Parliament was at liberty, under the terms of the 1782 settlement, to oppose military action against the French and to enter into independent arrangements with the French government. Such a legal position, if it had developed, would have weakened Britain's military position, and undermined the war effort. It would have been theoretically possible, under the terms of the Bill of Rights of 1689, for the Irish Parliament to have denied George III the right to raise a standing army in Ireland, and thus reduce the availability of regiments for the European campaign.

The seriousness of the situation was not lost on the King, and the legislative Union of the two kingdoms became his priority in the wake of the 1798 Rebellion.[25] Subtle political negotiation and pressure were necessary in order to persuade the Irish Parliament to relinquish its independence and to adopt a new constitutional model. Irish parliamentarians would be required to accept a united Parliament with greater influence over the internal affairs of Ireland than the joint council, which was so fiercely opposed up to 1782. Constitutional change is rarely easy to achieve; however, a number of factors present assisted the new policy.

The turbulence of 1798, both in Ireland and in France, brought a realisation to the aristocracy and landed classes that revolutionary action by the lower classes could overthrow their power. In addition, the lack of equality enjoyed by Roman Catholics and dissenters in Ireland had fuelled the insurrection there. Emancipation and other issues, which caused popular discontent, had to be dealt with quickly in order to reduce the threat. Peaceful constitutional change, incorporating the hope of emancipation, was therefore vital in the short term to shore up the vested interests of the landed gentry in Great Britain.

The difficulty faced by Pitt, the British Prime Minister, was that Ireland was deeply divided over proposed changes to the legal rights of Roman Catholics within the constitution. The rights of practising Roman Catholics had been severely restricted following the Williamite revolution of 1688.[26] The suppression of Catholicism began as soon as William 'Prince of Orange'[27] arrived in England, having been invited by Protestant noblemen. The Prince assembled his supporters at Exeter Cathedral[28] and asked for their support in the defence of the Protestant religion.[29] Prince William carried a standard declaring "The Protestant Religion and Liberties of England" amalgamated with the motto of the House of Orange, "I will maintain".[30]

The succession of William III and Mary[31] as joint sovereigns in February 1689, secured the Protestant Ascendancy in both Great Britain and Ireland through the constitutional changes they implemented. The most notable legislative instrument from this period, the Bill of Rights of 1689,[32] remains the primary constitutional source in respect of succession to the Crown,[33] the supremacy of Parliament over Royal authority,[34] and the primacy of the Church of England as the established church.[35]

The Act of Union was seen by some of its proponents as an opportunity to reform the constitution and bring about the emancipation of Catholics. Successive British monarchs since 1689 had faced the dilemma of how to address the rights of Roman Catholics within Great Britain and Ireland, when the papacy refused to recognise the succession of William and Mary to the English throne. The influence of James II continued during the lifetime of his son, James III, who resided in Rome and continued to nominate bishops for the Irish Church until his death in 1766.[36] The Irish Parliament, fearful that the Protestant succession to the throne would be overturned, introduced an oath in 1709 which required public officials, including registered clergy, to renounce the right of James III to the throne.[37] This Act effectively made the Roman Catholic Church illegal, as the Pope denounced the oath and only 33 priests subjected themselves to it.[38]

The death of James III was viewed as reducing the risk to the Protestant succession, and there developed a body of opinion suggesting that Rome was no longer a political threat to the constitution. The Irish Parliament granted some concessions on the issue in 1793, passing legislation[39] enabling Catholics to stand for elections and vote.[40] However, they were still prohibited from sitting in Parliament.[41] The Irish Catholics had faired less favourably than their counterparts in Quebec, who achieved emancipation in 1784.[42]

Lord Cornwallis, the Lord Lieutenant, had sought the inclusion of Catholic emancipation within the terms of the Act of Union, as a means of reducing resistance from the Catholic majority; but his wishes were not realised, in the face of hostility to the proposal from prominent figures within the Irish government. A compromise was reached, whereby a promise was given by Pitt to introduce an emancipation Act following the Union of both Parliaments. Accepting this assurance, Catholic property owners actively supported the Union, whilst some members of the Orange

Order sought to preserve the 'Protestant constitution' by opposing the Bill.[43]

It would be a mistake to conclude that the restricted legal rights of Catholics in Ireland was the main motivation for the conception of the idea for the Union. The reality had more to do with political expediency. Concerns over possible future actions by an Irish Parliament and the military threat posed by the French, coupled with civil unrest, generated the political desire to have a speedy conclusion to this constitutional problem.

The passage of the Act was not a smooth affair in the Irish Parliament. The debate began on 22 January 1799, when Mr Secretary Dundas delivered the following message from the King to the House of Commons:

> His majesty is persuaded, that the unremitting industry with which our enemies persevere in their avowed design of effecting the separation of Ireland from this Kingdom, cannot fail to engage the particular attention of parliament; and his majesty recommends it to this house to consider of the most effectual means of finally defeating this design, by disposing the parliaments of both Kingdoms to provide . . . final adjustment as may best tend to improve and perpetuate a connection essential to their common security, and consolidate the strength, power and resources of the British Empire.[44]

It was argued that Union would adversely affect the constitution, trade and property of the country.[45] Indeed, the competency of the Irish Parliament to adopt "a measure invasive of the rights of the people, and subversive of the constitution" was questioned; and if the legislature did have such competency then "it would be the height of such folly to make such a sacrifice to the pride of Britain".[46] It was proposed that:

> The house should declare its resolution of maintaining the right of the people of Ireland to a resident and independent legislature, as recognised by the British Parliament in 1782,[47] and finally settled at the adjustment of all differences between the two kingdoms.

After a prolonged and heated debate, the proposal to accede to Union with Great Britain was defeated on 24 January by 111 to 106 votes.

Although the proposal was rejected in Ireland, Pitt introduced a number of resolutions in the British Parliament on 31 January 1799, which were subsequently passed. In effect, these paved the way for the desired legislative Union, and demonstrated to the Irish Parliament the determination of the British legislature. These resolutions, which eventually formed the basis of the Act of Union 1801, included the following proposals:[48]

> I. To concur such measures as may best tend to unite the two kingdoms of Great Britain and Ireland into one kingdom, in such manner, and on such terms and conditions, as may be established by acts of the respective parliaments of his majesty's said kingdoms.
> II. That the said kingdoms of Great Britain and Ireland shall . . . [unite] by the name of the United Kingdom of Great Britain and Ireland.
> III. The succession to the monarchy and the imperial crown of the said united kingdoms shall continue limited and settled, in the same manner as the imperial crowns of the said kingdoms of Great Britain and Ireland now stands limited and settled, according to existing laws . . .
> IV. That the said United Kingdom be represented in the same parliament, to be styled 'the Parliament of the United Kingdom of Great Britain and Ireland . . .
> V. That the churches of England and Ireland, and the doctrine, worship, discipline and government thereof, shall be preserved as now by law established.
> VIII. That for the like purpose it would be fit to propose that all the laws in force at the time of the union, and that all the courts of civil or ecclesiastical jurisdiction within the respective kingdoms, shall remain as now by law established . . .

The resolutions were moved on 7 February 1799 in the British House of Commons. Following debate in both houses, they were assented to; and on 11 April Parliament moved an address to the throne, which was carried without a division.[49] In Ireland, further consideration of the Bill was postponed until 1 August 1799, when it was again opposed.

A new Parliament assembled in Ireland in 1800, and the business of seeking a legislative Union was formally reintroduced on 5 February 1800 by a message from the Lord Lieutenant. The message stated that he was commanded by the King to lay before both houses of the Irish Parliament the resolutions of the British Parliament. A lengthy and acrimonious debate ensued in the Commons, concluding with a majority of 43 in favour of the adoption of the Lord Lieutenant's message.[50] Thus it was evident that the British Parliament in London had continued to recognise the independent sovereign nature of the Irish Parliament.

The intensity of the subsequent debate on the legislation can be judged by the events of 17 February 1800, when, as a consequence of the vehemence of Mr Grattan's speech (opposing), the Irish Chancellor of the Exchequer, Mr Corry, felt obliged to challenge his political opponent to a duel. In this combat five shots were fired and the Chancellor was wounded in the arm.[51] Despite winning the duel, Grattan and his political allies lost the debate. A total of 161 MPs voted to accept the Union; 115 opposed the legislation.

On 24 March 1800, the Irish peers adopted the whole of the Articles of Union, thus completing the parliamentary stages in Ireland. As a result, both houses of the Irish Parliament sent an address to the Lord Lieutenant for delivery to the King, containing the resolutions accepting the Articles. On 2 April 1800, King George sent an address to the British House of Lords, informing them of the decision in Ireland and recommending that they:

> Take such further steps as may best tend to the speedy and complete execution of the work so happy begun (1799), and so interesting to the security of his majesty's subjects, and to the general strength and prosperity of the British Empire.[52]

The King's address highlighted the urgency which the British establishment had placed upon the need for constitutional reform, and the importance parliamentary Union between Great Britain and Ireland was believed to have in terms of security and economic prosperity within the British Empire. Passage of the bill was easier in the British Parliament, although there were some heated exchanges. The Irish Parliament did not dissolve until Royal assent was given to the bill; it remained in session in order to ratify several alterations and amendments made in the British Parliament, in addition to making arrangements for elections of Irish members to the new Imperial Parliament.[53]

On 2 August 1800 the Dublin Parliament was prorogued and legislative sovereignty in Ireland passed into history. The Government of Ireland Act 1920, and the recent legislation restoring devolved government in Northern Ireland, did not restore parliamentary sovereignty in Ireland, but rather permitted the exercise of authority devolved from the Imperial Parliament of the United Kingdom. The parliament of the Irish Republic obtained sovereignty as a consequence of a proclamation by King George VI in 1948 conceding Crown sovereignty; and the parliament of the United Kingdom relinquished legislative sovereignty through a statutory instrument.

Following the Union, Irish Catholics looked to the new Imperial Parliament of Great Britain and Ireland to deliver the freedom to fully participate in all political privileges within the nation. Their hopes were quickly dashed. When Pitt placed the proposition before the cabinet council, it was strongly opposed by some ministers.[54] The King decided the issue, by declaring that the oath taken by him at his coronation precluded his assent to a policy which would have endangered the religious establishment.[55] George III effectively vetoed emancipation under the constitution as sovereign. He was strongly opposed to Catholic emancipation, despite the government's undertaking to the Irish. Indeed, he declared in January 1801 that, "I shall reckon any man my personal enemy who proposes such a measure."[56]

The Act of Union addressed a number of issues beyond that of parliamentary Union, which impacted indirectly upon the constitution. As a consequence of the provisions of the Act, King George issued a number of declarations on 1 January 1801 in respect of his title, the flag of the kingdom and the wording of the liturgy in the Anglican Church. The sovereign's new title within the constitution became "George the third, by the grace of God, of the United Kingdom of Great Britain and Ireland, King, Defender of the Faith."[57] The new Royal arms, or ensigns armorial, incorporated the Irish harp in a quarter of the shield.[58] Whilst the flag of the Union was to incorporate "the crosses of St Andrew and St Patrick quarterly per saltire counter changed argent and gules".[59]

In conclusion, it could be argued that the Act of Union had a major impact upon the constitutional framework of Great Britain and Ireland. The legislative Union created the national identity by which the United Kingdom is known throughout the world; the Union flag is recognised as the symbol of the British state; and the cultural impact which the concept of the United Kingdom generated remains to the forefront of modern political debate. The 1801 Act failed in many respects to create a United Kingdom. Failure to deliver immediate emancipation engendered mistrust in the British political establishment; when emancipation did materialise, sectarianism had taken root and political debate became stagnated upon religious prejudice and bias.

Despite the advent of legislative control by a London Parliament, Ireland retained its unique judicial system and civil administration. Laws passed by previous Irish Parliaments remained in force until they were specifically repealed by new legislation, which applied throughout the United Kingdom. Legal anomalies continued to exist and some such statutes remain in force: for example, it is still unlawful to kick a football on a Sunday in Northern Ireland, and those who do so are liable to a fine of 4d (2p).[60] The Act of Union has been dismantled in stages, as political and social changes have emerged. In 1870, the Church of Ireland was disestablished, and as a consequence lost the right to have four bishops in the House of Lords. The 1920 Government of Ireland Act replaced the main provisions of the 1801 Act, as the 26 southern counties obtained limited legislative jurisdiction and Northern Ireland was created. Hence, the United Kingdom is now that of Great Britain and Northern Ireland.

Two hundred years later, the constitutional and legal impact of the Act of Union has to be judged against communal division, fuelled by cultural friction. The legislative Union did not unite the people, but in many ways deepened suspicion and mistrust. The architects of the Act of Union could not have foreseen the strife, violence and pain that Ireland would have to endure as factionalism and sectarianism transformed the ideal of a united people within a single kingdom into a divided people within Ireland. It would be inaccurate to blame the modern Troubles directly upon the political decisions of 1799–1801, but the constitutional changes brought about during that period cannot be divorced from the political problems of Ireland in the twentieth century. It is perhaps too soon for history to judge whether the Act of Union minimised social problems in these islands or perpetuated them.

Notes

1 The Act of Union of Great Britain and Ireland became law on 1 January 1801.
2 The Proclamation by King George III (1 January 1801) declaring His Majesty's pleasure for the holding the first Parliament of the United Kingdom of Great Britain and Ireland stated:
> Whereas, in pursuance of the fourth article of the articles of union between Great Britain and Ireland, as the same have been ratified and confirmed by two acts of parliament, the one passed by the parliament of Great Britain, and the other by the parliament of Ireland and both entitled 'An act for the Union of Great Britain and Ireland.'

3 Laudabiliter, 1155. This letter gave Henry II papal authority over the island of Ireland and commanded all the inhabitants to obey him as their sovereign.
4 For an account of the expansion of the Norman influence in Ireland in the period 1171–1300, see Jonathan Bardon, *A History of Ulster*, Blackstaff, 1997, chapter 2, pp 25–45.
5 The Act for the union of Great Britain and Ireland 1800 (Parliament of Ireland) was given Royal assent in August 1800.
6 The Act of Union with Scotland in 1707, created a new sovereign parliament for Great Britain assembled at Westminster.
7 Act for the Union of Great Britain and Ireland 1800 (Parliament of Great Britain) received Royal assent on 2 July 1800.
8 This practice remains unto the present day, when the Lords spiritual and Lords temporal pay homage to the newly crowned sovereign during the latter stages of the Coronation ceremony.
9 13 Edward I.
10 For a full account of the sovereign authority of the early Norman kings, see Harvey (deputy Record Keeper of the Tower), 'Early Regulations for the Conservancy of the Peace', reproduced in Supplement E, Appendix to the First Report of the Constabulary Force Commissioners, 27 March 1839.

11 Ibid, pp 21–31.

12 Lord Glaisdale in *Town Investments Limited v Department of the Environment* (1978), AC 359 (HL), alluded to the constitutional relationship between ministers of the Crown and the Crown when he stated:

> With the development of modern government fresh departments were formed to be headed by ministers or secretaries of state. Just as all were originally appointed to carry out departmentally the royal will, so today all ministers are appointed to exercise the powers of the Crown . . .

13 The appointment of justices to administer justice and give relief to the people, outside the sheriff courts, commenced by statute de Justic. assign. quod vocatur Rageman, 4 Ed. I.

14 In *Fisher v Oldham Corporation* (1930), McCardie (J) held, "A constable . . . when acting as a peace officer, is not exercising a delegated authority, but an original authority . . . "
The original jurisdiction of a constable emanates from Anglo-Saxon law and custom. The role of a constable was extended in the period following the Magna Carta.

15 The constitutional settlement encapsulated in the Bill of Rights of 1688 placed some limited constraints upon the powers of a monarch; however, this was by mutual agreement, and the prerogative of a sovereign to ignore the provisions of the Bill of Rights has never been tested.

16 The Prince's Case (1601) 8 Co. Rep 1a.

17 F Ridley, 'There is no British Constitution', 41 *Parliamentary Affairs*, 1988, London, p 340.

18 An example of the sovereign power of Parliament can be found in the actions of the Irish Parliament meeting in 1695, which passed a bill "annulling all attainers and acts passed in the late pretended parliament of king James". See T Smollett, *The History of England*, Vol. 2, 1824, p 59.

19 Dicey 8th Ed. (1959, p. 40) discusses the sovereignty of Parliament, stating that within the British constitution, Parliament has "the right to make or unmake any law whatever". In this context, both the Parliament of Ireland and the Parliament of Great Britain had the power to pass legislation that overruled previous Acts and dissolved their respective legislatures and transferred their sovereignty to a new Parliament of the United Kingdom of Great Britain and Ireland.

20 Proclamation made at the coronation of King George III in 1760. Extracted from the *Dublin Almanac*, 1847, pp 366-383, Pettigrew and Oulton, Dublin.

21 Ibid, pp 366–83.

22 *History of Great Britain*, Vol. 3, Jones and Co, 1824, p 184.

23 Ibid.

24 Ibid.

25 For an account of the French intervention in the 1798 rebellion see T Pakenham, *The Year of Liberty*, Weidenfeld and Nicolson, 1998.

26 Prince William arrived at Brixham on 5 November 1688.

27 Prince William's title emanated from the principality of Orange in southeastern France. Louis XIV had invaded and seized this territory from the Dutch in 1682,

The Union

and at the time of William's arrival in England in 1688 there was a genuine fear that the French would invade Holland. Several days after William arrived in England, Louis ordered the invasion.
28 The Prince of Orange addressed the Nobles, Knights and Gentlemen of Exeter in the presence of his chaplain, Gilbert Burnett, on 12 November 1688.
29 See Macaulay's *History of England*, vol 3, 1849, chapter 10.
30 MW Dewar, *Why Orangeism*, Grand Orange Lodge of Ireland, 1958, p 10.
31 William III was married to the eldest daughter of the Catholic King James II.
32 10 Statutes 44. The Bill of Rights remains as law today, although in an amended form.
33 No heir to the throne could succeed if a Roman Catholic by faith.
34 For an analysis of the importance of the Bill of Rights 1689 to the supremacy of Parliament see C Turpin, *British Government and the Constitution*, Butterworths, 1995. One example of a restriction placed upon the Crown, was the requirement for it to obtain the consent of Parliament to maintain a standing army during peacetime.
35 The monarch, at his or her coronation, must take an oath to uphold the Protestant religion, and adopts the title 'Defender of the Faith.' The sovereign within the constitution is the Governor of the Church of England.
36 M Elliott, *The Catholics of Ulster: a History*, Penguin, 2000, p 169.
37 Oath of Abjuration Act 1709.
38 Elliott, p 165.
39 Catholic Relief Act 1793 (Irish Parliament).
40 Ibid. To be eligible to vote, the individual had to be a 40s freeholder.
41 In effect, Roman Catholics continued to be disenfranchised unless they voted for a Protestant candidate.
42 The Quebec Act of 1784 granted limited emancipation to Roman Catholics in the Canadian province in question.
43 Bardon, pp 238–39.
44 A similar address was delivered to the Parliament of Great Britain on 2 April 1799 by the Duke of Portland. See *The New Annual Register (1800)*, London, 1801, p 108.
45 Argued by Sir John Parnell, Irish House of Commons, 22 January 1799.
46 Such a view was expressed by George Ponsonby MP, brother of the Earl of Besborough, during the debate in the Irish House of Commons.
47 The parliamentary proceedings of 1782 had aimed to establish the independence of both legislatures, and were viewed by the parties to the arrangement as a final settlement.
48 The full text of the Resolutions are recorded in E Baines, *History of the Wars of the French Revolution*, Vol 1, Longman, Hurst, Rees et al, 1817.
49 *History of Great Britain*, Vol 3, p 280.
50 *The New Annual Register (1800)*, p 108.
51 Ibid, p 109.
52 Ibid.
53 Under the terms of the Act of Union, Ireland could return 100 members to the new Imperial Parliament, and the Irish peers elected 30 of their number to the

new House of Lords, four of whom were to be spiritual Lords.
54 Pitt's inability to unite the cabinet behind him on this policy, contributed to his decision to resign from office on 3 February 1801.
55 *The History of Great Britain*, p 293.
56 28 January 1801. Watson (1960), p 104, cited by Bardon, p 241.
57 The full text was published in 'Public papers', *New Annual Register 1801*, p 116.
58 Ibid, p 117.
59 Ibid.
60 Lords Day Observance Act (1695).

Norman Baxter is a recognised expert in the sphere of constitutional law, human rights and the criminal justice system. He was awarded a doctorate in philosophy by the University of Ulster, and has had a number of research papers published in international journals. He has recently produced an academic textbook in his field of expertise, which is due to be published in the early summer of 2001.

From Rebels to Unionists: The Political Transformation of Ulster's Presbyterians

Finlay Holmes

That many Presbyterians in Ulster were deeply involved in the United Irish movement in the 1790s, whose aims included "the total separation" of Ireland from Britain and which culminated in the rebellion of 1798, and that many of their children and grandchildren became ardent unionists, utterly opposed to any weakening of Ireland's links with Britain, are incontrovertible facts of Irish history. "The defection of the Presbyterians from the movement of which they were the main originators, and the great and enduring change which took place in their sentiments", observed the nineteenth-century historian Lecky, "are facts of the deepest importance in Irish history, and deserve very careful and detailed explanation."[1]

Lecky wisely considered that it would be an error "to attribute these changes to any single cause".[2] Among the explanations he offered were the success of Orangeism in providing "a new and rival enthusiasm in the heart of the disaffected province", the deterrent effects of General Lake's ruthless campaign to disarm and "pacify" Ulster in 1797; later, the reports of how, in Wexford, "rebels there were imprisoning and murdering Protestants, priests in their vestments leading them as to a holy war . . . how Protestants were thronging the chapels to be baptised, as the sole means of saving their lives".[3] While acknowledging that there was much in these reports that was exaggerated, Lecky believed that they had caused many Presbyterian United Irishmen to think again about the cause in which they had become involved. Reports from France and Europe were equally disillusioning, as the foreign policy and military adventurism of revolutionary France appeared increasingly indifferent to the rights of other nations.

These have remained prominent among explanations for "the great and enduring change" which took place in Presbyterian sentiments so far as disillusionment with revolutionary republicanism was concerned. Even before the disaster of 1798 many Ulster Presbyterians, including some who had been enthusiastic reformers, had distanced themselves from the United Irish radicals. In January 1793 the Rev Robert Black of Derry, once prominent in Volunteer and reform circles, claimed to be speaking for "the sober and rational part of the community" when he attacked "seditious spirits who wished to overturn the constitution".[4] Also in 1793, the Synod of Ulster, while reaffirming its opinion that constitutional reform was necessary, assured the Lord Lieutenant that they approved only of constitutional means of achieving reform, "rejecting with abhorrence every idea of popular tumult or foreign aid".[5] The United Irishmen, despairing of achieving adequate reform by constitutional means, were becoming convinced that they would have to resort to "popular tumult and foreign aid".

As Lecky suggested, the brutal disarming of Ulster in 1797 detached many Presbyterian supporters from the revolutionary cause. The experience of the rebellion itself, the sufferings which accompanied and followed it, completed the disillusionment of many and strengthened the position of their critics and loyalists in the Synod. The Synod, like other ecclesiastical bodies, including the Roman Catholic hierarchy, condemned the rebels, denouncing "the inexcusable crimes of a few unworthy members of our body whose conduct we can only view with grief and indignation",[6] and demonstrating Presbyterian loyalty by voting £500 for national defence. The contemporary Presbyterian historian William Campbell may have judged the Synod's behaviour "extraordinary", but even he acknowledged that the rebellion was the action "not of the body of Presbyterians but only of part, made mad by unexampled oppression".[7] This was not the line taken by the Synod, however. An address to the people under the Synod's pastoral care enjoined "loyalty to the king and attachment to the Constitution", declaring the rebellion totally unjustified. "Did not Christians of every denomination enjoy perfect liberty of conscience? Were not the shackles broken which had confined our trade? Was not private property secure and the land every day becoming more prosperous?"[8]

In 1779 the Synod, on the basis of reports requested from presbyteries, claimed again that only a "comparatively small number of their members had been implicated in treasonable and seditious practices".[9] Dr Ian McBride has listed 63 Presbyterian ministers and ministerial probationers suspected of involvement in the rebellion.[10] Not all of these belonged to the Synod of Ulster, of course. Four were from the Presbytery of Antrim, three were Seceders, five were Reformed Presbyterians or Covenanters, and the precise ecclesiastical allegiance of six others McBride is unable to determine. However, 45 associated with the Synod of Ulster were more than the "comparatively few" acknowledged by the Synod. Among those imprisoned were two former Moderators of Synod, while one well-known minister, the Rev James Porter of Greyabbey, had been hanged outside his meeting house.

Defeated rebels in Antrim and Down were still being rounded up when James McKey, a Mountpottinger loyalist who was keeping the Marquis of Downshire well informed about the situation on the ground, expressed his perceptive opinion that:

> ... we will have a much more settled country in a short time than ever your lordship saw it. For some years past there was something brooding in the minds of republicans and now that it has broke out and that it could not succeed they will become loyal subjects. [11]

He was to be proved right so far as many Presbyterians were concerned. The time was clearly right for those within the Synod and in government who wanted to encourage such a conversion on the part of Presbyterian United Irishmen. Prominent among them was the Irish Chief Secretary, Lord Castlereagh, chief architect of the Act of Union, whose own family background was Ulster Presbyterian. Writing to the Prime Minister, Lord Addington, in 1802, he enclosed a letter he had received from the Rev Robert Black on the subject of the Ulster Presbyterians and commented:

> ... the enclosed sketch will show you how much there is in the body which requires amendment and how much may be done by an efficient protection and support given on the part of government to those who have committed themselves in support of the state against a democratic party in the Synod, several of whom, if not engaged in the rebellion, were deeply infected with its principles.[12]

Castlereagh was also being advised on the subject of the Presbyterians by the Rev William Bruce, minister of Belfast's First Presbyterian congregation, and Alexander Knox, his former secretary. Knox described the situation as he saw it:

> This is perhaps a more favourable moment for forming a salutary connection between the government and the Presbyterians of Ulster than may arrive again. The republicanism of that part of Ireland is checked and repressed by the cruelties of the Roman Catholics in the late rebellion and by the despotism of Bonaparte. They are therefore in a humour for acquiescing in the views of government beyond which they were or (should the opportunity be missed) may be hereafter.[13]

The means which Castlereagh, guided by Knox and Black, adopted to achieve his ends involved a massively increased *regium donum*, the state grant for Presbyterian ministers, but given on new terms. It was to be paid to ministers as individuals and not as a block grant to the Synod, and the agent responsible for its distribution was to be appointed and paid by the government. The Rev Robert Black was appointed as the first agent. To receive his grant a minister had to take an oath of allegiance before two magistrates, and would be paid £100, £75 or £50 according to the size of his congregation. This system of classification of ministers was alien to Presbyterians, who regarded it as introducing a form of hierarchy into a church which emphasised the equality of all its ministers. It was an indication of Presbyterian demoralisation in the wake of the rebellion that they accepted these arrangements. These increased payments represented an enormous subvention for the ministers of a church which had been struggling to ensure that stipends did not fall below £40 a year.

Knox considered that these arrangements would make the Synod of Ulster ministers:

> . . . a subordinate ecclesiastical aristocracy whose feelings must be those of zealous loyalty and whose influence upon their people will be as surely sedative when it should be and exciting when it should be so as it was the direct reverse before.[14]

Earlier, Black had argued that the improved financial prospects of ministers "would tend to the future respectability of the clergy by facilitating them marrying into families of repute and influence".[15] It was intended that Presbyterian ministers would become a conservative rather than a radical influence in their congregations. William Drennan complained that the ministers were being bought and forecast that their congregations would desert them.[16] Seceders and Covenanters derided the Synod of Ulster ministers as hirelings, until the Seceders themselves accepted similar arrangements for their ministers. Only the Covenanters held out for ecclesiastical independence and their numbers did increase, but not dramatically.

If Castlereagh and Black imagined that they had tamed the Synod's ministers they soon discovered their mistake. A test of the new relationship between church and government came when the Synod decided to recognise as a suitable college for ministerial education the Belfast Academical Institution, founded by Belfast's commercial and professional élite, some of whom, like William Drennan, who gave the address at the opening ceremony, had had United Irish associations. Castlereagh immediately saw this as "a deep laid scheme to again bring the Presbyterian Synod within the ranks of democracy"[17] and he warned Peel, who now held the office of Irish Chief Secretary, of the "incalculable importance of not suffering Dr Drennan and his associates to have the power of granting or withholding certificates of qualification for the ministry of that church".[18] He let the Synod know that the government might withold *regium donum* payments from ministers who were not university graduates. In the Synod, Black threw the considerable weight of his influence against any arrangement between church and college, but without success. A majority in the Synod voted to appoint a professor of divinity to teach their ordinands in the Institution, which would provide courses in arts on the model of the Scottish universities.

During the debate in the Synod, the Rev James Carlile of Dublin, with reference to Castlereagh's warnings, asked the irreverent question:

> Who or what is this Lord Castlereagh that he should send such a message to the Synod of Ulster? Is he a minister of the body? Is he an elder? What right has he to obtrude himself on our deliberations? As long as I can raise my voice I will raise it against the principle of admitting civil governors as such to be heard in our deliberations . . . This day's discussion will tell whether we deserve to rank as an independent, conscientious, upright body, with no other end in view than the glory of God and the welfare of his church or whether we deserve that Lord Castlereagh should drive his chariot into the midst of us, and tread us down as the offal of the streets.[19]

The voice of Presbyterian radicalism had not been silenced.

Black's defeat on the Institution question marked the beginning of the end of his dominance of the Synod, and six months later he committed suicide, anticipating the tragic fate of his patron, Castlereagh. Black's mantle was to pass, within a few years, to another equally gifted orator, Henry Cooke. Cooke, who had supported the Synod's decision on the Institution question in 1817, began in 1822 to raise new queries about the church's relationship with the college. His concern was ostensibly theological, but the fact that, like Black, his political sympathies were conservative, has supported the view of John Jamieson, the historian of the Belfast Institution, that Cooke was continuing the campaign of Castlereagh and Black under a theological cloak.[20]

In his correspondence with Peel on the Institution question, Castlereagh had returned to a subject he had raised with Addington in 1802 – the possibility of an "internal fermentation" in the Synod of Ulster, in which the "democratic party" would be defeated.[21] That something like this did happen in the 1820s, in the conflict initiated by Cooke's attack on the Institution, has strengthened suspicions that this was a political conflict in disguise. Against this, it is undeniable that in Cooke's campaign against heresy in church and college a crucial theological question was at issue, the question of the divinity of Christ, which was being queried by some ministers and professors in the Institution.

In the eighteenth century the theological ethos of the Synod of Ulster had become latitudinarian, signalled by a gradual departure from the practice of requiring ministers to subscribe to the Westminster Confession of Faith at ordination. In the nineteenth century, however, Irish Presbyterianism began to feel the impact of Evangelicalism, a movement of renewal in European and American Protestantism, emphasising the experience of personal salvation. The great dynamic of Evangelicalism was the salvation of souls, but in the context of dechristianisation in the French Revolution it was sometimes perceived and patronised as a counter-revolutionary force. Evangelicals in Britain and Ireland saw the French Revolution and the 1798 Rebellion as manifestations of the anarchic consequences of human sin. Evangelical societies like the London Hibernian Society appealed for support on the grounds that evangelism would prevent revolution in Ireland.

In 1798 the Evangelical Society of Ulster was founded in association with the London Missionary Society to promote evangelism in Ulster. Drennan's sister, Martha McTier, attended some of their meetings and reported to her brother that the evangelists were preaching "a zealous religion subtly blended with loyalty".[22] It was this combination which triumphed in the conflict in the Synod of Ulster when the new evangelicalism, which was to characterise nineteenth century Irish Presbyterianism, triumphed over the latitudinarianism of the eighteenth century. Henry Cooke, apostle of conservatism in religion and politics, was victorious over the non-subscribing, anti-trinitarian Henry Montgomery, who was not ashamed to own that his kinsmen had been rebels in 1798.[23]

Cooke has commonly been credited or blamed for having completed the transformation of Ulster Presbyterians, initiated by Castlereagh and Black, from the radical republicanism of the 1790s to the unionism and conservatism of the nineteenth century. It is a thesis which requires qualification – Cooke's efforts to lead Ulster Presbyterians into the Tory political camp were by no means successful in his lifetime.

In 1829, the year of Cooke's triumph in the Synod, the burning issue in British and Irish politics was Catholic emancipation. The Synod of Ulster, in 1793 and in 1813, had expressed its support for emancipation, for full civil rights for all, irrespective of religious belief; but in 1829, when the concession of emancipation seemed imminent, Cooke, under pressure from diehard Protestant elements which had given him support in the conflict in the Synod, called for a special meeting of Synod to be convened to consider the current "critical" political situation. He was unsuccessful, even in his own presbytery. Only one presbytery, Ballymena, decided to call for a special meeting of Synod, and as requisitions from at least two presbyteries were needed if a special meeting of Synod was to be called, no such meeting took place and no official Presbyterian opposition to emancipation was articulated.[24]

Few Presbyterians approved of Cooke's campaign to support the Church of Ireland when it came under attack from a reforming Whig government in alliance with the O'Connellites in the 1830s. His publication of the banns of marriage between Presbytery and Episcopacy in 1834, at a huge Conservative and Protestant demonstration at Hillsborough, brought him savage criticism from within his own church. Clearly there were still Presbyterians to whom Cooke's support for the political and ecclesiastical establishment was anathema, though it is significant that his sharpest critic, 'John Knox, Junior', expressed "equal disgust and aversion" for "the lamentations of conservatism and the gross absurdities of repealers and radical reformers".[25]

Many Presbyterians who did not share Cooke's conservatism did share his unionism. As early as 1817, Henry Joy, proprietor of the *Belfast News Letter* and uncle of Henry Joy McCracken, though never himself a United Irishman, a reformer turned conservative like the Rev Robert Black, published his opinion that the experience of the 1790s had taught Irish Protestants that "adherence to the British connexion [sic], so long as the Papists form the majority of the island, is absolutely necessary to their existence".[26] One of the objects of the 1834 Hillsborough demonstration had been to oppose O'Connell's agitation for the repeal of the Union, which Cooke characterised as "just a discreet word for Romish ascendancy and protestant extermination".[27] Political polarisation in Ireland was intensified by the way in which political and religious loyalties were intertwined. Protestants perceived O'Connell's repeal movement as representing the interests of Irish Catholics, and identified their interests with the maintenance of the Union.

In 1841, when O'Connell visited Belfast to advocate repeal, Cooke challenged him to a debate on the issue. O'Connell declined the challenge on the grounds that as Cooke was the leader of the Presbyterians – which some Presbyterians would have disputed – he did not want to give the impression that he was against the Presbyterians. Cooke was hailed in Ulster Protestant circles as the victor, "the cook who dish'd Dan".[28] He was the principal speaker at a demonstration held in Belfast to celebrate "the repulse of the Repealer". In his speech, Cooke combined economic and religious arguments in favour of the Union.

"Look at Belfast", he cried:

> When I was myself a youth I remember it almost a village. But what a glorious sight does it now present – the masted grove within our harbour, our mighty warehouses teeming with the wealth of every climate – our great manufactories lifting themselves on every side . . . Look at Belfast and be a repealer, if you can.[29]

It was an argument which was convincing to a population experiencing industrial growth and it combined with the anti-catholicism of many Presbyterians to make them unionists. Significantly, for once, Cooke was applauded by the *Northern Whig* which preceded him in stating the economic argument in favour of the Union.

Even such a convinced liberal as Mary Ann McCracken, Henry Joy's sister, while never repudiating the United Irish vision of her brother, came to the conclusion that:

> . . . it would be necessary to lay aside natural feelings of National pride and love of independence, which is not easily done, in order to consider whether the people of this country might not have their liberty and happiness better secured by being an integral part of a great and powerful nation provided that ample justice towards Ireland was strictly observed and that Ireland would have a better chance of justice when the liberals of both countries were united in our parliament than when divided.[30]

Most Ulster Presbyterians may have become unionists by 1841, but they had not become Tories, as Cooke himself acknowledged in his correspondence with Peel, the Tory leader.[31] In 1840 the Synod of Ulster and the Secession Synod had united to form the General Assembly of the Presbyterian Church in Ireland and Cooke had welcomed the union, arguing that, among other consequences, Presbyterian support for the Union would be strengthened. He told a largely Church of Ireland audience in Dublin in 1837, gathered to attack the Whig government's non-sectarian national educational system:

> I do not mean to attach to the members of the Church of Scotland in Ireland any undue value, but it is my conviction that, were any circumstances to pervert the Presbyterians of Ulster, the union of the three kingdoms would not be worth a twelve months' purchase.[32]

There was little doubt about Presbyterian support for the Union. It had brought them many gains. The aims of their Volunteer and United Irish forebears were being achieved in a gradual process of reform. The old

Protestant Ascendancy Parliament in Dublin had gone, as had the sacramental test against dissenters in public life. The power of landlords was diminishing with the extension of the franchise; there had been reform of tithe payments and municipal corporations. However, these were only beginnings and Presbyterians were far from satisfied with the pace and extent of reform; in particular they were at odds with Peel's Tory government which they blamed for the disruption of the Church of Scotland in 1843 and continuing restrictions on the legality of certain Presbyterian marriages. Their dissatisfaction led the General Assembly in 1843 to recommend that church members should exercise their franchise to "secure a full and adequate representation of the principles and interests of Presbyterianism in the British legislature".[33] Cooke, rightly interpreting the resolution as an attack on his political party, walked out of the Assembly in protest.

Cooke was out of step, politically, with the Assembly, as one of his critics, the Rev AP Goudy, grandson of James Porter of Greyabbey, spelt out:

> The Presbyterian Church is laid under a deep debt of gratitude to Dr. Cooke. He was made the instrument of accomplishing a great reformation in this church by extirpating the unitarianism which tinged and weakened the body. We shall never forget the gratitude that is due to him . . . But we do not hold his political opinions on very many subjects. At the same time we have every reason to believe that our opinions correspond with a large and increasing majority of Irish Presbyterians.[34]

Against opposition from Cooke, Ulster Presbyterians were at the forefront of the struggle for tenant right in the middle of the nineteenth century. James McKnight, editor of the newly founded liberal Presbyterian newspaper the *Banner of Ulster*, rejoiced in the General Assembly's support for the movement:

> Our Church is now in her natural position, namely as that of guardian and witness on behalf of the poor man's rights in opposition to the rich Man's tyranny . . . We can conceive of no alliance more unnatural or more degrading than that which has sometimes been brought into forced operation between our free Presbyterianism and the spirit of reactionary toryism.[35]

Significantly, however, for McKnight the patriotic object of the tenant right movement was "that of elevating the masses of the Irish people, without distinction, to the realised dignity of British citizenship".[36]

Cooke's death-bed appeal to Presbyterian electors to vote Tory in the general election of 1868 to save the Church of Ireland from disestablishment was contradicted by the *Banner of Ulster*'s emotive reminder of their forefathers' sufferings: " . . . your fathers submitted to be hunted like partridges on the mountains rather than bow their heads to the yoke of Prelacy. Will you now vote for its continued ascendancy?"[37] A Presbyterian Liberal, Thomas McClure, was elected in Belfast. In Londonderry, however, although Presbyterian ministers were prominent supporters of the Liberal candidate, Richard Dowse, many of the members of their congregations voted Tory.[38] Pulpit and pew did not always agree, politically.

Whether they voted Liberal or Conservative, most Ulster Presbyterians had abandoned William Drennan's objective of a "total separation from Britain".[39] Drennan's son became an ardent unionist. Jemmy Hope, who died in 1846, was one of the few who remained faithful to the United Irish vision, although even he had doubts about O'Connell. The nineteenth century experience of Presbyterians was binding them, economically, politically and spiritually to Britain, perceived as a great Protestant, liberal, democratic nation, the world's leading industrial power, under whose Empire the work of the world evangelisation was advancing. If Linda Colley is right in identifying Protestantism as an essential element of Britishness,[40] then it is scarcely surprising that such self-conscious Protestants as the Ulster Presbyterians should have been enthusiastic supporters of the link with Britain. The increasing identification of Protestantism with unionism paralleled and was partly in consequence of the identification of Irish nationalism with Roman Catholicism.

Irish Protestantism and Roman Catholicism both experienced renewal in the nineteenth century, but Evangelicalism in Protestantism and Ultramontanism in Roman Catholicism, each emphasising and reinforcing distinctive and mutually exclusive aspects of their respective traditions, widened and deepened the gulf between them. The nineteenth century Evangelical Protestant crusade to evangelise Irish Roman Catholics intensified Roman Catholic hostility to Protestantism, while the Roman Catholic response to the crusade confirmed Protestant suspicions that Roman Catholicism was hostile to the gospel. Presbyterian anti-Catholicism was also nourished by relationships being developed between Irish Presbyterians and persecuted Protestants in Spain and Italy.[41] The sufferings of minority Protestant churches under intolerant Roman Catholic regimes in Spain and Italy increased Presbyterian anxieties about their prospects under a Roman Catholic majority in Ireland. Having suffered under the old Protestant Ascendancy, they were determined not to be subjugated under a Catholic Ascendancy.

The change in Irish Presbyterian sentiments was largely the result of changed historical circumstances. In the 1790s Presbyterian United Irishmen may well have believed that Roman Catholicism, apparently overthrown in France, was in terminal decline. Few could think that in the middle of the nineteenth century and certainly no one in Ireland. Now Irish Protestants were faced by a resurgent, self-confident, even triumphalist Catholicism, the Catholicism of Cardinal Cullen and the Syllabus of Errors. The advance of democracy had given a majority population new power. As Maureen Wall, University College, Dublin, historian, observed:

> The brutal truth was that the policy of equal rights for all and the brotherhood of Irishmen, if pushed to its logical conclusion, would inevitably lead to Catholic superiority and naturally no Protestant could contemplate such a prospect without grave misgivings indeed. This was the fundamental weakness of the whole United Irish position.[42]

Ulster Presbyterians were mystified by Gladstone's inability to understand their opposition to Home Rule for Ireland in 1886 and his appeal to them to "retain and maintain the tradition of their United Irish sires".[43] Replying on behalf of the Presbyterians who had hitherto been supporters of Gladstone's reforming policies in Ireland, JJ Shaw argued that they were not repudiating the tradition of their United Irish ancestors:

> Catholic emancipation, a reformed parliament, a responsible executive and equal laws for the whole Irish people. These were the real and declared objects of the United Irishmen. It was because they saw no hope of attaining these objects through an Irish parliament that they took up arms.[44]

These objects had been achieved, Shaw contended, under the parliament of the United Kingdom. In her recent study of the United Irishmen, Nancy Curtin appears to agree with him to some extent: "As the liberalism espoused by the United Irishmen emerged triumphant in Great Britain in the nineteenth century, Ulster radicals found even more reason to become reconciled to the union."[45]

In response to Gladstone's Home Rule Bill a special meeting of the General Assembly on 9 March 1886 resolved, almost unanimously:

> That we would deprecate in the strongest manner, as disastrous to the best interests of the country, a separate parliament for Ireland . . . or any

legislation tending to imperil the legislative union between Great Britain and Ireland or to interfere with the unity and supremacy of the Imperial Parliament . . . would, in our judgment, lead to the ascendancy of one class and creed in matters pertaining to religion, education and civil administration. We do not believe that any guarantees, moral or material, could be devised which would safeguard the rights and privileges of minorities scattered throughout Ireland against encroachment by a majority vested with legislative and executive functions.[46]

Thomas Sinclair, ruling elder and former Gladstonian Liberal, who seconded the Assembly resolution, insisted that they were not insensitive to "the rights of the Irish people and the wants of Ireland",[47] though it is doubtful if many Ulster Presbyterians appreciated or had much sympathy with the aspirations and feelings of Irish nationalists. Sinclair, a businessman, argued that Home Rule would be disastrous for the industrial northeast, because of the inevitably protectionist policy which an Irish government would adopt which

. . . would empty their mills, clear their rivers and shipyards, would stop their looms, would make the voices of their spindles silent and would cause a complete destruction of the industry that made the province so prosperous.[48]

No doubt there were many, even in Ulster, who had not shared in that prosperity and Sinclair could not have foreseen that his malign scenario would become a reality under the Union a century later, but it was a compelling argument for many Ulster Presbyterians in the nineteenth century. It was Sinclair again who articulated Presbyterian incredulity that Gladstone should think that they were still rebels, as in 1798:

Would it be a triumph of civilisation if, after having, by eighty-six years of gradual justice transfigured the Ulster rebels of '98 into the most loyal and devoted subjects of the realm, she were now, by a grand act of injustice, to turn back the shadow on the dial and invite the return of hours of darkness and despair.[49]

Again Sinclair was not to know that their determination to resist Home Rule would contribute, in time, to the return of hours of darkness and despair.

There were, of course, some Presbyterian Home Rulers, of whom the Rev JB Armour of Ballymoney is probably the best known, but they were a minority and even Armour did not advocate separation from Britain. There were also those who cherished and kept alive the memory of the

United Irishmen and 1798.[50] RL Marshall of Magee College, whose unionist and Orange loyalties were unquestionable, often remarked that many for whom unionism had become a religion, would relate proudly, in the right company and circumstances, how an ancestor had carried a pike in '98. Most Presbyterians, who cherish such memories, regard their United Irish ancestors as crusaders for political and social justice and not as Irish republicans and nationalists.

Notes
1 WEH Lecky, *A History of Ireland in the Eighteenth Century*, Chicago and London, 1972, p 386.
2 Ibid.
3 Ibid pp 386–7.
4 *Belfast News Letter*, 25 January 1793.
5 *Records of the General Synod of Ulster*, iii, pp 136–7.
6 Ibid, p 208.
7 W Campbell, Ms History of the Presbyterians, Presbyterian Historical Society, Belfast, p 101.
8 *Records of the General Synod of Ulster*, p 211.
9 Ibid, p 221.
10 IR McBride, *Scripture Politics: Ulster Presbyterians and Irish Radicalism in the late Eighteenth Century*, Oxford, 1998, pp 232–6.
11 J McKey to Lord Downshire, 15 June 1798, PRONI D 601/F/244.
12 Castlereagh to Addington, 21 July 1802, *Memoirs and Correspondence of Castlereagh*, London, 1845–53, iv, p 224.
13 Knox to Castlereagh, 15 July 1803, *Castlereagh Correspondence*, iv, p 288
14 Ibid, p 287.
15 Black to Castlereagh, 30 December 1800, *Castlereagh Correspondence*, iii, p 423.
16 Drennan to M McTier, 19 October 1800, *The Drennan Letters*, 1931, p 303.
17 Castlereagh to Peel, 9 November 1816, BM Add MS 401811 ff 219–20.
18 Ibid.
19 *Belfast News Letter*, 1 July 1817.
20 J Jamieson, 'The influence of the Rev Henry Cooke on the political life in Ulster', unpublished MA thesis, QUB, 1950, p 78.
21 Castlereagh to Peel, 9 November 1816, BM Add MS 401811 ff 219–20; Castlereagh to Addington, 21 July 1802, *Castlereagh Correspondence*, iv, p 224.
22 M McTier to Drennan, 27 September 1801, *Letters*, p 313.
23 *Irish Unitarian Magazine*, 1847, p 335.
24 RF Holmes, *Henry Cooke*, Belfast and Ottawa, 1981, pp 63–6.
25 'John Knox, junior', *The First and Second Blast of the Trumpet against the monstrous union of Presbytery and Prelacy*, Belfast, 1835, p 4.
26 H Joy (ed), *Historical Collections Relative to the town of Belfast*, Belfast, 1817, p xiii.
27 Holmes, *Cooke*, p 115.

28 *Northern Whig*, 7 January 1841.
29 Holmes, *Cooke*, p 148.
30 Mary Ann McCracken to RR Madden, 15 October 1844 Quoted by Ian McBride, *Scripture Politics*, p 215.
31 Holmes, *Cooke*, p 153.
32 Ibid, p 135.
33 *Minutes of the General Assembly*, i, p 224.
34 *Banner of Ulster*, 3 May 1844.
35 Ibid, 16 July 1850.
36 Ibid.
37 Ibid, 19 November 1868.
38 BM Walker, *Ulster Politics: The Formative Years, 1868–86*, Belfast, 1989, p 62.
39 Drennan to Bruce, undated, ATQ Stewart, 'A Stable Unseen Power', in J Bossy and P Jupp (eds), *Essays Presented to Michael Roberts*, Belfast, 1976, p 87.
40 L Colley, *Britons: Forging the Nation, 1707–1837*, London, 1992, pp 10–58.
41 Finlay Holmes, 'The Continental Mission', in J Thompson (ed), *Into All the World: A History of the Overseas Work of the Presbyterian Church in Ireland*, Belfast, 1990, pp 144–62.
42 Maureen Wall, 'The United Irishmen' in JL McCracken (ed), *Historical Studies*, 5, 1965, p 134.
43 JJ Shaw, *Mr Gladstone's Two Irish Policies, 1869 and 1886*, London, 1888, pp 7–9.
44 Ibid, pp 9–10.
45 Nancy Curtin, *The United Irishmen*, Oxford, 1998, p 284.
46 *Minutes of the General Assembly*,1886, p 13.
47 *The Witness*, 12 March 1886.
48 Ibid.
49 Ibid, 21 May 1886.
50 See Ian McBride, 'Memory and Forgetting: Ulster Presbyterians and 1798' in T Bartlett, D Keogh and K Whelan (eds), *The 1798 Rebellion* (Forthcoming publication). Dr McBride allowed me to read his essay in typescript.

Finlay Holmes taught church history in Magee Theological College, in Union Theological College and in the Faculty of Theology of the Queen's University of Belfast for 33 years. Among his publications are a biography of Henry Cooke and a history of the Presbyterian Church in Ireland. He was Moderator of the General Assembly of the Presbyterian Church in Ireland in 1990–91.

Home Rule, Partition and the Northern Nationalists, 1870–1930

Eamon Phoenix

The rise of the Irish Home Rule movement is inseparable from the name of Isaac Butt. An Ulster Protestant barrister and former Orangeman, Butt came to see modest devolution under the Crown as the only guarantee against Fenianism and revolution.

Yet Butt was never a full-blooded nationalist, but rather, "a far-seeing conservative" trying to serve the best interests of the United Kingdom by seeking the reconciliation of Britain and Ireland through Home Rule.[1]

Butt's moderate Home Government Association, formed in 1870, briefly appealed to a section of Irish Protestant conservatives, disillusioned by the disestablishment of the Church of Ireland. However, as Butt's ineffectual and patrician leadership was overthrown in favour of the more aggressive policy of Charles Stewart Parnell in 1879, Protestant support dwindled and the 'Irish Party' became a vehicle for the aspirations of the Roman Catholic majority in the island as a whole.

The growing success of the Home Rule cause was accelerated by the Third Reform Act of 1884 which extended the vote to the agricultural labourer and the urban worker. This Act was to pave the way for both an Orange and a Green political resurgence in Ireland. Until the emergence of Home Rule in the 1880s, Protestant voters in the north had been divided into supporters of the two main British political parties, Conservative and Liberal. Most Ulster Catholics, on the other hand, rallied to support the Home Rule Party, particularly from 1885 when the Parnellites captured 17 of the province's 33 seats. But despite this much-vaunted 'invasion of Ulster', the mass of Ulster Protestants were determined to thwart any attempt by the Liberal Prime Minister, William Gladstone, to grant Ireland self-government.

Parnell's electoral victory finally convinced the 'Grand Old Man' of the essential justness of the Home Rule cause. His first Home Rule Bill of 1886 failed, however, in the teeth of a combined unionist opposition in the House of Commons. A second bill in 1893 was thrown out by the Tory-dominated House of Lords, which now became the greatest obstacle to nationalist aspirations.

The first Home Rule crisis forced a rapid realignment in Ulster politics as the mass of Presbyterian Liberals reconstituted themselves as Liberal Unionists and began to forge an alliance with their former Tory adversaries. Typical was the case of the Tyrone landlord and former Liberal leader, Hugh de Fellenberg Montgomery of Fivemiletown. Noting in August 1885 that "the RC voters in the country districts are, with exceptions that one may count on one's fingers, all enrolled in the [Parnellite] National League", Montgomery declared his hostility to Home Rule and, by 1905, had become a leading member of the Ulster Unionist Council.[2]

But while such key defections were important to the new emerging Unionism, by far the most significant result of the Home Rule crisis in the north of Ireland was the revival of the Orange Order. Formed in north Armagh in 1795 against a background of sectarian faction fighting, the Order's anti-Catholic overtones had tended to repel the better off during the nineteenth century. From the 1880s, the gentry and middle-classes returned to its banner, realising its potential as a powerful cross-class alliance against an all-Ireland Home Rule scheme. Under their first parliamentary leader, Colonel Edward Saunderson, a Cavan landlord who had migrated from Liberalism to 'Orange Toryism', the Ulster Unionists declared their determination to use force rather than submit to "the degradation of Ireland" under a national parliament in Dublin. In their campaign, the northern loyalists were assured of the powerful support of the British Conservative Party to which the Union became "almost a sacred thing".

From 1885, therefore, until the Treaty settlement of 1921, the Union was the single dominating issue in Irish politics. Religion and politics were virtually synonymous, and Catholic Unionists, such as Denis Henry, KC (later Lord Chief Justice of Northern Ireland), and Protestant Home Rulers, such as Rev JB Armour of Ballymoney, were rare exceptions to the rule.

The Parnellite split of 1890–91 led to the dramatic break-up of the party he had welded into a disciplined phalanx. The next decade was to witness a bitter 'civil war' within the Home Rule movement. Such internecine feuding, together with the Conservatives' long ascendancy at Westminster (from 1895 to 1905) relegated Home Rule to the margins of British politics. Conservative attempts to undermine the Home Rule demand by a policy of 'kindness' in these years had little success, though Wyndham's Land Act (1903) marked a vast, bloodless revolution, peacefully transferring the land from landlord to tenant. With the Land Question satisfactorily resolved, the issue of national self-government, often equated in nationalist eyes with national independence, now moved up the political agenda.

The ending of Conservative rule coincided with the reunification of the antagonistic strands of constitutional nationalism under the chairmanship of John Redmond. Redmond, a Wexford barrister and ardent imperialist, believed passionately in the concept of 'Home Rule within the Empire.' "Let us", he declared early in his career, "have national freedom and imperial unity and strength." As such, he was strongly opposed to the separatist stirrings which marked the dawn of the new century. The Gaelic League, formed to revive Irish as a spoken language, had, from the 1890s, steadily promoted the idea of a separate Irish cultural nation. Of a similar stamp was Arthur Griffith's tiny Sinn Féin party, whose novel policy of an Anglo-Irish 'dual monarchy' even attracted some northern Protestants like the essayist Robert Lynd.

In the background, too, flickered the 'Fenian Flame' of the militant separatist Irish Republican Brotherhood which was being revived in Belfast after 1904 by two men, Bulmer Hobson, a County Down Quaker, and Denis McCullough, a Falls Road Catholic.[3] To Rev James Hannay, the Belfast-born rector of Westport (better known, perhaps, as the novelist, George A Birmingham), the Gaelic revival and the propaganda of non-violent Sinn Féin were sure signs of "an intellectual and moral awakening in Ireland".

The Irish Parliamentary Party, however, still commanded the allegiance of the mass of Irish Catholics. It was led in the north by the young Belfast barman turned journalist, 'Wee Joe' Devlin. Born in 1871 into a working-class family in Hamill Street, he rose to become a Home Rule MP and finally, in 1903, general secretary of the United Irish League (UIL), the main Home Rule organisation. For the next 30 years until his death in 1934, this 'pocket Demosthenes' dominated the nationalist scene by the sheer weight of his personality and consummate political intellect.

Devlin's revival of the sectarian Ancient Order of Hibernians (AOH) after 1905 has led to the somewhat distorted image of the Ulster Home Rule leader as a 'ghetto boss', assiduously cultivating an atavistic sectarian vote. But this view is unfair to a politician who did much to improve the lot of the Catholic and Protestant working classes of Belfast. His successful exposure of the sweated conditions in the city's linen mills led to the application of the Trade Boards Act to the industry after 1909, with a consequent improvement in working conditions. Yet he underestimated the extent to which his identification with the 'Hibs' reinforced Protestant fears of 'Rome Rule'.[4]

The Liberal landslide of 1905, and the subsequent constitutional crisis in Britain over the powers of the House of Lords, conspired by 1910 to force the Prime Minister, Herbert Asquith, back to the 1886 position of reliance on the votes of the Irish nationalists. One immediate result was the

Parliament Act of 1911 which finally removed the veto of power of the House of Lords. Nationalist Ireland confidently predicted that 1914 would be the 'Home Rule Year' and John Redmond would preside over an all-Ireland Parliament in Dublin's College Green.

But the two years between the introduction of the Third Home Rule Bill in 1912 and the outbreak of World War One were to see the emergence of determined Ulster Unionist resistance to the notion of an Irish Parliament. The Unionists were led by Edward Carson, a Dublin lawyer and compelling orator, and Captain James Craig, a Belfast stockbroker whose massive, blunt features seemed to personify "the very soul of Ulster intransigence". Carson's aim, however, was not to get special treatment for the north, but rather to maintain intact the Union of Britain and Ireland. He hoped to use the solid resistance of almost 800,000 Ulster Protestants as a weapon in this struggle, convinced – wrongly, as it turned out – that "Home Rule without Ulster would be impossible." Craig, his origins among the Orange grassroots of east Ulster, had long seen partition as a means of preserving the identity of "his own people". To this end he had been instrumental in setting up the Ulster Unionist Council in 1905 as a means of giving the northern movement a more regional and more militant focus.

From the outset, the unionist campaign was supported by powerful interests in British society, in the Conservative party – now led by Bonar Law, the Canadian-born son of an Ulster Presbyterian minister – in the army, the aristocracy, and big business. "There are things stronger than parliamentary majorities," declared Law darkly in 1912, underlining the extra-parliamentary nature of the unionist campaign.

The introduction of the Third Home Rule Bill, in April 1912, was accompanied by rising tension with sectarian outbreaks in Ulster at Castledawson, where Hibernians attacked a Sunday School procession, and in the Belfast shipyards where loyalist militants drove Catholics from their jobs. By January 1913, loyalist opposition had been galvanised into the Ulster Volunteer Force (UVF) while the leading Presbyterian journal, *The Witness,* asserted that resistance to Home Rule, even in arms, was "a sacred duty". At first Home Rulers dismissed the new force as 'Carson's Comic Circus', Devlin assuring the government that the threat from the UVF was "grotesquely exaggerated" and regarded by the northern Home Rulers "with absolute contempt".[5]

In January 1913, in a strategic move, Carson dropped his demand for the unbroken Union in favour of nine-county exclusion. As DW Miller puts it, from that moment the Ulster Unionists "would vote against Home Rule for Ireland until the end of time, but they would only fight for Ulster". Asquith and Lloyd George – never passionate Home Rulers in the Gladstonian mould – warned Redmond of the need for a compromise if serious bloodshed was to be averted.

The result was Lloyd George's 'county option' scheme of February 1914. The proposals allowed any Ulster county to opt out of Home Rule for a six-year period by means of a plebiscite. While nationalist Ireland endorsed the scheme as virtually guaranteeing Irish unity, Carson rejected it as "a sentence of death with a stay of execution for six years". For a brief moment the government considered a show of force against the Carsonites, but the Larne gun-running of April 1914, together with the 'Curragh Incident', which threw into question the loyalty of the army high command, destabilised an already weak Asquith cabinet. Military supremacy now lay with 'Carson's Army' of 90,000 armed recruits. This factor, more than any other, was to ensure that the British government would continue to pursue some form of exclusion or partition to deal with the Ulster problem.

The impact of the UVF was no less dramatic on Irish nationalism. As one historian observes, by challenging the authority of the sovereign Parliament at Westminster, and by reintroducing the gun as the final arbiter in Irish politics, "Carson rekindled the Fenian Flame".[6] The revolutionary Irish Republican Brotherhood, watching in the wings, was quick to take advantage of the situation and, by late 1913, had launched a nationalist counterweight in the shape of the Irish Volunteers, initially under Redmond's nominal control. The nationalist army's main concern was to ensure the implementation of all-Ireland Home Rule and by June 1914 it had swollen to some 170,000 men, a quarter of them concentrated in Ulster. The Buckingham Palace Conference in the last days of peace, in July 1914, failed to resolve the Ulster impasse, and in Churchill's colourful phrase, became bogged down in "the muddy byways of Fermanagh and Tyrone".

The outbreak of the Great War was marked by what the Royal Irish Constabulary termed "a mutual cessation of political strife" in Ireland as both Redmond and Carson pledged unequivocal support for Britain's war effort. As the storm clouds gathered, the Irish leader's success in forcing a reluctant Asquith to place the Home Rule Act on the statute book proved something of a hollow victory. Not only was its operation suspended for the duration of the war, but Asquith made it clear that any final settlement must include partition.

In a desperate effort to win British goodwill for the future, Redmond – ever the imperialist – was to make his greatest mistake in a speech at Woodenbridge, Co Wicklow, in September 1914 in urging Irishmen to enlist in the British army and "go wherever the firing-line extends". Redmond's speech misread the mood of nationalist opinion and split the Irish Volunteers. A small anti-war section – by far the most active militarily – broke away under Professor Eoin MacNeill, Antrim Glensman and Gaelic Leaguer. This section now passed into the hands of the IRB which was to use it as the strike force of the 1916 Rising.[7]

Thousands of Redmond's Volunteers joined the rush to the colours in the first years of the war and fought bravely alongside their former UVF adversaries on the battlefields of Europe. Amongst the Irish contingent were several thousand members of Devlin's National Volunteers from west Belfast. "We have succeeded in making national self-government the law of the land," Devlin assured them as they marched off to the front in November 1914. However, James Connolly, the Belfast-based leader of the Irish Citizen Army and a supporter of a separatist uprising, struck a discordant note in his paper, the *Worker's Republic*:

Full steam ahead, John Redmond said,
and everything is well chum.
Home Rule will come when we are dead
and buried out in Belgium.[8]

Redmond's political standing was further weakened by the formation of a coalition government in 1915, which included Carson and Bonar Law. Home Rule, it seemed to many nationalists, was now at the mercy of its most implacable foes. It required only the 'blood sacrifice' of the Easter Rising and the crop of martyrs it produced to seal the Home Rule Party's fate.

Pearse, MacDermott and the IRB inner circle had intended the Rising as a successful national revolt by the Volunteers and élite Citizen's Army. But, in the event, with the struggle narrowed to Dublin, the secret cadre of revolutionaries realised that they had no prospect of military success. However, they calculated that an armed stand – however futile – would almost certainly provoke the British into harsh reprisals; by their martyrdom they might convert Irish nationalists to the cause of an Irish republic.

The insurgents judged accurately. The Rising had at first engendered feelings of strong hostility. But its aftermath – internment, martial law, and above all, the execution of 16 of the leaders – worked a sea change in Irish public opinion. As one Redmondite observer wrote: "A few unknown men, shot in a barrack yard had embittered a whole nation."[9] Even in the north, where the Rising was confined to a brief mobilisation of Volunteers at Coalisland, nationalist opinion quickly swung from condemnation of the rebels to admiration for their cause. As the Tyrone county inspector of police noted, the executions "changed the whole feeling . . . the Sinn Féiners from being objects of contempt and derision becoming heroes".[10]

Ulster unionist opinion, on the other hand, was united in condemnation of the rebellion as a 'stab in the back' of the empire in its titanic crisis. For its part, the City of Derry Grand Orange Lodge passed a resolution of "abhorrence and detestation" of the events in Dublin while "deploring the loss of so many gallant soldiers".

In a desperate effort to retrieve the initiative, the Nationalist leaders allowed themselves to be stampeded in May 1916 into the disastrous Lloyd George scheme for six-county partition. The resourceful 'Welsh Wizard' led Redmond to understand that exclusion would be temporary, whilst giving Carson a written guarantee that it would be permanent. The proposals fell through, sabotaged by the southern Unionists in the cabinet, but not before the Home Rulers, and Devlin in particular, had become tarred by the brush of partition in the Irish Nationalist mind. The 'Black Friday' conference in St Mary's Hall, Belfast, which endorsed the Lloyd George scheme in June 1916, was to split northern nationalism irrevocably and paved the way for Sinn Féin in the north.[11]

By 1917, nationalist sentiment was crystallising around a new republican Sinn Féin party led by Eamon de Valera, the senior surviving commandant of the Rising, and dedicated to a policy of abstention from Westminster. In the north, however, the burning issue for Nationalists remained partition rather than 'Home Rule v Republic'. Many Ulster Catholics opposed the abstentionist tactic, arguing, with much force, that such a policy would make the "naked deformity of partition" more likely. This fear underlay the Home Rule victories over Sinn Féin in the South Armagh and East Tyrone by-elections in the spring of 1918.[12]

Redmond died in March 1918 as the Irish Convention, set up by Lloyd George to assuage American opinion, concluded its futile deliberations. The Convention was fatally damaged by the abstention of Sinn Féin and the adamant demand of Ulster unionism for partition, but the willingness of Lord Midleton's Southern Unionists to countenance Home Rule ensured their place in an independent Ireland after 1922.

British policy during the last months of the war and, in particular, the government's threat to impose conscription in April 1918, gave an immense impetus to Sinn Féin which was widely credited with having prevented this 'blood tax'. This was the background to the post-war general election of December 1918, the first test of the ballot box since 1910. Sinn Féin, pledged to an all-Ireland republic, swept 73 of the 105 Irish seats. The Home Rule Party was reduced to half a dozen seats in

Ulster – thanks to the 'green pact' with Sinn Féin brokered by the Roman Catholic Primate, Cardinal Logue.[13]

Carson and Craig, bent on a policy of partition for the north-east, now led the largest Irish grouping at Westminster with 26 seats, 23 of them in north-east Ulster. Carson's migration from his Trinity College bailiwick to Duncairn, a "slum constituency in Belfast", symbolised this new *realpolitik*. In the Falls Division, however, Joe Devlin defeated the Sinn Féin leader, de Valera, by a margin of almost three to one, though Ulster nationalists remained hopelessly divided between constitutionalism and Sinn Féin for the next decade.

The three years between the 1918 election and the Anglo-Irish Treaty of 1921 form a watershed in modern Irish history. In accordance with their election manifesto, the Sinn Féin MPs, meeting as Dail Eireann, set up an alternative government to that of Dublin Castle, with de Valera as President. But while the new cabinet achieved striking success in several areas, its hopes of raising the question of Irish self-determination at the Paris Peace Conference were soon dashed. As the peace strategy faded, an astute Devlin predicted "a fierce conflict between government and Sinn Féin".[14]

Indeed, that conflict slowly developed into an Anglo-Irish war between the Volunteers, re-styled as the Irish Republican Army (IRA), and the Royal Irish Constabulary (RIC), soon to be reinforced by the notorious counter-terror forces, the 'Black and Tans' and 'Auxiliaries'. A small war by international standards, the conflict was marked by acts of savagery on both sides. The IRA, confronted with vastly superior forces, waged a guerrilla war with the limited objective of wearing down Britain's will to remain in Ireland.

At Westminster, the return of a Tory-dominated coalition, headed by Lloyd George, ensured that partition would become a fixed idea of British policy. Sinn Féin's "blessed abstention" from Parliament – to borrow Churchill's phrase – meant that the balance of power now shifted from the Irish nationalists to the Ulster Unionists who held three junior ministries. Craig, as Parliamentary Secretary to the Ministry of Pensions was, therefore, well placed to influence the shape of the forthcoming Home Rule settlement.

The task of forming an Irish settlement posed thorny problems for a coalition whose members had held diametrically opposed views on Home Rule a mere five years previously. The Cabinet Committee which drew up the Partition Act in late 1919 was tempted to include the historic nine-county province in the new Northern Ireland. Liberals argued that the large Catholic population (43 per cent) might make Irish unity more probable. In the end, however, the Lloyd George cabinet gave way to Craig's pragmatic view that a six-county bloc would provide a more 'viable' area for permanent unionist control. The scattered unionists of Cavan, Monaghan and Donegal felt "betrayed and deserted" at this breach of the 1912 Covenant, but had to face the toils alone.[15]

The Government of Ireland Act (1920) – the Fourth Home Rule Act – divided Ireland into two areas, each having its own regional parliament and government with control over domestic affairs. At the same time, the measure seemed to envisage eventual Irish unity by providing "a bond of union" in the shape of a low level Council of Ireland. The Act represented a major triumph for Craig who had secured his six counties. In the words of his brother, Captain Charles Craig MP, the provision of a devolved parliament would place unionism "in a position of absolute security for the future". On the nationalist side, only Devlin, a solitary figure at Westminster, saw the dangers of the 'Partition Act'. He railed against it as portending both "permanent partition" and "permanent minority status" for northern Catholics. Not without justification, the West Belfast MP attacked the glaring lack of safeguards in the Act for the minority. Whereas the Southern Unionists were granted weighted representation in a Dublin Senate, the northern upper chamber was to be a mirror image of the Unionist-dominated House of Commons. The need for such checks and balances, he told the Commons, was underlined by the tragic sectarian bloodshed in north-east Ulster in the summer of 1920 against the backcloth of the Anglo-Irish war.[16]

The Dail responded to anti-Catholic violence with the 'Belfast boycott', directed against certain banks and businesses, but this tended only to reinforce the embryonic border.[17]

It was not until late 1922 that murder, arson and expulsion from homes ceased to be a daily occurrence in the new state. Over 450 people, the majority of them members of the nationalist community, died violently during 1920–22, while some 8,000 Catholic workers were expelled from their employment. In a reference to these events, Lloyd George was to admit to Churchill: "Our Ulster case is not a good one." The upsurge of violence had two important effects. First, it seemed to confirm nationalist fears of being subjected to the rule of a unionist majority in a separate state. Secondly, the mounting unrest led Lloyd George to endorse Craig's scheme for a new auxiliary police force, the Ulster Special Constabulary, formed in October 1920. The USC, drawn from the former UVF, largely ensured the establishment of the border in face of IRA resistance, but its sectarian ethos earned it the enduring hatred of the nationalist population.[18]

In May 1921, following elections in the six counties, the new Northern Ireland Parliament was established, with Sir James Craig as its first Prime Minister. "From that moment," wrote Churchill perceptively, "Ulster's position was unassailable." During this formative period Sinn Féin failed to produce a coherent strategy to avert partition. Irish unity came a poor second to national status in the revolutionary scheme of things. This was certainly the case during the Treaty negotiations of October–December 1921. Arthur Griffith and Michael Collins, the leaders of the Irish delegation, tried to secure the 'essential unity' of Ireland, but were forced in the end to settle for dominion status for the 26 counties. A Boundary Commission was to revise the disputed 1920 border. The prospect of the Commission and the belief that it would so reduce the north's territory as to produce Irish unity by contraction, largely explains why the Sinn Féin leaders signed the treaty of 6 December 1921.[19]

While Craig protested at what he saw as a perfidious breach of trust by London, the Treaty evoked grave misgivings among northern nationalists. Sinn Féin, declared HC O'Doherty, the Nationalist Mayor of Derry, to the Dail cabinet two days after the document was signed, "have given away what we have fought for for . . . 750 years . . . We will be ostracised on account of our creed".[20] Most nationalists supported the terms, however, in the hope that "essential Irish unity" might yet be achieved.

For the border nationalist majorities, Article 12 – the Boundary Clause – was to prove "a tangled web of ambiguity". The problem here was that while it referred to "the wishes of the inhabitants" – implying large-scale transfers of territory to the new Free State – this was countered by "economic and geographic conditions". In the case of south Down, the Commission chairman, Judge Richard Feetham, was to decide that Belfast's need for a water supply outweighed the demand of a clear nationalist majority. Four years later, in 1925, the much-vaunted Boundary Commission collapsed, leaving the Northern Ireland state intact and partition more deeply entrenched.[21]

The resulting Tripartite Agreement of 3 December 1925, by which the Free State government of WT Cosgrave formally recognised the 1920 border and agreed to the abolition of the Council of Ireland, in exchange for financial concessions, under Artlcle 5, came as a crushing blow to the border nationalists of Tyrone, Fermanagh, south Armagh and Derry city. This feeling was captured in the headlines of the *Ulster Herald* in Omagh on 12 December 1925: "Border Nationalists Deserted."

The supreme irony of the Home Rule crisis of 1912–21 was that the only part of Ireland to enjoy self-government was that area which had strenuously resisted it. But for the northern nationalists, the outworking of the Home Rule struggle brought an abiding sense of isolation and abandonment by both nationalist Ireland and the British government. Successive Unionist administrations after 1922 saw little need to assuage their political enemies, while, by the 1930s, the minority had virtually opted out of the state, forming a kind of state within a state, complete with its own social, cultural and educational infrastructure.

As proportional representation was swept away for local and Northern Ireland elections by 1929, and discrimination became institutionalised in the government and civil service in the early 1930s, a British Conservative peer, Lord Rankeillour, was unconvinced by Craigavon's rebuttal of nationalist grievances. "All the same", he told the Stormont Prime Minister in 1932, "I cannot think the position in Northern Ireland is a happy one." The minority, he felt, would "remain under a sense of inferiority . . . [realising] that they were more comfortable under Westminster".[22] The fact was that the minority problem remained unaddressed by both Westminster and Stormont until it imploded violently on the world's television screens in 1968. One effect of Westminster's belated intervention was the abrupt dissolution of Northern Ireland's unique 'Home Rule' experiment in March 1972.

Notes

1 Michael Hurst, *Parnell and Irish Nationalism*, London, 1968, pp 19–20; David Thornley, *Isaac Butt and Home Rule*, London, 1964, pp 379–83.
2 John Magee, 'The Monaghan Election of 1883 and the Invasion of Ulster', *Clogher Record*, v 8, 1974, pp 147–66; Patrick Buckland, *Ulster Unionism and the Origins of Northern Ireland 1886-1922*, Dublin, 1973, pp 5–19.
3 Denis Gwynn, *The Life of John Redmond*, London, 1932, p 52; FX Martin (ed), *Leaders and Men of the Easter Rising: Dublin 1916*, London, 1969, pp 95–101.
4 Eamon Phoenix, *Northern Nationalism: Nationalist Politics, Partition and the Catholic Minority in Northern Ireland 1890-1940*, Belfast, 1994, pp 2–6; AC Hepburn, *A Past Apart: Studies in the History of Catholic Belfast 1850-1950*, Belfast, 1996, pp 157–72.
5 RFG Holmes, 'Ulster will Fight and Ulster will be Right: the Protestant Churches and Ulster's Resistance to Home Rule', *Studies in Church History*, v 20, pp 321–35; Phoenix, op cit, pp 9–10.
6 Michael Laffan, *The Partition of Ireland 1911-1925*, Dublin Historical Association, 1983, pp 31–2.
7 Alvin Jackson, *Ireland 1798-1908*, Blackwell, 1999, pp 197–202.
8 *The Worker's Republic*, 8 April 1916.
9 M Laffan, 'The Unification of Sinn Féin', *Irish Historical Studies*, v 17, March 1971, p 353.
10 Phoenix, op cit, pp 19–21.
11 Ibid, pp 21–35.

12 Ibid, pp 46–7.
13 Ibid, pp 49–55.
14 Devlin to John Dillon, 15 May 1919, Trinity College, Dublin, Dillon papers, 6930/224.
15 Ronan Fanning, 'Anglo-Irish Relations: Partition and the British Dimension in Historical Perspective', *Irish Studies in International Affairs*, v 2, no 1, 1985, pp 10–13 (Royal Irish Academy).
16 Laffan, op cit, p 65; Phoenix, op cit, pp 76, 87–105.
17 Ibid, pp 91–2.
18 Michael Farrell, *Arming the Protestants: the Formation of the Ulster Special Constabulary and the Royal Ulster Constabulary, 1920–27*, Brandon, 1983, pp 30–54.
19 Phoenix, op cit, pp 150–3.
20 Minutes of Conference between a Northern nationalist delegation and the Dail Ministry, 7 December 1921, PRONI D2991/B2.
21 Phoenix, op cit, pp 288–336.
22 Rankeillour to Craigavon, 26 November 1932, Public Record Office of Northern Ireland, CAB 9B/205/1.

Dr Eamon Phoenix is Senior Lecturer in History at Stranmillis University College. A well-known broadcaster and journalist on historical and political issues, he is the author of several books on modern Irish history, including *Northern Nationalism: Nationalist Politics, Partition and the Catholic Minority in Northern Ireland 1890–1940* (Ulster Historical Foundation).

A Question of Degree? The Union, Unionism and the Belfast Agreement

Arthur Aughey

There was some truth in the claim that intellectual engagement once meant acknowledgement of the claim (even by resistance to it) that 'We are all Marxists now.' Perhaps it could be said with some justification of political life today that 'we are all Gladstonians again'. There is, though, a certain irony in why this should be so. If the Irish question dominated politics at the end of the nineteenth century, then the British question dominates it at the beginning of the twenty-first. The fate of Ulster unionism under the dispensation of the Belfast Agreement of 1998 is both intimately bound up with an answer to the British question and the Irish question. As at the end of the nineteenth century, so too now at the beginning of the twenty-first, Ulster unionism's relationship with this neo-Gladstonian project is as ambiguous as ever. How could it not be? Traditional fears of the consequences of Gladstonian principles remain as strong today as they did a century ago, despite the willingness of David Trimble to associate the Ulster Unionist Party with their contemporary expression.

New Britain?
The spirit of the Grand Old Man, in the form of the 'New' Labour government, has this time won the Home Rule argument. In this case, the forces of constitutional conservatism have experienced a defeat and the forces of constitutional liberalism have had their historical revenge. Reform of the structure of British governance has been undertaken which will affect radically the future of the Union. The familiar Gladstonian premise, which 'New' Labour professes to share, is that devolution of power to the nations of Britain is the best means to secure the unity of the United Kingdom. However, the question which tormented Gladstone's policy of Irish Home Rule, one might think, still looms large. It was neatly posed by the title of an article by a latter-day Gladstonian, Vernon Bogdanor: 'Devolution: Decentralisation or Disintegration?'[1] In the Panglossian world of 'New' Labour this has become something of a non-question. Devolution will both decentralise power and disintegrate an excessively integrated system of government. Both are positive. Disintegration of British politics does not mean dissolution of the Union.

What it now means is British de-nationalisation in the sense in which WL Miller understood it: "the opposite of uniformity and homogeneity".[2] That "opposite" is complex, but can be taken to mean an act of self-determination within the Union which does not entail (necessarily) a slide towards independent statehood outside the Union. This has been defined by a number of commentators.

"It is generally accepted," argued Archie Brown, "that nations living in their historic homelands have a right to self-rule if a majority of their citizens want it."[3] Brown's careful use of the term "self-rule" suggests an act of self-determination which falls short of the dissolution of the British Union. The subtle politics of the issue were expressed with equal subtlety in Neil McCormick's formulation:

> . . . the members of a nation are as such in principle entitled to effective organs of political self-government within the world order of sovereign or post-sovereign states; but these need not provide for self-government in the form of a sovereign state.[4]

This formulation is taken to be particularly apt in the British case, where it has been difficult to envisage a coherent or neat constitutional settlement.

For Blairite neo-Gladstonians, then, it has been a mistake to look for a simple, one-dimensional answer to the British – or multinational – question. What really mattered was an intelligent grasp of what the constituent nations wanted. Once that was known, the system should adapt accordingly. In the jargon of contemporary constitutional reformers, that perspective translated into the expression 'asymmetrical devolution', meaning that different degrees of self-rule within the Union were appropriate for Northern Ireland, Scotland, Wales and possibly even England, and that these degrees of self-determination were compatible with the security of the Union. As a slogan, argued Brown, asymmetrical devolution certainly lacked the resonance of 'Bread and Justice' in revolutionary Petrograd. But that had to be "the price of union – and a price well worth paying".[5] Asymmetrical devolution or a modern version of Home Rule all-round, of which the Belfast Agreement can be seen as a particular example, represents a distinctively British attempt to reconcile the potentially destructive ambiguities of change in a multinational Union. Indeed, Karl Mannheim once thought that Britain had "a peculiar genius for working out in practice the correlation of principles which seem to be logically opposed to each other".[6] Making a success of asymmetrical devolution is the sort of practical constitutional correlation of logical opposites which the Union needs to achieve today if it is to survive centrifugal nationalist enthusiasms. It is worthwhile tracing the genealogy of this particular British 'genius', for it helps us to understand the distinctive asymmetry of the Belfast Agreement which causes problems for Ulster unionism.

Old Britain

The character of asymmetrical devolution emerges from an ideological contrast between nationalism and Britishness. For nationalists constitutional logic is simple. The national people is the sovereign people. The nation, the natural unit of self-government, is only obliged to obey the law because its identity is reflected back to it by the personnel of its government (one's own kind) and by the purpose of state power (advancing the national interest). Any other order of things is logically incoherent. The origins of this idea lie in the French Revolution. As Ernest Barker once put it, France said to the Bourbons: "You are wrong in proclaiming, 'L'Etat c'est moi'; she said to herself, and she said to the world, henceforth we proclaim, 'L'Etat c'est la nation'."[7] This was revolutionary stuff. And despite all the attempts to provide a venerable identity for political nationalism, one has to look no further than the French Revolution for its central idea. Tom Nairn proposed "that a mobilizable nationalism is not only a matter of having common traditions, revered institutions, or a rich community of customs and reflexes". Nationalism is not a question of cultural identity. Rather, the "mobilizing myth of nationalism is an idea of the people".[8] Nairn thought that Britain lacked a coherent national identity precisely because it had not and, because of its archaic monarchism, could not absorb the republican ideal of popular sovereignty. Indeed, much of Britain's identity had developed in opposition to this European form of integral nationalism. Nairn was right, but rather like Evelyn Waugh's Lord Copper, only up to a point. The British Union proposed an alternative to the French idea of nationalism which was not merely its negative. Indeed, it was an alternative which, until recently, a broad intellectual consensus thought to be preferable to the Franco-European model.[9]

The key characteristics of this British alternative had been rehearsed in Lord Acton's famous article 'Nationality', published in 1862. In the *ancien regime*, argued Acton, the rights of nationalities were neither recognised by governments nor asserted by the people:

> Beginning by a protest against the dominion of race over race, its mildest and least developed form, it grew into a condemnation of every State that included different races, and finally became the complete and consistent theory, that the State and the nation must be co-extensive.[10]

In the history of national theory, two distinctive political forms emerged. First, there developed the "right of national unity which is a product of democracy". Second, there developed "that claim of national liberty which belongs to the theory of freedom".[11] For Acton, these two views of nationality were connected in name only and in reality stood opposed. They corresponded to the French and to the British systems respectively. The latter was distinguished from the former because:

> ... it tends to diversity and not to uniformity, to harmony and not to unity; because it aims not at arbitrary change, but at careful respect for the existing conditions of political life, and because it obeys the laws and the results of history, not the aspirations of an ideal future.[12]

This was Burkean constitutionalism, suspicious of popular politics, revised and re-applied to the theory of modern nationalism. For Acton, the co-existence of several nations in the same state indicated a more progressive idea of nationhood than the simple unity which was the ideal of modern nationalism. Coping with the challenge of nationalism was a test for all states, but Acton was convinced that it was a test which had been solved in Britain.[13] Dissenting, Gladstonian Liberals like Ernest Barker did not agree wholeheartedly with the conservative Catholic Acton. What they did agree on was the beneficence of a British 'solution' which eschewed nationalist excess and political uniformity.

In *National Character and the Factors in its Formation*, Barker argued that nationhood was not the physical fact of one blood. It was an effort of the imagination which had created a common tradition. And it was out of such a common tradition that one could speak of the British nation. While acknowledging the intellectual force of Acton's essay on nationality, Barker took issue with him on the character of the multinational state. This was, in effect, a surrogate criticism of the old Austro-Hungarian Empire for which Acton (and, later, Arthur Griffith) expressed some sympathy. He thought Acton's understanding was defective for a number of reasons. First, the sort of multinationalism with which he seemed content – the Hapsburg model – "either pits each nation against the rest to secure its own absolutism, or allows itself to become the organ of one of the nations for the suppression of the others".[14] Second, Acton had assumed that nationality existed in two different forms. First, there was nationality as only a social fact which revealed itself "in common thoughts and feelings, custom and dress, language and possibly literature". Second, there was nationality as a political as well as a social fact, where "it issues in a common organization, possessed of authority, which expresses a common and independent will". This was too neat. It showed its limitations clearly when applied to the British case. For Barker, democracy, which Acton treated with aristocratic disdain, had transformed the fate of British multinationalism. An autocratic state might have united under the single will of the monarch a number of nations that were required to remain in the first degree, that is as mere social groups. This was no longer possible in the era of popular politics. In stating his reason why this was so, Barker expressed the key notion of liberal unionism. A state which is multinational would fall apart into as many democracies as there are nationalities by the dynamic of popular will, unless there was a countervailing political will to secure the state. It was all a question of degree.

"There is a sense" Barker thought, "in which the Scottish and the Welsh peoples are nations of the first degree, content with the social expression of their quality." But this was only a half truth. The whole truth was what distinguished modern Britishness from other forms of multinationalism. "On the other hand, the members of these peoples are also members of a nation – the British nation – which is a nation of the second degree." The Scots and the Welsh would not be content with a social expression of their identity, he thought, if they did not possess a political expression of it in the British state. However, Barker also accepted that Scotland had some of the attributes of a state and if these attributes were less visible in Wales, they could not be said to be absent there either. He also accepted that it might be difficult for a nation like the Scots to remain satisfied with being a nation of the first degree if they were to become disenchanted with their experience of nationality in the second degree. If the Scots desired independent statehood they would have their way. Britishness was not about imposition. It was about consent and solidarity. Both, he thought, had indeed been achieved in the practices of the United Kingdom. Britain "can be both multi-national and a single nation, and teach its citizens at one and the same time to glory both in the name of Scotsmen or Welshmen or Englishmen and in the name of Britons".[15] All that is supposedly new in Blair's principles of constitutional reform had been stated by Barker 70 years ago.

Ulster Unionism

Barker made the case for the multinational Union with admirable clarity. It remains the only sustainable democratic case for the Union. But Barker could only do so by omitting Ireland altogether, just as Linda Colley was to do two generations later in her influential history *Britons*.[16] The reason for this is simple. Gladstonianism assumed the Irish question to be also a question of degree. After 1922, the Irish question no longer appeared to be a matter of degree (there was no half-way house). It appeared to be a matter of absolutes – either Union or separation. Ireland, nationalist and unionist, and for opposing reasons, was the absolute exception to the Liberal rule of degree. Historically, Ulster unionists felt that the rule could only be applied to Ireland insofar as their concerns were ignored or overridden. There, the benign principle of consent seemed to transform itself potentially into the principle of coercion, because their interests were excluded. Unionists were compelled to make the British multinational case for themselves. They are still compelled to do so. In the aftermath of the Home Rule crisis, Ulster unionists made their own rule the exception. Their crime in the Gladstonian scheme of things seemed to be one of loyalty. In sum, it was to demand absolutely the second degree of nationality (Britishness) at the expense of the first degree (Irishness).

Unionists have always defended the proposition that the Union had brought into existence a new multinational political (British) identity, which could not be decomposed into its component parts without the consent of all its citizens. In 1912, for instance, Thomas Sinclair argued that "a minority within the United Kingdom should not be measured by mere numbers alone". Rather, its place in the constitution was to be tested by "its association with the upbuilding of national character, by its fidelity to law and order, and by its sympathy with the world mission of the British Empire in the interests of civil and religious freedom". There was no doubt in Sinclair's mind that, albeit a minority in Ireland, Ulster unionists were an integral part of the British constitutional nation. "Tried by all these tests," he concluded, "Ulster is entitled to retain her full share in every privilege of the whole realm."[17] The simple demand was that unionists should not be deprived of the protection of British law and British citizenship for a dubious status within the Irish national people. This was especially so since they felt that the Irish people would not be content to glory to any degree in the name of Briton, but would wish to expunge absolutely all trace of Britishness.

In the violent press of these matters at the beginning of the twentieth century, it is arguable that unionists ignored or suppressed acknowledgement of nationality in the first degree (Irishness). This would be entirely justified criticism if it were not for the fact that the nationalist Ireland, emerging after 1918, never recognised unionist nationality in either the first or second degrees (their Britishness). The fate of the narrow ground of Northern Ireland was to experience the historic outworking of the contradiction of the Catholic national people – a people of the first degree – seeking to fulfil their historical destiny as a people of the second degree (in a 32-county Irish Republic) and the British Protestant constitutional people – a people of the second degree – who identified themselves fully with the continuity of the British nation. That contradiction has constituted the particular question which British governments have tried to answer since 1972. They have tried to answer it in a very British (liberal) way. In short, they have tried consistently to transform the Ulster question from a question of absolutes into a question of degree. The Belfast Agreement is yet another attempt to achieve the same transformation.

Transforming the Question?

The intellectual origins of the Belfast Agreement can be traced to the Downing Street Declaration of December 1993 in which the British and Irish governments set out the principles of any future settlement in Northern Ireland. In the Declaration, and to the consternation of many unionists, the British government seemed to concede the principle of popular sovereignty to the Irish 'people' by declaring that it would legislate for any agreement between the Irish people as a whole. However, by way of balance, it also confirmed the status of Northern Ireland's place within the Union. On the other hand, the Irish government, to the consternation of many republicans, seemed to concede the principle of constitutional sovereignty to the people of Northern Ireland. The historic character of the Irish state has been defined not only by the gap between, but also by the claim to remove the gap between, the ideal of popular sovereignty (all Ireland) and the reality of its constitutional sovereignty (the 26-county Irish Republic). However, the Irish government acknowledged that the British concession of the metaphysics of self-determination for the Irish people (as a whole) meant Dublin conceding the formal legitimacy of Northern Ireland's position within the United Kingdom on the basis of consent.

The wording of the Declaration was that:

> ... it is for the people of the island of Ireland alone, by agreement between the two parts respectively, to exercise their right of self-determination on the basis of consent, freely and concurrently given, North and South, to bring about a united Ireland, if that is their wish.

This obtuse formulation suggested that it was possible to conceive of Irish self-determination no longer as a divisive absolute, but as a question of degree. Northern Ireland would remain part of the Union because in that part of Ireland there was no consent for Irish unity. But Northern Ireland's place within the Union would also depend on political and cultural changes which would secure for it the consent of nationalists. This was a subtle, perhaps sophistical, reformulation of the question. However, the whole structure of the Belfast Agreement is built on the assumption that the institutionalisation of that reformulation can deliver a satisfactory answer in which intractable absolutes can become manageable degrees.

Mannheim would have appreciated the Agreement's attempt to correlate principles which seem to be logically opposed. There is a superficial commonality with the other devolved institutions in the United Kingdom. On the one hand, 'New' Labour's constitutional reform is a policy designed to reconcile a view of devolution which, in the ambiguous words of former Welsh Secretary Ron Davies, is a process and not an event with, on the other hand, a view of devolution which, in the words of former Labour leader John Smith, represents a "settled will" which can stabilise a modified Union. 'Third way constitutionalism' is defined by the promise that there can be a 'loserless ending' which satisfies the broadest possible range of opinion. Nowhere is this more hopefully stated, publicly at least, than in the case of the Belfast Agreement. It aims to translate both the historic objective of nationalism, to bring about the end of partition in Ireland, and the historic unionist ambition, to strengthen the Union of Great Britain and Northern Ireland, into a mutually acceptable political code. It assumes that politics can move from self-defeating certainty towards what has been felicitously called 'creative ambiguity'. It supposes acknowledgement of a common interest amongst those of whatever class and whatever religion who have a stake in peace, security and stability. Everyone, at least insofar as they subscribe to the principles of the Agreement, can be a winner.

Those sceptical of 'New' Labour's constitutional changes, just like those sceptical of Gladstone's over a century ago, think that it makes optimism (or deceit) the basis of British policy. The journalist John Lloyd shares that scepticism. The centre of the strategy, he thought, cannot hold and will collapse in Scotland and perhaps ultimately in Wales, to the advantage of nationalism, even though it is designed to defeat the nationalist threat.[18] He believed that this was an absolute certainty in Northern Ireland because there it was designed to accommodate the nationalist threat. That remains the view of those who understand the 'correlative principles' of the Agreement to be a big lie. Its complex arrangements, argue unionists opposed to the Agreement, are designed to conceal the betrayal of principle which has taken place. This view now appears to be held by a majority of the unionist electorate. How do we account for this?

The claim embodied in the Agreement is that it represents a "balanced accommodation" between unionism and nationalism in Northern Ireland.

That is a claim to political virtue and rationality. The history of Northern Ireland has conditioned unionists to be suspicious of that virtue and to be sceptical of that rationality. The origin of this traditional – and absolute – judgement has lain in this. Experience suggests that nationalists do not want a stable settlement. On the contrary, the unionist assumption has been that nationalists desire only a dispensation which will erode Northern Ireland's Britishness. A further assumption has been that nationalists can never accept the democratic legitimacy of Northern Ireland. They have never acknowledged the justice of partition or the right of unionists to exercise their own form of self-determination. For unionists, the obstacle to reason has always been the nationalist expectation that somehow the 'wrong' of partition will be rectified. This was the politics of absolutes in which there was no point trying to reach agreement with one's opponents. There can be no loserless endings. Something or someone has to give. The fatalistic tendency in unionist politics, summed up for so long in the demeanour of James (now Lord) Molyneaux, has always believed that that someone will be them.

In the referendum in May 1998, however, a very slight majority of the unionist electorate suppressed their suspicions and suspended their traditional fatalism for a contract with the future. More in hope than expectation they were prepared to accept the Agreement's charm of potential, that here was a way to end honourably the squalid violence of the last 30 years. Perhaps here at last was a chance to change the code of politics in Northern Ireland from absolute matters to ones of degree. Their relationship with the Agreement, then, like Gustav Streseman's description of the Weimar constitution, was an affair of reason, not of the heart. It had been an emotionally painful decision to accept and the Agreement had a whiff of appeasement about it. Nevertheless, an intellectual calculation of constitutional security was a crucial factor. It was that calculation which swung the balance in David Trimble's favour. The devolved Assembly could act as a counterweight to a Gladstonian officialdom seen as generally unsympathetic to unionist concerns. The referendum result, of course, was only the beginning of the battle for the hearts and minds of the unionist electorate. That battle would take place not on the ideal promise of the Agreement but on the practical implementation of the Agreement. In short, the real contest within unionism was this. The wager of David Trimble and his supporters was that in the course of the implementation of the Agreement the 'soft no' vote would come to see the advantages of political stability. They would come to understand that the Agreement really did lay the basis for genuine and mutually beneficial compromise which respected their identity. The calculation of Trimble's opponents, both within his party and outside it, was that the 'soft yes' vote would come to understand the implementation of the Agreement to be capitulation to a nationalist and republican agenda.

The implementation of the Agreement has witnessed a steady shift of 'soft yes' opinion into the anti-Trimble camp. One can point to a range of particular reasons for this: the failure of the IRA to decommission; the character of the Patten Report on police reform; the establishment of a Human Rights Commission without a unionist voice; the release of terrorist prisoners while paramilitary activity continues; the refusal of Sinn Féin to accept the flag of the state which it helps to govern. These are, however, particular manifestations of a larger concern. It is that the real 'process' is not balanced at all between Britishness and Irishness. Rather, it is a process intent on the replacement of Britishness by Irishness. The process sold to unionists was that their consent would be decisive. The Union, albeit a significantly reformed Union, would be 'safe'. This implied a process of normalisation within Northern Ireland as a part of the United Kingdom which would develop forms of cooperation with the Irish Republic consistent with that status. However, the trend of opinion within unionism has come to understand the 'process' of the Agreement to coincide with an iron law of appeasement moving inexorably towards the achievement of nationalist goals. In other words, what has influenced the migration of soft yes opinion is the sense that it is not the active consent of unionists in Northern Ireland which is being sought, but merely acquiescence in political arrangements which promote nationalist advantage. The major focus of this concern throughout has been the issue of police reform. The major lesson taken from the issue of police reform is that moderate nationalism will always coalesce around maximalist demands, even if that threatens the destruction of moderate unionism. There appears to be little evidence of nationalist absolutes becoming questions of degree. And that has encouraged unionists to re-assert their own form of absolutism.

Even David Trimble alluded to this in a speech to the British–Irish Association at Oxford in September 2000. He argued that Unionist opinion was becoming increasingly hostile to the assumption that the 'logic' of the Agreement meant accepting meekly whatever interpretation their opponents cared to put on it. This, he warned, was fostering a dangerous political alienation, for it appeared to discount unionist opinion altogether. It appeared to say, which the reported view of the Irish Foreign Minister Brian Cowen seemed to confirm: "We've allowed you the Union. But we're damned if we'll allow you to be British." This interpretation of events may appear rather self-serving as well as self-pitying. And there is some truth in that charge. There is a tendency for unionists only to see things changing and changing to their disadvantage. Rarely does attention focus on what stays the same to the discomfort of their opponents. However, there is an older political logic of at work. It is this. If you show a degree of cooperation you get taken for granted. If you show an absolute bloody-mindedness then the British government might just take notice.

Conclusion

Perhaps the (Northern) Irish question will always elude the assumptions of Gladstonianism, especially in its Barkerian formulation. In Great Britain constitutional issues can perhaps best be understood as questions of degree. Certainly, the relatively benign and accommodative multinationalism of the British state has encouraged a relaxed politics of identity. Despite the absurd claims of the Parekh Report, this remains the case.[19] What has been reasonably effective in sustaining the United Kingdom in Scotland and Wales – a dual sense of nationality – and in England – an absentminded confusion of Englishness with Britishness – has never worked in Northern Ireland. Ireland was the exception which always proved the British rule. Neo-Gladstonianism, the great hope of retaining the cohesion of the British state, may yet work in Edinburgh, Cardiff and London. In Belfast, accommodation of the sort prescribed in the Agreement has so far remained notable by its absence. The subtlety of a politics of degree has not yet displaced the simplicity of the politics of absolutes.

Notes

1 V Bogdanor, 'Devolution: Decentralisation or Disintegration?', *The Political Quarterly*, Vol 70, No 2, 1999, pp 185–94.
2 WL Miller, 'The De-nationalisation of British Politics: The Re-emergence of the Periphery', *West European Politics*, Vol 6, No 4, 1983, pp 103–29.
3 Archie Brown, 'Asymmetrical Devolution: The Scottish Case', *Political Quarterly*, Vol 69, No 3, 1998, pp 215–23.
4 Neil MacCormick, 'Liberalism, nationalism and the Post-sovereign State', *Political Studies*, Vol XLIV, 1996, pp 553–67.
5 Brown, ibid, p 222.
6 J Kent, 'William Temple, the Church of England and British national identity', in Weight, R, and Beach, A, (eds), *The Right To Belong: Citizenship and National Identity in Britain, 1930–1960*, IB Taurus, 1998, p 29.
7 Ernest Barker, *Essays on Government*, The Clarendon Press, 1945, p 53.
8 Tom Nairn, *The Break-Up of Britain: Crisis and Neo-Nationalism*, second edition, NLB, 1981, pp 294–5.
9 I Buruma, *Voltaire's Coconuts or Anglomania in Europe*, Weidenfeld and Nicholson, 1999; C Laborde, 'The Concept of the State in British and French

Political Thought', *Political Studies*, Vol 48, 2000, pp 540–57.
10 John Emerich Edward Acton, The History Of Freedom And Other Essays, Macmillan, 1909, p 385.
11 Ibid, p 288.
12 Ibid, p 289.
13 Ibid, p 296.
14 Ernest Barker, *National Character and The Factors In Its Formation*, Methuen, 1928, p 16.
15 Ibid, p 17.
16 Linda Colley, *Britons: Forging the Nation 1707–1837*, Pimlico, 1992.
17 Thomas Sinclair, 'The Position of Ulster', in Rosenbaum, S, (ed), *Against Home Rule*, The Kennikat Press, 1970, p 173.
18 J Lloyd, 'The new Tory federalists', *New Statesman*, 20 February 1998, pp 10–11.
19 Commission on the Future of Multi-Ethnic Britain (2000), *The Future of Multi-Ethnic Britain* (The Parekh Report), Profile Books, chapters 2–3.

Arthur Aughey is Senior Lecturer in Politics at the University of Ulster at Jordanstown. He is a member of the Northern Ireland Advisory Committee of the British Council and a patron of The Friends of the Union. He has written extensively on British politics and particularly on Northern Ireland. He has completed a study of Britishness to be published by Pluto Press in the summer of 2001.

Unionism among the Paramilitaries

Steve Bruce

Introduction

The first thing to note is that the politics of the Protestant paramilitary organisations have never been popular. The vast majority of unionist voters in Northern Ireland throughout the Troubles have continued to support the Ulster Unionist Party or the main alternative, Ian Paisley's Democratic Unionist Party. Various paramilitary forays into electoral politics have rarely had any impact; the main effect of the small parties associated with the Ulster Volunteer Force (UVF) and the Ulster Defence Association (UDA) has been to prevent right-wing unionist politicians plausibly threatening a violent response to political initiatives.

The Political Evolution of the UVF

When Augustus 'Gusty' Spence and a handful of Shankill Road loyalists formed the Belfast arm of the UVF in 1966, they were acting simply as ultra-unionists. Spence was active in the west Belfast branch of the Ulster Unionist Party (UUP) and the UVF's re-formation had been encouraged by a small number of disaffected unionists who were concerned about the security of the state. Spence was sentenced to life imprisonment in 1966 for a sectarian murder and was thus already in prison when the Troubles began in earnest in 1970.[1] Gradually his political thinking developed. He became critical of the Unionist Party and of the Stormont regime, partly because it was not willing to defend itself and partly because he felt that he and his men had been 'used'. Spence happily adopted the nationalist view that the Unionist party's tenure had been 'fifty years of misrule' and became almost socialist in his general views. He also came to advocate negotiations with nationalists. Though highly critical of the Provisional IRA, he accepted that Catholics had to be given some say in running the place and was one of the first loyalists to accept that Sinn Féin should be involved in talks: "If people are democratically and constitutionally elected then you have to take account of them, if you are a democrat. Sooner or later someone will have to talk to them."[2] Yet for all that, he remained committed to the Union with Great Britain.

In the 1970s few UVF men were much impressed by Spence's democratic socialism or his acceptance of Catholics in the Northern Ireland state. First, no-one joined the UVF for politics lessons. Second, except for his short period on the run in 1974, Spence was isolated from the organisation and the UVF's leadership was dominated by people who thought he had 'gone soft'. Third, UVF political thinking in the 1970s was naive and erratic. As a senior UVF man put it:

> We never had an overall goal. I never really knew what I was fighting for. If you was a journalist or that I might come out with some wee thing but I never really knew. A journalist would phone up and ask what we were thinking. We'd take down some book and take a few sentences out and jumble them up and give it to him as our policy.

In the summer of 1973 some UVF men promoted the short-lived Ulster Loyalist Front. This Shankill Road group had two local councillors and concentrated on the legal system. It wanted the return of jury trials and the release of internees. Prisoners were also a major concern of the next initiative: the Volunteer Political Party (VPP). Launched in the aftermath of the successful Ulster Workers' Council strike, on a mix of heady confidence from the strike and disillusionment with mainstream politicians, the VPP was a curious animal. It was created by men who thought the UVF should be doing something positive to complement its terrorism. It had a membership – all Volunteers were enrolled – but, as the *Combat* editorial announcing the party admitted, it had no policy:

> Another requirement is the formulation of a policy document which embraces all shades of opinion within the organization. In order to achieve this as quickly as possible we ask all interested personnel to submit to the Political Executive their proposals.[3]

One of those active in the VPP later admitted that it was not a real party: "It was about the prisons. What we wanted was to get attention for the prisoners, get conditions improved. That was my policy: the men in Long Kesh. That was really all." After fighting one election the VPP dissolved itself.

Spence's influence grew in the late 1970s when a coup left the UVF in the hands of people who had been close to him in the very early days. On his release in 1983, Spence began to work closely with Hughie Smyth, the sole elected councillor for the Progressive Unionist Party (PUP). When released, Billy Hutchinson also became active in the PUP, as did David Ervine. Both had been close to Spence in prison. Gradually the PUP began to develop a coherent and distinctive voice, which, taking the well-known distinction between ethnic and civic models of nationalism, we could call 'civic unionism'.[4] The PUP spokesmen were firmly opposed to the religio-ethnic unionism of Paisley's DUP (and the largest part of the UUP). They no longer talked of the 'rights of the Protestant people' but stressed the rights of equal citizenship. In 1985 the PUP issued *Sharing Responsibility*, which called for the protection of a bill of rights and a system of devolved government that ensured minority influence by mechanisms similar to those put in place 15 years later by the Belfast Agreement.

While they were still engaged in terrorism the UVF could not be a direct political force, but it could chivvy unionist politicians. In 1991 it persuaded the UDA to join a ceasefire for the duration of inconclusive inter-party talks. The following year, when other unionist bodies were dismissive of the Sinn Féin representative who offered what appeared to be a slight shift in position,[5] the UVF issued a statement hinting that an IRA ceasefire would bring a matching response.[6] When the IRA announcement came on 31 August 1994, many loyalists were reluctant to accept it at face-value, but six weeks later Spence announced an end to all hostilities.[7]

The Political Evolution of the UDA

In the summer of 1971 the leaders of the Shankill, Oldpark, Woodvale and East Belfast Defence Associations came together to form the Ulster Defence Association. Unlike the UVF, the UDA was legal and though many members wanted to defend by attack, there were also trade unionists and community leaders involved. Distinguishing 'hawks' from 'doves' is misleading. Many were both and the UDA's first electoral foray was promoted by Tommy Herron, the brigadier of the East Belfast UDA. Herron was a gangster whose men tortured and murdered Catholics, but he saw the importance of working class representation and he encouraged his colleagues to get involved in William Craig's Vanguard.

Herron failed to get elected to the 1973 Assembly (he got only half the first preference votes of Mrs Eileen Paisley in East Belfast), but another UDA man, Glenn Barr, became prominent in Vanguard. Barr was a Londonderry shop steward who had organised Protestant workers to keep their industries working during strikes called by Civil Rights leaders in the first years of unrest. The loose network of shop stewards and union activists was the framework for both the Derry UDA and the area's section of the Ulster Workers' Council. Barr became vice-chairman of Vanguard and chairman of the 1974 strike coordinating committee.

Barr was in favour of negotiated independence, but it was some time before he could persuade his paramilitary colleagues. He briefly left the UDA in 1975 when it refused to support Craig's proposal for a voluntary coalition with the SDLP. He was invited back in 1977 and formed the New Ulster Political Research Group (NUPRG). He made it sound very obvious:

We need to create a system of government, an identity and a nationality to which both sections of the community can aspire. We must look for the common denominator. The only common denominator that the Ulster people have, whether they be Catholic or Protestant, is that they are Ulstermen. And that is the basis from which we should build the new life for the Ulster people, a new identity for them. Awaken them to their own identity. That they are different. That they're not second-class Englishmen but first-class Ulstermen. And that's where my loyalty is.[8]

The independent government would have an elected president, who would chose an executive (preferably of academic and professional people) answerable to committees drawn from an elected legislature. There would be a detailed bill of rights and a judiciary responsible for safeguarding civil liberties.

In November 1978 the policy was published as *Beyond the Religious Divide* and immediately attracted favourable comments. One supporter was Paddy Devlin, one of the SDLP leaders closest to Barr's trade union background. The publication of the report was followed by a year of speaking engagements in the USA, Ireland, Holland and England, as well as innumerable gatherings in Northern Ireland. Although NUPRG won the admiration of many disinterested commentators, it failed to convert any of the major parties. When all was said and done, unionists wanted either full integration with Britain or a return to Stormont and nationalists wanted either a united Ireland or (as a temporary measure) institutionally guaranteed power-sharing in a devolved government.

Barr was savagely criticised by orthodox unionists, but he was also undermined by UDA colleagues. One brigadier objected to funding political work. Others resented his prominence. A few disliked the policy. One such was John McMichael. McMichael had risen through the ranks of the Lisburn Defence Association to become brigadier of South Belfast. Nominally McMichael was NUPRG secretary but he privately opposed Barr. He was especially critical of the Northern Ireland Negotiated Independence Association, a committee formed to connect the NUPRG to other pro-independence groups, because there were "too many Taigs" involved, and he did his best to kill any possibility of cross-divide support for the Association by trying to have it re-named the *Ulster* Negotiated Independence Association.

Barr quietly withdrew from the UDA and McMichael became political spokesman. The change in direction became clear in 1981 with the formation of the Ulster Loyalist Democratic Party (ULDP). As its name – "Ulster" and "Loyalist" – made clear, the new party represented a step back. In response to criticisms that the UDA was a 'Prod Sinn Féin', the ULDP offered a more limited independence within the United Kingdom. As McMichael explained it:

> We found that although people feel anti-Westminster and anti-English they still have a great affection for the monarchy. So it would be independence within the EEC and the Commonwealth, which we think would be acceptable to many Roman Catholics.[9]

The next phase in the UDA's political evolution followed the Anglo-Irish accord. Against a background of political protest, public disorder and sectarian assassination, the UDA in January 1987 published *Common Sense*. Following an unusually even-handed interpretation of how Northern Ireland had got into its parlous state, the document suggested a written constitution that could only be changed by a two-thirds majority in a referendum, a bill of rights and a Supreme Court to safeguard the freedom of the individual. That much was carried over from *Beyond the Religious Divide*. What was new was the clear deal offered to Catholics: they would be given power-sharing under a new name in return for a full commitment to supporting the Northern Ireland state. There would be no return to majority rule, but neither would there be the anathema of institutionalised power-sharing. Instead there would be proportionality at every stage of government.

As had been the case with *Beyond the Religious Divide*, the proposals were hailed in editorials as "brave" and ignored by unionists. McMichael's assassination a year after the report's publication froze the UDA's political activities and very few people noticed.

The departure of the 'Supreme Commander' Andy Tyrie, in March 1988, brought to an end the UDA that was more than just a terrorist organisation. In the next two years, all but one member of the ruling Inner Council was removed by police action or internal power struggles. Although the organisation re-stated its commitment to *Common Sense* (and tried to elevate John McMichael to martyred hero status), its energies shifted to murder. A revitalised UDA returned to a killing rate not seen since the early 1970s and, in August 1992, it was proscribed.

In 1989 the ULDP became the UDP, as the word 'Loyalist' was dropped, and it was briefly chaired by Ken Kerr. Like John McMichael, Kerr was a UDA brigadier and a member of the Inner Council, but his area was Derry, not a loyalist stronghold, and he was neither powerful nor popular. In May 1990 he was succeeded by Gary McMichael, the son of John, a young man who was not involved in the UDA. In 1993 Kerr lost his council seat but McMichael won one in Lisburn. Although Gary McMichael gradually became more articulate and competent, as he was thrust into the limelight, some in the UDA felt that their organisation was being over-shadowed by the PUP and approached Barr to see if he would return. When it became clear that the UDA would not return to its old independence policy, Barr declined to get involved.

Paramilitary Electoral Performance

Having examined in some detail the political thought of the UVF and UDA, we can review their electoral performance. The contrast with Sinn Féin is marked. Since Bobby Sands won a Westminster seat in 1981, Sinn Féin's percentage of the vote has grown steadily and it is now one of the four main parties in Northern Ireland. In 1997 it had 74 local councillors (compared with the 91 of the DUP or the 120 of the SDLP). In the 1998 elections to the Assembly, Sinn Féin won 18 seats, which entitled it to two ministries in the new executive.

Parties associated with the loyalist paramilitaries have not matched this performance. The two councillors of the United Loyalist Front were elected as independents. One of them, Hugh Smyth, was elected to the 1973 Assembly and then to the Convention, but again as an independent. Ken Gibson, the VPP candidate in 1974, failed to draw any significant number of votes away from the candidate sponsored by the alliance of the mainstream unionist parties. Smyth built himself a very strong base of personal support on the Shankill, but the PUP did not export well. Two candidates in the 1981 local elections polled in the low hundreds and one of them was eventually elected to Carrickfergus Borough Council in 1989, but that was the extent of the PUP's success until the ceasefires.

Although he was nominally a Vanguard candidate, everyone knew that Tommy Herron was a UDA boss. He and Tommy Lyttle failed to get elected to the 1973 Assembly when unknown candidates without paramilitary associations were elected. Barr was the only UDA man in either Assembly or Convention, but he was a Vanguard official and the least 'military' public figure in the UDA. He never contested an election under UDA or NUPRG colours.

The first open test of the popularity of UDA politics came in January 1981. A vacancy arose in Belfast City Council, and with only five months before the next scheduled elections, the DUP argued for filling it by nomination. The other parties decided to contest it but the Ulster Unionist withdrew, claiming to have been threatened. Sammy Millar of the UDA and NUPRG was elected on a very low turnout. When the full elections came around, the NUPRG tested the waters further by fielding two more candidates. Both lost. Three months later a well-known UDA man stood in an East Belfast by-election and lost to the UUP.

Despite this, John McMichael abandoned Barr's caution and, in February 1982, stood in the Westminster by-election caused by the murder of South Belfast MP Robert Bradford. The UUP's Martin Smyth won with 40 per cent of the vote. McMichael got just two per cent of the unionist vote in a constituency that included several thousand working class loyalists in the Roden Street, Sandy Row and Village areas. Many of them would have been members of the UDA.

The publication of *Common Sense* made no difference to the ULDP's political fortunes, and could hardly be expected to when the violent protests against the Anglo-Irish accord had undermined the UDA's claims to be taken seriously as a constitutional political force. However unionists felt about the accord, those who regularly voted were not going to support people who petrol-bombed the homes of police officers; those who liked the notion of burning out 'the SS RUC' did not vote. McMichael's idea of creating a new alliance of rural conservatives and working class Belfast loyalists in the Ulster Clubs got nowhere because there was no collapse in confidence in the major unionist parties.[10]

In the 1990s the UDP matched the PUP in that it had one local councillor; when Kerr lost his Derry seat, Gary McMichael won one in Lisburn. McMichael made his father's mistake of contesting a Westminster by-election, for the seat of Upper Bann. David Trimble won with 20,547 votes; McMichael got 600!

The 1994 ceasefires changed many aspects of the environment for the UDP and PUP. The first improvement in their fortunes owed everything to a generous election system. In May 1996 elections were held for a Forum and for places in the formal negotiations on the future of Northern Ireland that eventually led to the Belfast Agreement. Ninety members were to be elected from the Westminster constituencies but to ensure that the parties with paramilitary links were included in the process, these seats were to be augmented by 20 members, two each from the ten parties gaining the most votes province-wide. Neither the PUP nor UDP won enough votes for constituency seats, but their province-wide poll (respectively 3.5 and 2.2 per cent of the vote) was enough to give each two seats from the regional list.

In the Westminster elections of 1997 the PUP fielded candidates in three constituencies and the two best known – Billy Hutchinson in South Antrim and David Ervine in South Belfast – did well, taking 3,490 and 5,687 votes respectively. The third candidate, Willie Donaldson, took 1,751 votes in East Antrim. It is worth noting that, unlike Hutchinson and Ervine, Donaldson was not a former terrorist, but a well-known working class figure who had sat as an independent before joining the PUP. The UDP did not field any candidates.

The elections for the Assembly set up by the Belfast Agreement were more difficult for the small parties; there was no additional member top-up. The PUP won two seats. Ervine was elected third out of six candidates in East Belfast. Billy Hutchinson was elected in fourth place in North Belfast. The UDP did not win any seats.

The final election in this series was the European Parliament election in 1999. As usual Paisley topped the poll (28 per cent of the vote), with John Hume of the SDLP a close second and Jim Nicholson of the UUP taking the third seat. Sinn Féin came a close fourth. David Ervine of the PUP came fifth with 3.3 per cent of the vote (ahead of independent unionist Robert McCartney and the Alliance party).

We can summarise this record as follows. In contrast to Sinn Féin, the political parties associated with loyalist terrorism have been unpopular. Although sometimes lionised by middle-class commentators seeking signs of hope in unlikely places, they have made no significant inroads into the voter base of the UUP and DUP.[11] Until the 1998 Assembly elections, they were confined to the occasional success with electorates so small that well-known individuals could win irrespective of policies. With the brief exception of Kerr in Derry, those successes were confined to Belfast and its commuting environs of Lisburn and Newtownabbey. Before the ceasefires, the UDA's fronts fielded more candidates and did better than those of the UVF. After the ceasefires, although neither organisation made any great headway, the pattern was reversed. The PUP proved markedly more popular than the UDP: in the 1998 elections for the new Legislative Assembly, it won more than twice as many votes.

Loyalist Politics Post-Ceasefires

It is always difficult, in the absence of detailed survey data, to be sure why people support one party rather another. Hence what follows is inevitably speculative, but it is speculation based on over 20 years of close involvement with loyalism. What I hope to do is explain why loyalists have been relatively unsuccessful and why, in the case of the PUP, this changed somewhat after the ceasefires.

Product

The first point is obvious: it helps to have a distinctive agenda. Loyalists could not find political space by emulating Sinn Féin's relationship with the SDLP. Sinn Féin competes with the SDLP not just by wanting some different things, but also by wanting the same things more aggressively.

The Union

Though less easy to do now that it is in government, through the 1980s Sinn Féin was also able to attack the SDLP as the party that had sold out. The loyalist parties could not find political space by being more Orange than the UUP because that role had already been ably filled by the DUP.

The only possibility of successful loyalist intervention in a crowded field rested on finding something new and at the start of the Troubles there were only two conceivable political innovations: socialism and independence. Most of the paramilitaries I have interviewed have said something to the effect that, were there no border issue, they would be left-of-centre. Before the Troubles, the Northern Ireland Labour Party had four MPs at Stormont, all elected from Belfast (where the party gained almost as many votes as the Unionist Party) and all elected from areas where the paramilitaries recruited strongly. But once the constitutional issue had been raised again, socialism was not a plausible alternative. It was tarnished by association: some Catholics were socialists. It was also tarnished by its own principles: socialism promoted working class solidarity and a large part of the Belfast working class was Catholic. Anything even vaguely left-wing was thus vulnerable to unionists' assertions that socialism equals nationalism.

This left independence, but its problems were legion. There were misgivings about the economic viability of such a small country on the fringes of Europe; Gibson of the UVF made that point. But worse, there was no sign that the minority would be any more enthusiastic about an independent Ulster than it was about a British Ulster. That it was an innovation at all meant that it was suspect to the majority. For obvious reasons, unionism dreams of restoring the past. Things were very good when all of Ireland was British. Then they were good because Ulster was still British. As any future will be less unionist than the past, the most successful unionist politicians are those whose manner and style, as well as politics, are most obviously tied to the past. Even when it is presented as the last chance to hold on to the present, innovation is suspect because it is an admission that something must be given up.

Awareness that independence was not popular led the UDA to move back to a more conventional unionist position, but in so doing it came to compete with the DUP and the right-wing of the UUP. In contrast, the PUP, by taking seriously its own civic unionist rhetoric of *Sharing Responsibility*, has found empty space as, in the words of one activist, "the Alliance party for the proles". The PUP leaders are enthusiastic supporters of the Belfast Agreement. Though they are committed to the Union, they accept the rights of others to campaign against it, provided they do so by exclusively democratic means. At times during the lacklustre campaign for a 'Yes' vote in the referendum, they seemed like the only real supporters of the Agreement on the unionist side.

Given that, as of October 2000, unionist opinion seems to be running against the Agreement, this distinct position may prove a liability but it does give the PUP leaders a very clear line which they can pursue consistently.

Personnel

It seems paradoxical, but the PUP has prospered relative to the UDP by having its clearly more liberal political agenda presented by individuals with the more illiberal personal records. One of the most interesting consequences of the ceasefires (and of the period of negotiations leading up to them) is that they changed being a terrorist from a handicap into an advantage.

Sinn Féin has never been much handicapped by being associated with the IRA but the loyalist parties were. This can be traced back to the fundamental difference between pro- and anti-state terrorism.[12] Throughout the Troubles most unionists have continued to support their social institutions and the institutions of the state, and have been extremely critical of their paramilitaries, at best sometimes tolerated as a necessary evil. Loyalist paramilitary politics were most acceptable when presented by people least obviously involved in terrorism. During the 1970s, Barr and others in the UDA managed to be taken somewhat seriously by disguising their closeness to those responsible for terrorism and by stressing their links to more legitimate groups such as the Loyalist Association of Workers and Vanguard. When John McMichael became political leader, the mass media initially allowed him to pretend that he was marginal to the UDA's terror campaign. In contrast, the UVF's politics were clearly coming from people intimately involved in terrorism and were not even entertained by unionists.

The IRA gave UDA politics back to 'civilians' by murdering first John McMichael and then, shortly before it called its ceasefire, Ray Smallwoods (who had been convicted for the attempted murder of Bernadette McAliskey). As a result of those deaths and the sacking of Ken Kerr, the leadership of the UDP passed to Gary McMichael who had no terrorist involvement and had never been in the UDA. Only one member of the UDA's first negotiating team had any serious terrorist form: John White, who had been sentenced to a number of life sentences and had been in prison so long that his relations with the current UDA leadership (other than that of west Belfast) were at best distant.

In contrast, with the exception of Smyth, the leaders of the PUP were former UVF terrorists who had served long sentences for serious crimes (almost all were lifers) and held senior positions in the organisation. Spence had founded the UVF, commanded the prisoners in the Maze and served 18 years. Billy Mitchell had been on the Brigade Staff in the 1970s and was a lifer. Ervine had served ten years for explosives offences and had been the senior 'non-military' UVF man in east Belfast. Hutchinson was a lifer and a former officer commanding the Special Category prisoners in the Maze.

In brief, at the point where the loyalist paramilitary organisations were allowed to go public, the UVF's political arm was led by core former UVF men. The UDA's political wing was led by a civilian.

This gave the PUP men a number of distinct advantages over the UDP leadership. First, they became the darlings of the media and of liberal unionists because they were better able to challenge conservative unionists who fell into the old martial rhetoric to put up or shut up. That they could speak with the authority of men who had inflicted great damage on others and served long sentences 'for God and Ulster', and could do so in the deliberately coarse language of people who were at the sharp end of the Ulster conflict, played a considerable part in protecting the backs of Trimble and the liberal unionists. The PUP leaders could also respond authoritatively to right-wing unionists who objected to the inclusion of Sinn Féin in the talks process on the grounds that one should not 'talk to terrorists'. The DUP's stance was criticised from all sides. Paisley's involvement with the UVF and UDA in the 1974 strike, with the UDA in the 1977 strike, and his leadership of various organisations like the 'Third Force' was repeatedly brought up, but such criticisms had much greater force for the Protestant working class when they were made by former paramilitaries than when they were made by nationalists.

Their standing as serious terrorists also allowed the PUP leaders to win the confidence of the UVF far more convincingly than could the UDP with UDA members. In the run-up to the ceasefires, and since, they have had to face lengthy and acrimonious arguments with UVF men, but they went into those meetings with the status of serious 'players' who had 'done their bit' for the struggle. Many UVF men disagreed with them. After all, they were breaking a lot of unionist taboos. But their critics could not easily dismiss them as being of no account. Even their one failure worked to their advantage. Most of the UVF was persuaded to give peace a chance. Part of the Portadown UVF, led by Billy Wright, broke away to form the Loyalist Volunteer Force and was supported by a very small number of middle ranking UVF men in north Belfast. When the LVF committed sectarian murders, the PUP was able to speak for the 'responsible' UVF and create a clear distinction in the public mind between the good terrorists and the bad terrorists, a distinction that was reinforced by LVF attacks on leading UVF men who supported the PUP and by threats to Ervine and Hutchinson.

In contrast, the UDP has had greater difficulty asserting its authority over the UDA and persuading the UDA to control its members. Although the UDA acted firmly in 1994 to discipline the South Belfast brigadier who argued against the ceasefire (he briefly joined Billy Wright in the LVF before leaving Northern Ireland), it could not maintain control over its units, especially the west and north Belfast men loyal to Johnny Adair. Twice during the long talks process, UDA prisoners threatened to withdraw their support. There was well-supported speculation that UDA men were involved in a number of murders claimed by the LVF, and in January 1998 the UDP delegation had to withdraw from the talks before it would have been suspended. Although it was allowed back in late February, the suspicions remained. When Adair was released from prison in September 1999 he affirmed his support for the peace process but he also encouraged his men in sectarian attacks, made a pointed show of support for the Orange protesters at Drumcree, encouraged dissident loyalist groups and launched an attack on the UVF that led to him being returned to prison in August 2000.

The differences between public perceptions of the UVF and UDA should not be exaggerated. Very obviously most unionists despise all paramilitaries alike. The UVF has been linked to a number of murders since 1994, but none of these killings was obviously sanctioned by the UVF leadership. In contrast, between 1994 and 1999, the UDA was responsible for seven murders and is thought to have had a hand in some of the 16 murders committed by the LVF (including that of Portadown solicitor Rosemary Nelson). Especially after the LVF murdered Richard Jamieson, the UVF commander in Portadown, in January 2000, there was a clear perception in the minds of those at all sympathetic to loyalist politics that, while the UVF was doing its best to maintain its support for the peace process in the face of provocation from dissidents, the UDA was divided and ambiguous.

That they were former terrorists, who had the support of the core of their former colleagues, gave the PUP leaders an additional advantage that can be seen if we pursue the 'Alliance party for the proles' motif. In 1974 the Alliance party was the repository of the British government's (false, it turned out) hopes of building a moderate centre. That it was seen as the middle of the road party, in practice unionist but unwilling to take a principled stand on the border, made it unpopular with the Protestant working class and it remained a thoroughly middle class party. Twenty years later, and aided by a much-changed political climate (with apparently both the extreme unionist and the physical force republican options exhausted), the PUP managed to present similar policies but in a very different tone of voice. As the party led by people who used to kill for the Union, the PUP was able to emulate the success of right-wing Republican president Richard Nixon, who in the 1970s managed to open diplomatic relations with the Soviet Union and China when no Democratic party politician could have been seen compromising with communism. Rightwing unionist opposition to the Belfast Agreement has been based on the argument that, whatever the deal looks like on paper, the real deal is the sell-out of unionism. The PUP has been able to criticise this as a lack of confidence in the power of unionism, an admission of weakness, a mark of fear, and has presented its position as one of strength and faith in the Union. In the run up to the referendum on the Belfast Agreement, the PUP presented two facets. It was in favour of the accommodations but it was also still firm on the Union. One leaflet was entitled 'The Union is Secure' and it concluded: "A **YES** vote will affirm that **you wish to keep the Union secure** and maintain your British heritage and way of life. A **NO** vote will indicate that **you wish to leave the defence of your British heritage** to others". That Hutchinson could say: "If I have to die for my Britishness, I will die"[13] and be believed, allowed the PUP to present its liberal unionism as the policy of strong men who were the equals of republicans, not as weaklings bowing to an inevitable defeat.

Conclusion

This is a story about small differences. Although the involvement of the PUP and UDP was essential in helping London and Dublin shift the centre of the republican movement from the IRA to Sinn Féin, the loyalists are neither an essential nor a major part of unionist politics. Loyalists remain constrained by the dominance of the constitutional issue and by the UUP's greater claim to the left and the centre and by the DUP's better claim to the right on that issue. That most unionist voters continue to have faith in those expressions of the conflict within unionism about the extent of necessary compromise, means that they have little need to overcome their revulsion for those who commit vile crimes supposedly in support of the community that likes to contrast itself with the nationalists by claiming to be especially loyal and law-abiding. That, in August 2000, the UVF and UDA repeated the murderous feuding of 1974 will have done nothing for the electoral prospects of either the PUP or the UDP.

But the small difference is a revealing one. The choreography of the peace process requires that recent history be divided into two clear periods: before and after 1994. In the 'before' period, when terrorists were terrorists, the loyalist politicians who were most successful were those who were seen as most marginal to the terror organisations. In the 'after' period, what had previously been a stigma became a considerable asset. Because they had the stronger ties to their former terrorist colleagues, the PUP was better able than the UDP to convince voters that it represented the end of terrorism (or at least the hope of the end of terrorism).

Notes

1 Spence's UVF were responsible for three killings (John Patrick Scullion, Peter Ward, and Matilda Gould) in 1966. See cases 1–3 in David McKittrick, Seamus Kelters, Brian Feeney and Chris Thornton, *Lost Lives: The Stories of Men and Women who Died as a Result of the Northern Ireland troubles*, Mainstream 1999.
2 *Shankill Bulletin*, 31 May 1985: 6.
3 *Combat* 1 (14) 1974: 1.
4 Arthur Aughey, *Under Siege: Ulster Unionism and the Anglo-Irish Agreement*, Blackstaff Press, 1989.
5 Paul Bew and Gordon Gillespie, *Northern Ireland: A Chronology 1968–93*, Gill and Macmillan, 1993, p 266.
6 *Irish News*, 27 June 1992.
7 Paul Bew and Gordon Gillespie, *The Northern Ireland Peace Process 1993-1996: A Chronology*, Gill and Macmillan, 1996, p 72.
8 Padraig O'Malley, *The Uncivil Wars: Ireland Today*, Blackstaff Press, 1983, p 319.
9 Ibid, note 9, p 333.
10 A sad footnote that tells us a lot about the extravagant fantasies that surrounded loyalists paramilitaries: this failed attempt to create a new movement seems to have been the grain of sand on which the Ulster Independence Movement activist Jim Sands fabricated his pearl of an extensive murder conspiracy that Sean McPhilemy promoted in his film and book *The Committee*. For a critical commentary see Steve Bruce, 'Loyalist Assassinations and Police Collusion in Northern Ireland: An Extended critique of Sean McPhilemy's The Committee, *Studies in Conflict and Terrorism 23* (January 2000) pp 61-80.
11 We might go further and note that unionist politics in the Stormont days always had space for one or two maverick independent working class unionists. To date only the European election result shows any sign of the PUP making any greater dent in unionist voting patterns.
12 Steve Bruce, *The Red Hand: Protestant Paramilitaries in Northern Ireland*, Oxford University Press, 1992.
13 *Irish News*, 17 February 1999.

Steve Bruce is Professor of Sociology at the University of Aberdeen and is a noted authority on loyalist politics and paramilitarism. His publications include *The Red Hand: Protestant Paramilitaries in Northern Ireland* and *The Edge of the Union*.

The Union: A Republican Perspective

Danny Morrison

The icon that has always summed up the Union for me is the Union Jack, a foreign flag that usually caused a shudder of fear, unease or alienation. Of course, the Union cannot be summed up as simply as that, as if a flag were all it was. The fact is that the link with Britain has been detrimental for nationalists and, I would argue, has not generally made unionist people any more secure or happy either.

I was born in 17 Corby Way, Andersonstown, in 1953 into a two-bedroom Housing Trust dwelling. But we moved to No 2 Corby Way, which had three bedrooms, just before my mother gave birth to Susan, her third child. My father was a painter at the shipyard, taking as much overtime as possible. When he was laid-off he had to go to work in England for months on end.

In our new house I now had my own bedroom, whose window had a view of south Belfast. On the 'Twelfth' I could see the tents pitched at Finaghy Road, but as far as I know no Protestants lived in our area. Nor can I recall ever seeing the RUC on patrol in Andersonstown, though the barracks – a two-storey building with a little gravel courtyard, with a flagpole flying the Union Jack through the four seasons – sat unmolested at the junction of the Glen Road and Andersonstown Road, doing little trade.

My mother's parents came from the Dromore area of County Down. They were married in 1905 and moved to Belfast where they had a shop around the Newtownards Road area, before moving to the Grosvenor Road in west Belfast. The Grosvenor was then a mixed working-class area that had experienced serious civil strife towards the end of the nineteenth century and also at the time of partition, though it would be many years before I learnt the history of my parents' families.

My maternal grandmother's birthplace, a small cottage in the townland of Islanderry, was available as a holiday home during the summer, and we got eggs and milk from a farmer, Geordie Dempster – probably the first Protestant I ever met. He had two sisters, Aggie and Maggie, whose eccentric ways frightened me. I can't recall exactly of whom I asked what was the difference between Catholics and Protestants, but the answer left me none-the-wiser: "Protestants use contraceptives and get divorced, and we Catholics don't." Whatever contraceptives were!

My mother's eldest sister, May, married late in life to Hugh Downey, also from Dromore, though he had moved to Belfast where he worked as a barman and a trade unionist. I was too young to know him other than as an ailing old man, but he had also been a Labour MP in Stormont, representing the Docks area during World War Two and I think the family were proud of that. When I was on the run in the 1970s I stayed in my Aunty May's. In her living room was a glass cabinet full of hard-back *Hansard* reports from the time Hugh served in Parliament.

His was the first corpse I had ever seen. My mate, Seamy Lavery, begged to come to the wake with me because, as he put it, "I've never seen a dead Mister before."

Around 1943 my Uncle Harry, who was in the IRA and on the run, had asked my Uncle Hugh if he could give some publicity to the prisoners in Crumlin Road Jail, who were being ill-treated. Hugh persuaded Jack Beattie, a Protestant, to read out the communication in Stormont. As a result of this, the next election in Hugh's constituency, which was a mixed one, was fairly bitter and Hugh lost his seat. I remember, not many years ago, Sam McAughtry writing somewhere of how as a young man, working in the cause of *true* Labour, he had helped defeat Hugh Downey, and I felt annoyed, even then, after 50 years!

In 1961 or 1962 there was a headline in the *Irish News* about the IRA – possibly its announcement about the end of the border campaign. I have absolutely no idea from where I picked up the following guiding piece of information – possibly from eavesdropping or innuendo – but I pointed to the headline and proudly announced to my friend Brendan, "My Uncle Harry's in the IRA!" My mother pulled me backwards by the shoulder of my jumper at high speed into the scullery, shook me several times and warned me never to say that again.

Again, it was only later that I learnt the full story about her brother Harry: how he had been arrested by the RUC in 1946 and illegally handed over to the Gardai at a border checkpoint; and was charged, convicted and sentenced to death for the killing of two special branch officers (for which a co-accused had already been hanged). An international campaign appealing for clemency was launched and his barrister, Sean McBride, by good fortune, was elected to Leinster House as part of a coalition government which then introduced an amnesty for political prisoners – including Harry.

My association with Dublin probably also came about because of Harry. That is where he decided to stay after his release from Portlaoise Prison. He and his wife Kathleen settled there in the mid-1950s. Kathleen was from Kerry and each summer, for a few weeks, she, Harry and their kids

The Union

went to visit Kathleen's parents. They left us their house in Santry, close to the airport. It was whilst driving to Dublin and being stopped along with other cars, and behind trucks and goods vehicles, and having to produce papers at Killeen, and being asked if we had any jewellry, spirits or cigarettes to declare, that I became aware of a physical phenomenon called 'the border'. I heard of 'the border' before I heard of 'the Union'. My Uncle Seamus, who drove us, would curse under his breath and we kids in the back would always be nervous.

Dublin was the capital of Ireland. I saw the filled-in bullet holes in the GPO where the 1916 Rising was declared. We walked the streets and visited the usual tourist sights. Dublin was associated with a sort of freedom, though my Uncle Harry, in fits of pique, would still curse Fianna Fáil and the Gardai, behaviour I found inexplicable, given that he chose to live here. In 1966 I was part of a school drama group which made it to the finals in a competition in the Gaiety Theatre. In the minibus going down I learnt rebel songs from my mates, while only having a small understanding of what it was all about. These experiences helped form my attitudes and inchoate value system, until I matured and had a more objective basis for my political convictions.

At home we listened to the Home Service more than Radio Eireann (still marked Radio Athlone on our wireless). RTE was difficult to receive without an expensive outdoor television aerial, and so it was that we had a weird relationship of dependency on and aloofness from things British. There was a deep irony in our situation: for example, my father and other fathers had to go to England, not down south, to find work, and many unemployed young people joined the British army (later, after 1969, bringing their skills into the IRA). We liked and could identify with *Coronation Street* and the Beatles; we disliked the monarchy. We disliked the British army, but went to the pictures six times in a row to see *The Great Escape*. Other neighbours had a much greater sense of and pride in their Irishness – the GAA, the Irish language movement, etc – but I think they were in the minority and that the majority of people just felt a sullen sense of defeat because of partition, or were fatalistic in their attitudes.

Later, I read that the reform of the education system by the post-war Labour government created the opportunity for working-class Catholics in the north to avail of free third-level education, and that it was these individuals who were responsible for enlightened Catholic thinking and, later, for the founding of the Civil Rights movement. I think that is too simplistic.

In 1963 we moved from Andersonstown to a street off the Falls Road. Our area was called Iveagh or Broadway, and still contained a scattering of Protestant families, some of whom, including the Stephenson boys, I ran around with. On the Falls Road was Broadway Presbyterian Church which had a large congregation for two services each Sunday. Up until 12 July 1965 the area around the church was decked in red, white and blue bunting, and the Orangemen marched from the Donegall Road on to the Falls. We stood and watched while they played 'God Save the Queen'.

If I were to attribute my political awakening to a single incident it would have to be the time that Ian Paisley threatened to come onto the Falls and remove the Tricolour from the window of the Sinn Féin office, if the RUC did not do so first. It was September 1964, the month of the general election which brought Harold Wilson's Labour government to power. I was 11 and had just begun secondary school, which meant I had to get a bus from the Falls to Andersonstown. I couldn't understand what was going on. An older school friend told me stories about Paisley that made my hair stand on end. I was terrified of him.

The RUC, using sledge hammers, smashed their way into the Sinn Féin office and seized the Tricolour. Another flag was put in its place, leading to another RUC raid, which sparked riots that lasted for several days. We couldn't get to school because the buses were withdrawn. Some of the older boys from school had been arrested and were charged with riotous behaviour. But the outrage and grievance was obviously restricted to a small area, because the Sinn Féin candidate in that election actually lost his deposit and James Kilfedder, an Ulster Unionist, was elected as MP for West Belfast.

The incident blew over, but from then onwards Ian Paisley never seemed to be out of the news. He was a bogey man. He saw a threat when none was there.

The IRA had decisively lost the 1956–62 border campaign, and while republicans were respected in the areas they lived, no one saw them as delivering the promised land. It had all been tried before and had ended in defeat. Unionism was solid. People tried to get on with their lives, but, it seemed, they weren't even allowed to do that. No one was trying to overthrow the Union and it was a huge surprise to Catholics to learn that they were working to Rome's agenda to overthrow the Protestant faith.

From the mid-1950s in the USA the Civil Rights movement had began making inroads on behalf of American blacks. I don't know who thought of borrowing the idea. But I remember 5 October 1968 like it was yesterday: BBC television lifting the footage caught by the lone RTE cameraman covering the banned Duke Street march that day; and the photographs on the front of the *Sunday Press* showing a massive crowd, baton charges and water-cannons.

The Union

My diary for that week reads:

Derry civil rights march today. Gerry Fitt got hurt. No. 1, Mary Hopkin, 'Those Were The Days'. Fighting broke out in Derry today [Sunday] again. Police were appalling during the fighting. Four petrol bombs were thrown at police . . . Arkle is not to race again . . . Phoned up for a job in the 'Irish News'. Already taken. The cabinet support police action in Derry . . . Queen's University students march today. Also, Paisley in Shaftsbury [sic] Square. Last nite [sic] a petrol bomb was thrown at Protestant church on the top of the road. No clash between Paisley and students today.
[17th November] Marching in Derry. fighting broke out.
[And it continues: 2 January 1969] Peoples Democracy march set out for Derry. Major Bunting was waiting for them and there was some fighting . . .
[4 January] Fighting in Derry. 89 injured. Mass fighting. Bunting's car was burned.[1]

And so, at the age of 15 or 16, I became a news junkie. I went to the Falls Library and learnt what disenfranchisement meant. I discovered that the word 'gerrymander' was derived from Elbridge Gerry, a governor of Massachusetts, who in 1812 redrew the boundaries of electoral districts in such a way as to give one political party undue advantage over others (as the Ulster Unionists were doing in Derry), in order to preserve control. One district in Essex County, Massachusetts, looked like the shape of a salamander, which inspired a journalist to coin the name gerrymander to describe the practice.

When Prime Minister Terence O'Neill made his famous speech about "Ulster at the crossroads", we watched it on television as we ate dinner and held our breaths. I knew it was fairly momentous. My da made my younger sister keep quiet. I had become more and more interested in news and current affairs – the student uprising across Europe, the anti-Vietnam War protests – but I had a good measure of my own ignorance and rarely put forward an opinion.

I was studying for my O' levels and worked several nights a week in the International Hotel as a waiter. City councillors used to drink here and I remember being astonished one night to see Gerry Fitt, who was still our hero, drinking in the bar and having a laugh with a unionist whom he had been fighting with just hours earlier on television. I also went to weight-lifting with an older friend from the next street, Martin Taylor. He had been at the marches and told me about the atmosphere and the fighting and what it was all about. (In 1972 Martin was interned on the prison ship *Maidstone*, but escaped by swimming across Belfast Lough with six others.)

Back in 1969 the Shankill and the Falls were connected by a score of side streets, buses traversed both roads, people from the Falls shopped on the Shankill, I played squash in a hall on the Woodvale Road and I had a sister who worked in the Co-op on the Shankill. But people from either community still had a major problem overcoming their suspicions and distrust.

I had wanted to be an electronics engineer and fell in with a group of hams who built valve transmitters from cannibalised radios. We used to go on the air on the medium waveband close to Radio Ulster's frequency when it closed down at midnight. Slowly, we got to know each other and met up. And that's how I ended up having Protestant friends from the Shankill and Tiger's Bay.

I wrote about this for *The Observer*, and about the thoughts I had at the time when visiting 'Buttons' and Johnny Doak:

> Our Protestant friends and us can talk about everything under the sun but politics or religion . . . I would love to know what they really think of Paisley (what if they think he is wonderful?) or our side's demand for civil rights (what if they think we are troublemakers, rocking the boat?). What do they think of the outbursts of rioting – which could be nothing but could be something. Does Johnny really love the Queen?
> When we visit on Sunday nights Johnny puts on the Dave Allen Show. This could be a good sign – his liking a successful Irish man from the Free State – or ominous: Allen specialises in jokes aimed at the Catholic clergy.[2]

When the Troubles broke out definitively, in August 1969, I gave my transmitter to the republicans who were getting organised and armed behind the barricades. My transmitter was one of those used to broadcast Radio Free Belfast from rooms above the Long Bar in Leeson Street, which was owned at that time by Paddy Lenaghan, father of Mary McAleese who went on to become the President of Ireland. A few days later a pirate station came on the air based in the Shankill Road, from which we were now permanently separated by barricades. I recognised the signal as Johnny's and I never saw him again. He died about ten years ago.

For my generation August 1969 changed everything. We had taken to the streets to protest at the 'Battle of the Bogside' and the mobilisation of the B-Specials, whom it was feared would take over in Derry from the exhausted RUC. The Stormont government's perception of that week and ours was the difference between night and day. Their intelligence, indicating that the protests were part of an uprising, was so, terribly wrong. In fact, looking back, one of the major problems has always been this failure to understand, empathise, communicate. The conflict was fuelled by rumour-upon-rumour.

It was obvious that there was going to be an IRA split because of the lack of defence of nationalist areas by the leadership of the time, which had placed all its eggs in one basket – the reform of the northern state. The 'Official' republicans said that they wanted to unite the Protestant and Catholic working classes, which was an attractive idea were it not for the fact that it was working-class people from the Shankill, the RUC and the B-Specials who were burning us out.

I was attracted to the traditionalists (the 'Provisionals') with their simple, fundamentalist message that the state of Northern Ireland was irreformable. Protestants and Catholics had been deliberately kept divided. The republican analysis was that the Union, and British backing for the Union, was the problem. Working-class unionists couldn't help themselves. Of course this was a patronising attitude, but it was a convenient one because it meant baulking at other possible (and unpalatable) conclusions: namely, that unionists were really born-and-bred bigots and there could be no meeting point between us; or, that there was some legitimacy to their resistance to Home Rule and, furthermore, the passage of time conferred a degree of recognition of their sensibilities and aspirations. But in those early days I was beguiled by the quasi-Marxist notion that we could actually liberate the unionist people by sapping the will of Britain and its commitment to the Union by forcing the British government to negotiate a phased troop withdrawal.

And when we united Ireland the Irish people wouldn't be so stupid to discriminate against 'former unionists', the way Stormont had treated us! Hadn't Presbyterians established the United Irishmen, been among the first internationalists and fought and died for freedom, liberty and equality! Yes, the Brits were to blame for everything, and when the Brits were forced out the unionists would throw in their lot with the Irish people.

Of course this facile analysis didn't cover all contingencies, especially the human emotions that the conflict engendered, when people take up sides and get into trenches and see only the trench opposite and all who occupy it, and those in the hinterland beyond, as being 'the problem'. And when people lose their lives, causes become fundamentalist.

History is personal. I was now a 17-year-old republican, secretly selling *Republican News* from underneath my coat. Ted Heath became Prime Minister in June 1970, a natural ally to the unionists. Within weeks the British army imposed a curfew, searching for arms that had never been used against them. Those three days, the deaths, the house-wreckings, shifted many attitudes. Nationalists curfewed in their homes felt humiliated when two unionist MPs toured the subjugated area from the back of an open British army jeep.

It was extremely difficult trying to study when the political situation was deteriorating all the time. The IRA now felt it had the context and enough support to launch something of an armed struggle. It was probably amazed at how a dynamic came into play; how the organisation could regenerate itself after every loss; at the magnitude of its impact on the political situation; how it adapted to a propaganda war; how it adapted morally. It is extremely difficult, even now, to separate what drove me emotionally from what was reasoned.

One see-sawed between incidents, between bad IRA bombings and British army excesses, both of which involved the loss of civilian life.

In July 1971 the north's Prime Minister, Brian Faulkner, offered to the SDLP (then in opposition) the chairs or vice-chairs of various committees. Paddy Devlin described it as Brian Faulkner's "finest hour", but shortly afterwards the British army shot dead two civilians in Derry and the SDLP withdrew from Stormont. Years later, Gerry Fitt and Paddy Devlin were to turn on the SDLP because it was allegedly too green or nationalist, but, in truth, it was Fitt and Devlin in poor election showings who were subsequently to be seen to be out of touch with grassroots' opinion.

It was said that force could achieve nothing, yet within a year the SDLP and the Dublin government at Sunningdale were able to argue for a power-sharing administration and a council of Ireland. Clearly, the IRA campaign had, at a terrible price, nonetheless strengthened the negotiating hand of Irish nationalists.

Brian Faulkner and his supporters had recognised that nationalists could no longer be ignored; but the reaction from within unionism generally to the Agreement of 1973 is one that has been replicated time and again, whenever major reform or power-sharing comes on the agenda, and is the basic flaw at the heart of unionism. Firstly, Faulkner was opposed internally and his party split, with the Ulster Unionist Council rejecting Sunningdale by 427 to 374 votes. Then, when he formed a new party, his former colleagues in the Official Unionist Party supported the overthrow of the power-sharing executive by the Ulster Workers' Council strike. They had no compunction about associating with loyalist paramilitaries or supporting the setting-up of illegal roadblocks to enforce the strike. Sir Edward Carson had made a good mentor.

When Ireland was a unitary state, albeit within the British Empire, the unionist ascendancy had no problem with the concept of a united Ireland – provided they controlled it. Unionist opposition to the extension of the franchise to the nationalist majority speaks for their attitude towards democracy. Their reaction to the prospects of Home Rule was to foster sectarian divisions and fear, and to set up an illegal paramilitary army and threaten civil war. Sir Edward Carson in 1912 pledged to fight England in order to remain a part of England.

It is undeniable that unionists viewed the Union on their terms only and were prepared to challenge the will of the majority of British people as expressed at Westminster. The exclusion of Cavan, Monaghan and Donegal by the Ulster Unionist Council was a major mistake, because it meant that from the outset the Northern Ireland state was based on a sectarian headcount. Maintaining that dominant position became a preoccupation of Stormont government policy – the "Protestant Parliament for a Protestant People" syndrome – and informed attitudes towards the franchise; public housing; investment; the location of industry; the role of the RUC and the Orange Order; and Stormont's relations with the nationalist community, the Catholic Church and the government in Dublin.

How legitimate were the fears of unionists that Home Rule meant Rome Rule, or that the natives would take revenge for the plantation, for centuries of discrimination and oppression? Given the limitations in the Home Rule proposals, unionists would have been fairly secure and still been a major influence in political and civic life. And still in the Union. And nationalist grievances would have been fairly palliated. Has the Union, since partition, alleviated unionist insecurities or made them feel safer? Was the state of 'Northern Ireland' with its Protestant Parliament for a Protestant People one to be proud of? It always made me and my people feel vanquished, excluded and resentful and it drove many to arms because no political solution appeared possible, or permissible, just as at the time of writing progress is still proving elusive.

In many respects, the Union, to paraphrase something that Jack Lynch once said, is always that wall against which unionists will put their backs. As long as the Union with Britain is unconditionally guaranteed, the strongest demagogue in the unionist camp will always be in a position to prevent progress and represent conciliation and compromise as the slippery slope to a united Ireland. It would take a courageous leader to stand up to such a charge. Unfortunately, no such leader has taken the helm.

As an Irish republican I do not believe that Britain has any right to be in Ireland. Her presence has distorted the political landscape and determined relationships between its people in a negative, confrontational fashion. Britain's relationship with Ireland has not been a happy one. Nevertheless, we cannot turn back the clock and we have to face certain realities. I would not want to see unionists forced into a united Ireland against their will. But nor do I accept a unionist veto on my expressions of my Irishness. Furthermore, in my compromise with unionists, I expect formal recognition of my Irishness.

It is highly disingenuous of unionists to portray republican acceptance of the Belfast Agreement as republican acceptance of British rule, the Union, its flags and emblems. In each crisis associated with the working-out of the Belfast Agreement it is unionist difficulties and sensitivities that, because the Union is the status quo, tend to take priority. Take the example of the reaction to prison releases under the Belfast Agreement. Understandably, these early releases have been highly distressing for many relatives of the dead. On the other hand, for hundreds of mostly nationalist and republican families the killers of their loved ones – British soldiers and RUC men, protected by the state and defended by unionist politicians – never served a day in jail for the lives they took, the homes they destroyed. Why doesn't their distress at these injustices, carried out by the state in defence of the Union, weigh equally?

No one has a monopoly on suffering.

I think that unionists are making a disastrous mistake if they fail to recognise the major shifts in republican thinking and if they continue to make impossible demands of Irish republicans. I believe that the war is over and that all of us lost and suffered in that conflict.

We have to build a new society. It has to be a society where we respect and recognise each other as equals. I want a united Ireland, a 32-county, democratic, socialist republic, but I am not so naïve as to believe that it will come about unless it makes sense socially, politically and, of course, economically. That is the challenge that faces republicans. I believe it will happen.

Yes, republicans view the Belfast Agreement as transitional. There is no big secret or conspiracy about that, nor should it cause unionists to scream treachery and reach for their Lee Enfields. They have to accept that republicans have the same aspirations they always had, just as republicans have to accept that unionists want to maintain their Britishness. The difference, however, is that the Union cannot be maintained at the expense of nationalist rights. Nationalists demand equality and justice, two considerations which were never among the founding criteria of this state, which thus makes the working-out of the Belfast Agreement something of an experiment and probably provisional.

I believe that the continuation of the Union is actually an albatross around the neck of unionists preventing them from thinking creatively, imaginatively, yet, at the same time, leaving them perpetually insecure and with a siege mentality because their hosts, the British public, care little about the north of Ireland, and their fellow nationalists are always going to remain suspect.

Notes
1 Danny Morrison, personal diary, October 1968–January 1969.
2 *The Observer*, 1 August 1999.

Danny Morrison is the former editor of *An Phoblacht/Republican News*. As a prominent member of Sinn Féin, he was elected to the Northern Ireland Assembly in 1982 as a member for Mid-Ulster. He gave up political activism to devote himself to writing and reviewing fiction full-time, with some political commentary in the likes of the *Irish Times*, the *Guardian* and the *Washington Post*. He has written three novels and is currently working on a fourth.

The Union in Limbo: Europe, Britain and the Unionist Community

Antony Alcock

At the end of the World War Two five reasons were put forward for European integration. Four were fairly obvious and well known: to prevent future wars; to cooperate for the common economic good by removing barriers to trade and free movement of goods, services, capital and labour; to unite against a common enemy (in this case the Soviet Union and communism); and to control the Germans. Little was said about the fifth: the need to solve the problems where borders divided cultural communities from their kin, ie minority problems. Indeed, Hitler's exploitation of German minorities in Poland and Czechoslovakia was held to be an important cause of the war.

Fifty-five years after the beginning of the process of European integration, most Europeans would still feel satisfied in regard to the first four reasons. There is no prospect of war between members of the European Union; the EU is one of the three most prosperous areas in the world, which many other nations and peoples would like to join; the Soviet Union – and its empire – has collapsed and communism become discredited; the Germans are locked in to the European Community economically and politically. But enormous progress has been made in regard to the fifth reason as well.

For the first 25 years after the war, minorities were a taboo subject. They were still suspect. Self-determination, the slogan used in international forums to speed the process of decolonisation, meant only one thing in Europe – separation of minorities from their host states and thus a threat to the latter's integrity. In some countries assimilation of minorities – snuffing out their identity – was still the name of the game. Since then things have changed dramatically, and the reason is the process of European integration. Three aspects of this process have been significant.

The first was simply the recognition of existing state boundaries, which provided the territorial stability upon which to build mechanisms to ensure that minorities lived and flourished in their host state as they would do if they lived in their kin state, or were independent. The second has been the adherence of all western European states to the vast corpus of human, political, cultural, educational and welfare rights and standards postulated by Council of Europe Conventions and European Union Directives. The third has been the rise of regionalism, which found its greatest expression in the Council of Europe's 1978 Bordeaux Declaration, of which paragraphs 1–5 read in part:

> 1. ... the Region is a fundamental element of a country's wealth. It testifies to its cultural diversity. It stimulates economic development. When based on universal suffrage regional institutions guarantee the necessary decentralisation. They ensure the solidarity and the co-ordination of its local communities.
> 2. As heirs to the history of Europe and the richness of its culture, the regions of Europe are an irreplaceable and incomparable asset of European civilisation. They are both the symbol and the guarantors of that diversity, which is the pride of the European heritage in the eyes of humanity and to which every European both bears witness and contributes.
> 3. Every European's right to "his region" is part of his right to be different. To challenge this right would be to challenge the identity of European man and ultimately of Europe itself.
> 4. ... Far from weakening the state autonomous regional political institutions reduce the burden upon it and enable it to concentrate more effectively on its true responsibilities. As a result of decentralisation, the administration becomes more human and personal and lends itself better to control by the citizens and their elected representatives.
> 5. A state which was not able to recognise the diversity of the regions of which it is made up would be incapable of a genuinely positive approach to the diversity of the European Community.[1]

Many of the European Union's regions today, such as Bavaria, Lombardy, Venice, Naples, Aragon, Castile, Scotland and Savoy, were states in their own right in the past; others, like Catalonia, the Basque country, Brittany, Wales or Galicia, were centres of culture different from that of their host state. All have welcomed the trend to decentralisation in western Europe, which now has four federal states (Austria, Belgium, Germany and Switzerland) and three states with powers devolved to its regions (Britain, Italy and Spain). To these must be added Finland, with the Swedish population of the Aland Islands controlling what is in effect a state within a state. The regions in these countries are in the forefront of the struggle to have a European Union based on its regions rather than its states, and thus more democratic and more responsive to its citizens. The establishment, under the 1992 Maastricht Treaty, of a new European institution, the Committee of the Regions, was the first and belated acknowledgement that Europe's regions had a part to play in the construction of Europe. And because, at least in western Europe, most of these regions, except in Britain and France, have legislative, executive and financial powers, they are not only largely able to control their own economic, social and cultural development, but are eager to forge cross-border partnerships involving not only neighbouring regions, but even others some distance away. Indeed, the western continent of Europe has become a grid of interlocking regions, whose cooperation, like in Tyrol north and south, has served to bring together minorities separated from their kin by political frontiers, and achieved significant economic and social progress, without the fear of having decisions imposed on them by bodies other than their host state and the European Union itself.

Two significant results of all these developments are, first, that ethnicity is in only a few cases seen as a threat to state integrity, and therefore local ethnic political parties are able to concentrate less on defence of ethnic identity and more on becoming strong regional parties, arguing that they are not merely parties in a province or region of a state but in a province or region of the European Union. The second result is that an autonomy which provides a region with strong legislative, executive and financial powers can now be considered almost everywhere an acceptable alternative to self-determination.[2]

Of course violence as a means of obtaining or ensuring separatism has continued to exist – in the Basque country, Corsica and Cyprus – but in these conflicts the issue is government, not identity. So where does Britain, Northern Ireland and the unionist community fit into all this? The answer is that they don't. They are not part of the battle for a new democratic Europe – the British because they have thrown in the towel, and the people of Northern Ireland because they are sidelined.

As is well known, the people of Britain, but particularly the indigenous English, who comprise some three-quarters of the United Kingdom's population of 57 million, have had great difficulties in coming to terms with the process of European integration. In two definitions culture has been described as a way of doing things[3] or a motive for doing things.[4] The English have developed their own political culture for nigh on a thousand years at their own pace and at their own volition, uninterrupted by foreigners. In the late 1940s the British vetoed giving powers to the Council of Europe binding on Member States because of the possible clash on policy with the House of Commons, thus ensuring unanimity was necessary in the Council's Committee of Ministers. Thereafter they suspected that they were not being told the truth when successive Prime Ministers informed them that by 'going into Europe' they were only participating in a Common Market rather than embarking on the road to a unified state (Macmillan); that they could always veto what they did not like (Heath); and that the Euro was about economics not politics (Blair). If Dean Acheson was right to say in the 1950s that Britain had lost an

Empire and had not yet found a role, and British politicians were pointing to Europe to fill the vacuum, the record of the past 30 years is that the English have still not accepted the role its élites have tried to force on them, with the result that Britain has come to be labelled 'the awkward partner' in the European Community/Union, with the issue of Europe splitting not only the nation but also the two leading political parties.

In July 1988 the President of the European Commission, Jacques Delors of France, predicted that within ten years the European Community would be the source of 80 per cent of (our) economic legislation and perhaps even (our) fiscal and social legislation as well.[5]

When Tony Blair became Prime Minister in 1997 his policy was for Britain to be 'at the heart of Europe', and it is now clear that the many constitutional – and other – reforms on which he has embarked were deliberately designed to make Britain much more like 'Europe'. Among the reforms since carried out were devolution (to Scotland, Wales and Northern Ireland), reform of the House of Lords, incorporation of the European Convention of Human Rights into British law, and making the Bank of England independent in regard to monetary policy, rather than have it controlled by the elected government. To which should be added the Prime Minister's original, but now postponed, wish for proportional representation (PR) in voting, and eventual replacement of the pound sterling by the Euro. Blair's policy has also involved almost automatic acceptance of European Union legislation on every conceivable subject adopted by qualified majority vote (QMV) of the Union's Council of Ministers, a trend that had already set in under Mrs Thatcher, with the 1986 Single European Act; John Major, with the 1992 Maastricht Treaty; and Blair himself, with the 1997 Amsterdam Treaty. And at every meeting of the European Council of Heads of State and Government ever more has been promised: if the original intention of the European Community/Union was to create merely a 'level playing field' for European business and commercial activity, the aims now, openly declared, are for an eventual common foreign security and defence policy, a European police force operating on national territories, a harmonised system of European criminal law and legal procedures, and a new Charter of Rights.

If the Scots, Welsh and Irish in Northern Ireland have seized upon devolution as a means of controlling their economy and society and enhancing their cultural identity, the unrelenting assault on British institutions has left the indigenous English deeply demoralised. The political culture of the 'Crown-in-Parliament', developed over the centuries, has been undermined. For of what use is the monarchy if what is wanted to bring draft legislation into law is not the Queen's signature but the *nihil obstat* of the European Court of Justice? Of what use is Parliament when, faced with the task of scrutinising cascades of European legislation, its views can be overturned or ignored by QMV in the Council of Ministers? The role of the judiciary used to be to apply at once legislation passed by a democratically accountable legislature. Now it can set aside Commons' legislation pending appeals regarding that legislation to the European Court,[6] or declare it incompatible with European law and thus leave it up to the government to take the necessary action.[7] And as Parliament loses influence, the role of the MP is downgraded: to be a Member becomes a stepping stone, good on CVs, to more lucrative posts in quangos and City boards, rather than a career based on a desire to serve the public and to shape the destiny of the nation.

As for the present draft Charter of Rights awaiting adoption by the European Council, Article 51 states that the fundamental rights contained therein can be suspended if they get in the way of "objectives of general interest being pursued by the Union". When the European Commission tried to silence an official, Bernard Connolly, for revelations in his book *The Rotten Heart of Europe*,[8] the European Court of Justice's Court of First Instance ruled that "the general interest of the Communities" overrides freedom of speech. Constitutional lawyers have pointed out that this amounted to a *raison d'état* argument that violated the 1950 European Convention of Human Rights which was drafted – largely by British lawyers – to check authoritarian governments and make it impossible for abusive regimes to suppress human rights by claiming *raison d'état*.[9] An example of the misuse of *raison d'état* was the suspension of relations between the EU and Austria following the entry into the coalition government in Vienna of the Freedom party, one very critical of the European Union. This suspension (since lifted, having achieved nothing) was shamefully and slavishly followed by the British government. There have even been proposals that political parties like the Freedom party could be banned from the European Parliament if they were judged to be anti-democratic by the European Court of Justice.[10] But the devastating point about the Charter is that despite British government denials, even if it is decided that the Charter is not legally binding, the European Commission has said the European Court of Justice would indeed draw on it as a basis for decisions, a view supported by a number of Member States, including France.[11]

Previously an English High Court judge, on the basis of the European Convention of Human Rights, ruled that two Sikh terrorists could not be deported back to India from Britain, where they were alleged to pose a threat to national security, on the grounds that their human rights might be endangered on their return.[12] And it is, after all, European law which now requires, in cases when facts established indicate the presumption that there had been harassment or discrimination on the grounds of sex in the workplace, that the burden of proof would no longer, as traditionally, lie with the plaintiff, but that the defendant, whether an individual or a company, must prove that the action complained about did not occur, thus reversing a legal tradition dating back to the days of the Roman Republic![13]

But quite apart from the impositions of Europe, back home an assault has begun on British traditions and institutions that has continued unabated.

With regard to schools, one would find it hard to disagree with Nicholas Tate's devastating article 'They come not to praise England but to bury it.'[14] In it he doubts the strength of commitment in the education system to taking matters of national identity seriously. He referred to a survey in which 57 per cent of French children were glad to be French, whereas only 35 per cent of English children were proud of their nationality. In the schools it was "racist" to devote 50 per cent of the history curriculum to British history; a lecturer instructing teachers that their role was to educate a generation of cosmopolitans; a college principal referring to her students' inability to observe Remembrance Day as it involved "an implied unity which I'm not sure everyone can sign up to"; that history teachers have redefined their role as providing pupils with skills and concepts rather than as giving them a narrative in which to live their lives. Tate went further:

> In a recent survey of the views of European history teachers' associations, England was part of a small minority that did not consider heritage important, did not want to pay attention to national heroes and queried whether national identity was even a legitimate concept in a diverse society.

Identity, however, is not only an ethnic matter, but involves a sense of community which has nothing to do with jingoism, racism or xenophobia.

Unless, of course, that sense of community feels imposed upon, which is the point about the immigration issue today. England has always welcomed immigrants – Huguenots in the seventeenth century, Jews in the nineteenth, West Indians, people from the Indian sub-continent, Chinese and Ugandan Asians since World War Two, to name a few. There was work for them; they were hard workers; those that were refugees, as opposed to economic migrants, were mostly happy to be assimilated into the largely British cultural background. Britain needs immigrants now, but the rate of inward migration today is so enormous that they can no longer be easily absorbed. No longer individuals but whole families come, gravitating to their own kind who have gone before them, creating ghettos, described as "self-contained",[15] in the name of a supposed superior "multicultural society", encouraged by those who love every culture but their own, to remain culturally apart. The result is that in some areas there are primary schools where hardly a child speaks English. What future do such children face, not only in education but later in the workplace?

And then there is the criminal justice system and the police. Already there are plans to restrict the system of trial by jury. Far from an Englishman's home being his castle, people who defend themselves or their property from attack are far more likely to end in the dock than the criminal, who would almost certainly obtain compensation for any hurt that he suffered in the commission of his crime. The police, undermanned, overworked, accused of individual and institutional racism at every opportunity, struggle unavailingly against rising crime, not only in decaying inner-city centres but in country market towns. In the name of European harmonisation British citizens can actually be *prosecuted* for selling goods in pounds and ounces rather than grams; in gallons rather than litres.[16]

'New' Labour and the Prime Minister continually make it clear that they have no interest in or use for British history and traditions. The English might at various times in their history have been threatened by defeat, demoralisation or impoverishment, but never before have they faced being robbed of their national identity and heritage by their own government in order to be reduced to a rootless, alienated, dumb, dispirited rabble, to be moulded into the form decided by their new European masters.

Essential for the dumbing down process, and preparing for the new multicultural Europe, is to ditch the British past and to focus on the new Britain, in particular its multicultural identity. This was why the Runnymede Trust was commissioned by the Home Secretary to prepare the report *The Future of Multi-Ethnic Britain*. Its apparent implication, that the overwhelmingly (93 per cent) white inhabitants of the kingdom needed to re-examine their cultural identity and traditions in order to accommodate the other seven per cent, mostly from other incoming Commonwealth cultures, rather than that the incomers should adjust to the culture and traditions of their host state was initially welcomed by the Prime Minister and his government as a "timely contribution" to the national debate.[17] Later they backtracked in view of the hostility of a public outraged at the call for British history to be revised, rethought or jettisoned. As William Hague put it:

... they hate who we are, where we have come from and where we are going ... using genuine public concern about race relations to rewrite our past and abolish our present ... only a government led by a Prime Minister embarrassed about the country he lives in and the people who elected him could have welcomed this dangerous nonsense as a "timely contribution" to our national debate.[18]

A few days later the Mayor of London, Ken Livingstone, suggested that the statues of two generals in Trafalgar Square be removed on the grounds that no one knew who they were.[19] The message, that if one does not know what something is it should be replaced by something that is known, besides showing contempt for the nation and its past, is hardly a good advertisement for encouraging education and the acquisition of knowledge.

When this author was travelling and living on the continent in the 1950s and 1960s he was particularly struck by the respect and liking shown to the British by the smaller nations – the Belgians, Dutch, Danes, Norwegians and Swiss – for the part played in World War Two. Historically, of course, England (or Britain) has continually intervened to save the Europeans from themselves: from conquest by fanatic Spanish Catholicism in the sixteenth century; from conquest by royalist, republican and imperial France in the seventeenth, eighteenth and nineteenth centuries; and from the brutality of the Kaiser's Germany and the criminality of Hitler's in the twentieth. The French have never forgiven the British for not surrendering in 1940, and they know very well from where might come the real challenge to their hegemony in Europe's present 'new order' if Blair is not successful at home. However, in reality, the French are in no danger at all.

In one of the best books to be written about Europe in recent years, *Democracy in Europe*,[20] Larry Siedentop argues that three models of the state are in competition to become that for the European Community as a whole. The French model is based on power, power from the top – the President and the executive. This power is supported by a closed political class, an élite bureaucracy; the legislature has a lesser role and a lesser ability to provide checks and balances on the executive. The French model is thus based on the will of the executive. It does not require and is therefore least likely to foster a culture of consent. It is impatient of opposition once it has settled on a course of action considered 'rational'. The French political class prizes outcomes more than conciliations, coherence more than consent. As Siedentop points out, these traditions stretch through from the *ancien régime* and Napoleon through to the Fifth Republic, which is why the only hope for the ignored is direct action and why there are so many revolutions in French history.

The German state, on the other hand, is federal in form, creating different spheres and layers of authority and designed to limit the central power. The British model, however, is based on tradition – informality, precedent, custom, *de facto* rather than *de jure*, consensual ('common sense') rather than formal, hence the unwritten constitution. But this model cannot be exported; there are no clear constitutional ideas. It therefore cannot provide guidance for the construction of the European Union.

Because of the German willingness to leave the leadership of Europe to the French, and since Britain did not participate in the establishment of the European Community and has been the 'awkward partner' ever since it did join in 1973, it has been France that has led Europe. France has become the model for European government and therefore Brussels, as Siedentop has put it, has become an appendage of Paris. Whereas Britain wanted a gradual approach on economic integration and wanted interdependence, France and Germany were agreed together to use their political will to create a new order. The French have the enormous advantage of knowing what they want, and the Union is their creation – the Coal and Steel Community, the Common Agricultural Policy, the Euro – have all served French interests and there is no differentiation between French and European interests. Unfortunately, the other side of the French model is that it is run by a privileged and unaccountable élite, with all the propensity to corruption. And the same has happened in Europe. For four years running, the Court of Auditors rejected the European Commission's accounts but it was ignored. The Commission was only brought down when a Dutch official, Paul von Buitenen, exposed years of sleaze and corruption perpetrated by French nationals in the European civil service.[21]

All the British traditions that oppose this French model – particularly control of executive by the legislature and the principle of democratic consent – are in the process of being emasculated. In view of all this, no one should be surprised at the development of events in Northern Ireland and how the British-Unionist community has been affected.

As this author has written elsewhere,[22] what makes the Northern Ireland conflict unique is that whereas in many countries the central government seeks to retain control of an area where its supporters are in an ethnic or political minority, in Northern Ireland the central government wants to get rid of an area where its kin are in a majority.

For a long time now Westminster has wished the unionists would go away. After all, against Carson's advice, the British government of the day set up Stormont, thus making the province different from the rest of

Britain, so that it could come to an arrangement with the Dail about an 'agreed Ireland'. Then the traditional British parties stopped campaigning in the province, leaving the unionists isolated in the fight against Irish nationalism. That Westminster did not care a jot about the province could be seen a few years later, with the languid acceptance of the claim to Northern Ireland in Articles 2 and 3 of the new 1937 Irish Constitution. But the unionists did not go away (luckily for Britain during World War Two!), and a few years later, with the onset of the Troubles, Britain had (reluctantly) to intervene. In the next stage, 1970–98, if unionism could not be ignored, at least it could be humiliated by the imposition of direct rule, the abolition of the B-Specials, the 1985 Anglo-Irish Agreement and the 1995 Frameworks Documents.

The scene was then set for the third stage, and it is therefore well worth recalling what the situation was when the negotiations opened in 1996 leading to the Belfast 'Good Friday' Agreement two years later.

On the one hand there had been 28 years of violence, which had not shaken unionist resolve, but was very expensive in terms of lives lost or shattered and damage to the economy. On the other hand electoral fortune had brought to the fore four relatively young political leaders – Tony Blair, Prime Minister of the United Kingdom; Bertie Ahern, Prime Minister of the Irish Republic; David Trimble, leader of the Ulster Unionist Party; and Bill Clinton, President of the United States. There seemed to be a real determination to end the conflict once and for all, on a basis of intercommunity peace and reconciliation; decommissioning of paramilitary weapons; release of prisoners; institutionalised power sharing; with recognition of Northern Ireland's place as an integral part of the United Kingdom externally and the introduction of police and judicial reforms internally.

For the unionists the Belfast Agreement brought what seemed to be a number of advantages. The Irish government withdrew the claim to Northern Ireland. With the establishment of an Assembly, the people of Northern Ireland, impotent for so long under direct rule, could regain a large measure of control over their economic, social and cultural development. As elsewhere in Europe, cross-border arrangements required ratification by both jurisdictions.

But the high hopes of the people of Northern Ireland, 71 per cent of whom endorsed the text of the Agreement in a referendum, soon faded. The reasons lay not in the text of the Agreement, but on the one hand the failure to implement certain of its sections, and on the other with the way other sections were being interpreted. Within two years goodwill had been replaced by the same intercommunal hatred and suspicion that had existed during the previous 28.

It soon became clear that the PIRA (Provisional Irish Republican Army) had no intention of disarming; that dissident republicans, disgusted at the continuation of partition, would continue to wage war on Britain and that they would receive weapons from sympathisers in the PIRA and funds from sympathisers in the United States; and that the British and Irish governments had no intention of forcing the issue. The policies of both governments were based on acceptance that the political wing of the PIRA, Provisional Sinn Féin, was a democratic party with an elected mandate and no arms to hand in; that it would be better to have Sinn Féin/PIRA in the political process rather than outside. The weakness in this position, for unionists, was that it gave the initiative to republicans, paving the way for the resumption of that appeasement of Irish terrorism that had characterised British and Irish government policy for the previous 30 years – nothing had changed! Every subterfuge was used to avoid enforcing decommissioning – putting back deadlines, agreeing to inspection of dumps by international observers – thus allowing the threat of a resumption of violence by republicans if they did not get their way on 'political progress'. Of course republicans can rightly ask why they should decommission weapons while loyalist paramilitaries not only did not decommission their weapons, but instead targeted innocent Catholics. But whatever the relationship between Sinn Féin and the military wing of republicanism, the fact that there had been no decommissioning meant to almost every unionist that they were sharing power with unreconstructed, unrepentant terrorists who could never bring themselves to say the war was over.

Not only that, but the release of terrorist prisoners had, within two years, been almost completed. What was the result? They returned to their community areas, taking over housing estates, enforcing a vigilante justice on those who, for whatever reason, displeased them. What could be more grotesque than that in the end the two main loyalist paramilitary groups should attack each other, forcing hundreds of families to leave their homes.

But over and above these problems, serious enough, another even more insidious movement was taking place. In the past unionists had been ignored, humiliated and imposed upon. Now they were to find that peace and reconciliation between Britain and the Irish, of whatever shade of green, would require their effacement, as the British and Irish governments took advantage of institutional reforms to launch a concerted attack on their identity.

The unionists have always been a frontier people, from their roots on both sides of the English/Scottish border to their role in Ireland. Psychologically they see themselves as guardians of the realm. They identify with the realm. But if they identify with the realm, the new policy of the London–Dublin axis is that the only way to appease Irish nationalism is to ensure the realm does not identify with them. Hence the assault on the symbols of the state: the Patten Report's recommendation to change the name of the Royal Ulster Constabulary, the organisation which, at the great sacrifice of over 300 killed and 8,000 injured, had held terrorism at bay, to say nothing of the removal of the Queen's portrait and the Union flag from police stations, despite the mandate given to Chris Patten that reforms should enjoy the support of a majority of the population; that the Union flag can only be flown on official buildings on certain occasions (although flying it on the buildings where Irish republicans are the Ministers may well prove a test of British government resolve); that oaths of loyalty to serve the Queen in the discharge of their profession need no longer be taken by the police, solicitors or members of the Bar.

As Jeffrey Donaldson so rightly put it,[23] the policy of every British government since 1972 has been the promotion of an Anglo-Irish process built around the mollification of Irish nationalism in both its terrorist and constitutional manifestations. The demotion, demoralisation and diminution of unionism has, in effect, been the official policy of successive British and Irish governments. Yet not one leader of the Ulster Unionist Party between 1972 and 1998 was able either to destroy or divert this anti-unionist policy.

Yet why should unionists be concerned about Dublin having a say in the affairs of Northern Ireland when one considers the role of the European Union in British daily life? Why complain about the inability to control paramilitary thugs, drug dealers and joy riders in Northern Ireland's ghettos when the people in the rest of Britain voice their doubts about the ability of the police to tackle public disorder? Why complain about 'guns in government' when the British government hugs terrorists to its bosom? In a world frantic in the pursuit of rights and where the words 'duty' or 'responsibility' never appear in speech or in writing, why complain about terrorists receiving payments, either for alleged infringement of rights or to help them integrate into society, far exceeding those to their victims? Why be concerned about oaths of loyalty to the Queen when the institution of monarchy is being rendered so irrelevant? Above all, why expect accommodation of the 60 per cent Ulster-British population of Northern Ireland and their culture, when modification of that of the 75 per cent indigenous English is being sought in order to accommodate the seven per cent of multicultural incomers?

The Frameworks Documents spelled out that Northern Ireland could remain part of the United Kingdom as long as Ireland was united economically. The Irish Foreign Minister Brian Cowen is reported to have told Mr Mandelson that Northern Ireland could remain part of Britain as long as there was no further evidence of Britishness in its governance.[24] This was vehemently denied in later speeches by Mr Cowen and Mr Ahern, who fell over themselves in accepting that the Ulster-British had the right to their identity.[25] No unionist need be deceived. It is the tone which sets the music, and the tone from Westminster and Dublin has been for years to denigrate the Ulster-British and their culture. In the attempt to destroy their identity and culture, the unionists of Northern Ireland can indeed claim – at last – full equality of treatment at least with the English of the United Kingdom. While these attacks have engendered a hostile reaction, only time can tell whether or not they will be resumed. In the meantime, both communities are in limbo as they await the next stage in British, Irish and European history.

Notes

1 Council of Europe, *Conference of Local and Regional Authorities*, (Bordeaux, 1 February 1978), Strasbourg, 1978.
2 M Magliani, *The Autonomous Province of South Tyrol – A Model of Self-Governance?*, Bozen/Bolzano, European Academy, 2000, p 146.
3 Sir E Tylor, *Primitive Culture*, London, 1871.
4 B Malinovski, *A Scientific Theory of Culture*, Chapel Hill, 1944, p 36.
5 M Thatcher, *The Downing Street Years*, Harper-Collins, 1993, p 742.
6 Factortame, European Court of Justice, Case C-213/89 in *European Court Reports* 1990, vol 6, pp I 2433–74.
7 *Daily Telegraph*, 7 August 2000.
8 B Connolly, *The Rotten Heart of Europe*, Faber and Faber, 1995.
9 Ambrose Evans-Pritchard in the *Daily Telegraph*, 16 September and 21 September 2000.
10 *Sunday Times*, 12 March 2000.
11 *Daily Telegraph*, 21 September 2000.
12 *Daily Mail*, 2 August 2000.
13 Directive 97/80/EC of 15 December 1997, published in *Official Journal* L O/4 of 20 January 1998.
14 *Sunday Times*, 27 August 2000.
15 Trevor Phillips in the *Sunday Telegraph*, 15 October 2000.
16 *Sunday Telegraph*, 9 January 2000.
17 Figures from *Annual Abstract of Statistics*, The Stationery Office, 2000, n 136, Table 5.6, p 34.
18 *Daily Telegraph*, 13 October 2000.

19 *Daily Mail*, 20 October, 2000.
20 L Siedentop, *Democracy in Europe*, Allen Lane (Penguin Press), 2000.
21 Paul van Buitenen, *Blowing the Whistle*, Politicos, 2000.
22 AE Alcock, *Understanding Ulster*, Ulster Society (Publications) Ltd, 1994.
23 *Belfast Telegraph*, 22 September 2000.
24 *Irish Times*, 5 May 2000.
25 Department of Foreign Affairs Press Release, Dublin, 27 May 2000; *Address by the Taoiseach to the 21st Plenary of the British-Irish Inter Parliamentary Body*, Salt Hill, Galway, 9 October 2000.

Antony Alcock is Professor of European Studies at the University of Ulster's Coleraine campus, specialising in the problems of culturally divided communities as well as the process of European integration. Amongst his most recent publications are *Understanding Ulster* (1994), *A Short History of Europe* (1998) and *A History of the Protection of Regional Cultural Minorities in Europe – from the Edict of Nantes to the Present Day* (2000).

The Union

Identity, Security, and Self-Determination: The Long Road towards an Agreed Ireland

Martin Mansergh

Insecurity and fear of change, like hope, are probably inherent to the human condition. Civilisation is about creating the security and stability that enable people to change and look forward to it as an engine of progress.

The legacy of history still weighs heavily on two communities in Northern Ireland, as a new dispensation ushered in by the Belfast Agreement starts to prevail. The essence of the Agreement is respect for different identities, a recognition of each community's need for security in the broadest sense of the term, and common acceptance of a method of self-determination, which reconciles, not without some fundamental compromise on both sides, previously conflicting British and Irish views, as to how that should be applied in Ireland and in Northern Ireland.

What should result in political terms is an agreed Ireland, which becomes more and more of a reality as the Agreement works and takes root. But to have a greater sense of the significance of where we may be going, it is necessary to look back down the long road that has already been travelled and at the causes of conflict, and at what we are seeking to put behind us, much of it rooted deep in the past.

There was for centuries a lack of security in the relations between the peoples of the islands of Great Britain and Ireland. But that was not always so. It is not certain whether Ireland was first settled from northern Britain, or from the continent. There are genetic indications of close links between the western seaboard and the Basque country in northern Spain, indicating that like most myths the Milesian invasion may have had some basis in fact, at a later point in time.[1] In the mythical Irish sagas with their epic conflicts, the waves of invasion and the conflict between different provinces had no very significant east–west dimension, though the west of Scotland figures prominently as a place of refuge and kingdom across the water. It has to be assumed that in every century there was significant migration in both directions across the Irish Sea, as well as between Ireland and Europe. There was, for example, a significant Hiberno-Norse settlement, originating from

Dublin, in Cumbria from the ninth century AD.[2]

The Roman Empire regarded Ireland as too peripheral and strategically unimportant to be worth conquering. Despite local conflicts between kings, it is a remarkable fact, compared to other countries, that Christianity was introduced to Ireland peacefully and without martyrs being created. That was to be reserved for later centuries. Christianity also radiated out from Ireland in a largely peaceful way, though some Irish monks suffered martyrdom on the continent. It was the Vikings who first introduced acute insecurity across the whole of north-west Europe, and Brian Boru won fame as High King of Ireland, when he defeated them at Clontarf in 1014, after which those who remained gradually integrated with the rest of the population. It is ironic, given their fearsome reputation, that they introduced the relative stability and security of town life into Ireland.

Significantly, it was not so much the Irish as an advance Anglo-Norman contingent under Strongbow that unsettled Henry II with the fear of a rival kingdom and led to the Lordship of Ireland. Ironically, in the light of later conflict, the initial submission to Henry by Irish and Normans alike was entirely peaceful. But that was not to last. Once involved, the affairs of Ireland demanded continued attention and resources, if potential threats were to be contained. As late as 1487, a rival pretender to the throne of Henry VII was crowned in Dublin, and, before that, Ireland had played a significant, if peripheral, role in the power struggles involving the Bruces of Scotland and later the Wars of the Roses, acting as a refuge and a springboard for the York dynasty in 1460–61. The degree of control exercised was intermittent and sporadic, and left large parts of Irish life relatively undisturbed. But throughout feudal Europe, even where more systematically organised, central control tended to be weak, relying heavily on cooperation with local powers, when not in conflict with them.

It was common to speak of two nations in medieval Ireland. The inhabitants of medieval towns like Dublin and Tralee were largely descended from settlers from England and Wales. The countryside outside the Pale, which was the real division in medieval Ireland, remained largely Gaelic-speaking, and Ulster, which had the fewest towns, most of all, though parts of Antrim were within the sphere of influence of the Lords of the Isles. In the course of time, as a result of intermarriage and a lot of common interests, and notwithstanding the Statutes of Kilkenny designed to keep them apart, the two nations gradually merged, the final impetus being provided by the post-Reformation upheavals and the new Protestant settlers of the sixteenth and seventeenth centuries.

Even the strongest cultural nationalists of the early twentieth century were conscious that 'the historic Irish nation', as it existed prior to the 'Flight of the Earls' in 1607 or Henry II's invasion, did not have a single homogeneous racial origin. The 'Irish race', with both explicit and subliminal ethnic connotations, is a term that has long since gone out of use. In a famous passage in the *Nation*, the Young Irelander Thomas Davis, who had an enormous influence on the Gaelic League and the Irish-Ireland Movement, to which so many founders of the state belonged, wrote purple passages on both the antiquity of the century's civilisation, and the successive waves of migration to the country:

> This country of ours is no sand bank, thrown up by some caprice of earth. It is an ancient land, honoured in the archives of civilisation, traceable into antiquity by its piety, its valour, and its sufferings. Every great European race has sent its stream to the river of Irish mind . . . However closely we study our history, when we come to deal with politics we must sink the distinctions of blood as well as sect. The Milesian, the Dane, the Norman, the Welshman, the Scotchman, and the Saxon must combine, regardless of their blood – the Strongbownian must sit with the Ulster Scot, and his whose ancestor came from Tyre or Spain must confide in and work with the Cromwellian and the Williamite. This is as much needed as the mixture of Protestant and Catholic. If a union of all Irish-born men ever be accomplished, Ireland will have the greatest and most varied materials for an illustrious nationality, and for a tolerant and flexible character in literature, manners, religion, and life, of any nation on earth.[3]

The issue later was less the acknowledgement of the mixture, than what element should prevail and absorb. There was a strong view from the 1890s that the Gaelic tradition was the most distinctive, and that it was the indisputable key to a separate nationality. But this created, post-partition, fears of a forced embrace amongst those who did not or could not identify with it. In the south, 100 years on, it has come to be accepted amongst all traditions as an important part of what we are, though there is no longer an overriding emphasis on it as the main end of education.

Much of the religious and ideological fervour of the Middle Ages was directed outward in crusades against the Moslem and the 'infidel', though outbreaks of 'heresy' were ruthlessly repressed. The wide-open split in Christianity occasioned by the Reformation added a new sharp edge and bitterness to dynastic struggles. To this day, Hans Küng argues: "No peace among nations without peace among religions."[4] Outside a small part of a narrow ruling élite, the Reformation did not catch on in Ireland, where central authority had limited power even over those of Anglo-Norman descent, and where there was no concept of how to bring religious change to a largely Irish-speaking population. Meanwhile, for decades, Philip II of Spain, who had been married to the Catholic Queen Mary I of England, sought to overthrow her sister, the Protestant Queen Elizabeth I. Ireland was fertile ground for the Spanish, but equally warring Irish chiefs under increasing pressure from Elizabeth's Lord Deputies in Ireland, who exercised savage ethnic repression of a kind not seen before, sought and welcomed Spanish assistance. It was the start of several centuries when Ireland appeared to possess potential European strategic significance, its disaffected state tempting first Spain, then France, then Germany, and, arguably to a more limited degree, the Soviet Union and maverick allies like Libya in respect of Northern Ireland. Only with independence did Ireland cease to be a strategic threat, guaranteeing that it would not let itself be used as a base for an attack on Britain, and the end of the Cold War finally disposed of latterly far-fetched theories about the military significance of Northern Ireland, enabling Britain to declare that it had no selfish strategic interest in Northern Ireland.

New settlement was a means of short-circuiting the centuries-old shortcomings of policy implementation from an English point of view. The Munster colony may have been a comparative failure, but the Ulster settlement of the early seventeenth century in sparsely populated land from which its leaders had fled took more solid root. King James may have been killing two birds with one stone, ridding himself of potentially troublesome subjects from Scotland, while pacifying Gaelic Ulster. English rulers then and for a long time afterwards had a self-serving contempt for a culture and civilisation that they saw as alien and which they feared, and whose representatives did not always cut a dignified figure in London. The plantation and accompanying Anglicisation was justified by reference to supposedly superior civilised values, epitomised allegorically in Shakespeare's *The Tempest*.[5]

The remainder of the seventeenth century saw periodic violent upheavals, as when in the 1641 Rebellion the Ulster Irish rose and tried to throw off the colony, and later in the reign of James II when 'Old English' and Irish tried to overturn the recent Cromwellian settlement. The sense of insecurity of property, status, religious freedom and identity at different times pervaded all groups. Many Protestants became refugees in 1641 and 1689, but Catholic garrisons were slaughtered in Drogheda and Wexford in 1649, and ultimately by the end of the century Catholic dispossession was nearly complete, after a battle on Irish soil at the Boyne in 1690 decided the fate of the three kingdoms. A fearful Irish Parliament in 1697 disregarded the kingly promises of the Treaty of Limerick, just as the 'Patriot Parliament' of 1689 was ready to override any misjudged magnanimity by James II. It was a life-and-death struggle for power and land, in which Protestants and Catholics behaved as if they had to win and subsequently consolidate a total victory, the uneasy compromises and *modus vivendi* of the early Stuart period being no longer acceptable.

The morality and legitimacy of the outcome was open to challenge, even in seventeenth century terms. John Locke, philosopher of the Glorious Revolution, originator of the principle of government by consent, who exercised enormous influence on the Enlightenment and on America and France in the eighteenth century, openly condemned the practice of expropriating land to pay for war. He argued that the charges of war, even if due to the conqueror, could scarcely give him a title to any country he conquered, for the damages of war could scarcely amount to the value of any considerable area of land in any part of the world.

Locke argued that people who are the descendants of those forced to submit to the yoke of a government by constraint have a right to shake it off "till their rulers put them under such a frame of Government as they willingly, and of choice consent to". Locke may have had primarily in mind the Norman conquest of England and justifications of a paternalistic absolutism derived from it, but his principles apply perfectly to post-seventeenth century Ireland.[6]

Unionists have argued that, if their rights are not secure after three centuries, then the same ought to be true of Americans and Australians vis-à-vis the original inhabitants of their country. But, where the descendants of later arrivals far outweigh the former, some acknowledgement or apology, justice and reparation do not demand a difficult sacrifice or carry with it present dangers. The Protestant settlements of English and Scottish origin have always remained a minority in Ireland as a whole, so that South Africa is in many ways a better analogy. Orangemen and others who constantly commemorate the victory at the Boyne and the lifting of the Siege of Derry seem oblivious to the dangers of constantly casting the nationalist community back into the role of the defeated and unjustly dispossessed of the seventeenth century, especially when compounded by the further political dispossession of partition.

The Israeli Ambassador to France, Elie Barnavi, has observed, writing about the Middle East:

Legitimacy is the master word. You have bought a house, you have paid in cash, it is duly registered, it belongs to you in all legality. But it is situated in hostile quarters, where they do not like your skin, or your lifestyle or your company. No property title, however indisputable, will durably protect your possession, if your neighbours refuse to accept you as the legitimate owner. Certainly, if you are more rich than them, your property can bristle with security, and you can keep your enemies at a distance. But your life will be hell. However, your neighbours are no better off. You live in an armed camp, but they live in a shanty town open to the winds. To make this quarter a habitable place, they have as much need of you as you of them, perhaps more. That is what is at stake in the negotiation.[7]

Even if some of the expressions would be different in an Irish context, that is also the essence of the political settlement to be implemented, because the Belfast Agreement recognises the legitimacy of constitutional choice and "the birthright of all the people of Northern Ireland to identify themselves and be accepted as Irish or British, or both, as they may so choose". Identity, security and self-determination are guaranteed for both communities, now that there is at last a frame of government, to which, in the language of John Locke, the nationalist community have willingly and of choice consented to, on the assumption that it is not taken away again and that the will of the people is not overridden or set aside. Democracy is not just about the absence of violence. It is also about implementing the decisions of the people.

Unionists have also claimed that Ireland was never politically united prior to the Norman invasion. That point can be argued, but, as a key Forum study noted, the modern practice of self-determination since World War Two has been to put the emphasis on democracy and territorial integrity, rather than satisfy different groups with ambitions for self-determination, and the right to self-determination belongs to the population and territory as a whole, not to particular ethnic groups. Professor Asbjorn Eide made clear in his study for the Forum for Peace and Reconciliation:

> . . . territorial change is fully legitimate when it is based on the consent of the parties involved. Such change may be held to be particularly justified when the existing territorial arrangements were achieved in ways which would have been unacceptable under contemporary international law.[8]

What he was in effect saying was that at a later date the partition of Ireland would have been internationally frowned on, like the partition of Cyprus has been or the notion of two states of China. The Federal Republic of Germany also adhered to the essential unity of Germany, even during the *Ostpolitik*. The fundamental legitimacy of the objective of a united Ireland, provided it is brought about by consent, and in peace and agreement, is fully incorporated in the Belfast Agreement, which also recognises the equal legitimacy of other choices. Self-determination can have more than one outcome, and is not confined to sovereignty.

In the course of the eighteenth century, it was the élites of Protestant Ireland who were able to appropriate the badge of Irish national identity, who enjoyed a high degree of security behind the entrenchments of the Penal Laws, and who were able, subject to vital British strategic and commercial interests, to determine their own and the country's future. They had the initiative, but from a long-term perspective did not use their opportunity.

Many Ulster Protestants, outside of the Ascendancy, were dissatisfied with their reward from 1690. Many emigrated to America, and were to the fore in the American War of Independence, whilst Scottish Highlanders of Jacobite fame, like Flora McDonald and her husband Allan, were on the loyalist side. The Irish or Scots-Irish, who helped overthrow the 'tyranny' of King George III, and who supplied, it is claimed, up to 16 Presidents of a republic that did not overcome its distrust of Britain till well after World War Two (in fact till the first Catholic President of Irish-American extraction, John F Kennedy, struck up a warm relationship with Harold MacMillan), are an awkward model for twentieth or twenty-first century Ulster unionism.[9]

Protestant Ireland can be divided into four categories in the 1780s and the 1790s: the reactionaries, the conservatives, the liberals and the radicals. The reactionaries favoured Protestant Ascendancy based on maintaining the conquest, with or without Union. The conservatives saw Union as the safer option, and in their own and the country's best interests, that would allow for eventual emancipation with less political danger. The liberals of Grattan's Parliament, behind the Volunteers and the largely theoretical sovereign legislative independence of 1782–83, saw a Catholic Ireland treated more generously as falling in behind the (mainly Protestant) leadership of property. The radicals of the 1790s sought to establish a new independent nation, led by a bourgeois intelligentsia, on the American and French models and on the basis of parliamentary reform, emancipation, and equality, on the assumption that religious bigotry and divisions could safely be regarded as a thing of the past.

It was a noble dream that ended in disaster. The force of sectarian fears and passions was roused on both sides and the deep underlying sense of injustice welled up, and against the background of fears or hopes of French invasion that led to the pre-emptive ruthless repression, a bloodbath ensued. Acute insecurity was the primary cause of the Wexford rebellion. Henceforth, no one could underestimate the potential power of

Catholic Ireland, which in succeeding generations was determined by mass political mobilisation or otherwise to correct the injustices of past and present. Security and respect for identity was only won very slowly by the Catholic population, through the terrible experience of the Famine, and vulnerability to eviction long after, while many leaders were sent into exile. The Union sought to superimpose a common British identity, but there was little genuine solidarity, except amongst the élites. The counter-equation of Irish first, with Catholic, then with Gaelic, was a way of undermining the legitimacy and self-confidence of the possessors (or dispossessors).

The Act of Union was a compact between the landed élites of Britain and Ireland, one of which, at least in a certain sense, could be said to represent the nation, the other of which did not. The right of a minority in every sense to sign away in perpetuity Ireland's legislative independence, even if it had been accomplished without wholesale corruption, was open to question. It was accompanied by a broken promise by the British government to the Catholics of Ireland, a cardinal mistake which had a serious alienating effect, making a hollow mockery of the promised equality of the two countries. The Union also led post-1815 to deindustrialisation outside the north-east (which managed to create a cluster effect), to the immediate loss of status as a capital for Dublin, and solidarity fell down abysmally when faced with the Famine. No parliament sitting in Dublin could have evaded its responsibilities by appeals to the iron laws of political economy or by adopting a laissez-faire response to Famine, and in any case the spirit of Grattan's Parliament had been much more interventionist and pump-priming. What seems wholly disproportionate were the commercial fears about potential rivals in Ireland by English industrialists, whose crushing competition and economies of scale succeeded in reducing Ireland, outside the north-east, to a largely agricultural economy, with a job of feeding and supplying cheap labour to 'the workshop of the world', and filling the ranks of the armed forces of the Empire.

The Union can be interpreted as a form of abdication by the Protestant interest, a recognition that it could not manage the affairs of Ireland on its own, and that it did not have the courage to risk sharing the burden between the three traditions that existed then. On the other hand, in certain respects, from the perspective of the two islands as a whole, the élite was brought in from the cold. The Anglo-Irish participated as much as the Scottish élites in the imperial adventure, officering in the army and navy, but there were few positive benefits for the rest of the Irish population, which was never properly integrated.

The Union, in fact, proved no more reliable a protector of landlords or the various minority monopolies, which were dismantled, one after the other, in the course of a century which saw the spread of democracy – reforms which satisfied the more radical Presbyterian tradition. Outside of the north-east, which participated in the Industrial Revolution and benefited economically from the Union, the Protestant interest was on the retreat, and the population was falling steadily from the first religious census of 1861, as it had probably been doing since about 1800. A small patriotic minority, continuing the traditions of Grattan or the United Irishmen, sought to shape a future in which all would have an equal part to play, but they ended up with a largely Catholic following. The policy of resisting change, springing from an often deep-seated economic, social and political conservatism, meant that, when faced with a full-blown democracy that was determined to win self-government, if necessary by force, if a majority were persistently denied and compromise proved futile, Irish unionism had in the end no more cards left to play. Much more favourable terms could have been had for the asking earlier.[10] Even the Treaty, with its imposed dominion status, could only delay the inevitable. As Mikhail Gorbachev told the East German leadership in October 1989, at a time of rising unrest, "Life punishes those who move too late."

Ulster Unionists, who were geographically more concentrated and relatively in a stronger position, and with fears under practically every heading, were determined not to be left a minority under a Dublin government, even if it were only a devolved administration corralled in a unitary British state. They were supported to the hilt by the Conservatives, who wanted to halt Home Rule not just as detrimental to imperial power, but also because they saw the Bill as the best means of toppling the Liberal government. (After all, they had gained 20 years of power, with one interruption, on the ruins of the first Home Rule Bill.) But the Liberals were not much more principled either, since they acceded to Home Rule, not because a large majority of Irish people had wanted it for 30 years, but because the Irish Parliamentary Party after 1910 held the balance of power at Westminster.

It seems astonishing today that a proposal for the equivalent of present-day Scottish devolution, involving no loss of British identity and no threat to Empire, should have brought Ireland to the brink of civil war in 1914. While economically the Union of the whole of Great Britain and the whole of Ireland had served the north of Ireland well and made Belfast the industrial capital of Ireland, Home Rule was actually compatible with the continuation of the Union. Partition did not serve the economic interests of Northern Ireland nearly as well. But all the insecurities derived from history, as well as contemporary economic considerations, were deployed with a considerable degree of hysteria to ensure that as much of Ulster as could be held was excluded from Home Rule. Many of the Protestant clergy fell over themselves in their opposition to it. But it has to be said that the papal *Ne Temere* decree of 1908 was as badly timed for Home Rule, as Louis XIV's revocation of the Edict of Nantes in 1685 was for James II's policy of toleration.

Exclusion involved throwing back a large nationalist minority, that had been looking forward to full participation in a Home Rule Ireland, into a position of subordination that was likened by Kevin O'Higgins to the position of Catholics prior to emancipation.[11] Neither unionists nor the Protestant Churches in the north have ever adequately addressed the enormous loss that absolute insistence on their choice and their rights inflicted on their northern Catholic and nationalist neighbours; or whether Home Rule, which was neither separation nor independence, and which was within the UK and within the Empire, was so terrible a fate that all-out resistance to it, with all the long-term effects that have ensued, was morally or politically or democratically justified. It is claimed that Home Rule would have led inevitably to dominion status and separation, but that would have been unlikely without widespread agreement. Unionist scepticism about the likelihood of Home Rule being fair or lasting or even an Anglophile dominion emerging, meant that they were soon faced with far more radical outcomes. Having been through all the pain of establishing and consolidating independence, and slowly reaping the benefits, there is no possibility of the Republic now turning back the clock under the auspices of the British–Irish Council, because some unionists or neo-unionists in the south might be having second thoughts (and concluding that John Redmond might not have been so bad after all).

As many objections that unionists could have to Home Rule applied to the unwilling incorporation of a proportionately larger nationalist minority in Northern Ireland, but that minority did not at the time have the same power or backing. Home Rule for the whole island was itself a compromise, and when it was denied there was little reason not to go for full separation. It could be argued that Irish nationalism in the 26 counties and Ulster unionism in the remaining six each largely achieved their own goals of self-determination, but going in opposite directions, at the expense of a substantial nationalist minority in the north that lost any security or self-determination it had, and of a small southern unionist and Protestant minority that still possessed substantial economic interests and had no option but to adapt as best it could. The struggle in the south to consolidate independence after the civil war, on the basis of a stable democracy and a viable economy, was a long and arduous one, that has only comparatively recently been crowned with striking success.

Once again, like the Ascendancy in the eighteenth century, the unionist community in Northern Ireland had a near monopoly of power that lasted for nearly 50 years, which gave opportunities that were not taken for consolidating their position by a measure of conciliation. Indeed, within ten years every safeguard contained in the Government of Ireland Act, 1920, had been scrapped or rendered inoperable: proportional representation, the Boundary Commission, the Council of Ireland, and guarantees of non-discrimination. On the other hand, the south, while striving in the early decades to achieve a reunited Ireland by agreement with the British government over the heads of unionists, tended to underestimate, as generations of nationalists before them, the complexity of the problem and the deep-seated unionist resistance to incorporation in what they saw as a poorer neighbouring state, based on the twin pillars of an objectionable religious ethos and an alien native culture, perversely choosing the isolated Republic in preference to a great cosmopolitan Empire/United Kingdom, and pursuing a protectionist policy inimical to the interests of industry and living standards in the north-east.

When a nearly 50-year-old majoritarian domination was challenged by insistent civil rights demands from the minority, no one had a compass to guide them out of the crisis. There was acute insecurity on both sides of the community: the Catholic fear of a pogrom; the Protestant fear for their whole way of life. The unionists sought more law and order. The British government thought at first majority rule with some structural reform was the only way Northern Ireland could function. The Irish government advocated a united Ireland with Stormont, that would temper one majority rule with another, superimposed. The British government at first rejected any Irish government input as unhelpful interference, and only gradually came to appreciate the indispensable importance of working in partnership. The republican movement thought unity could be achieved by forcing a British withdrawal as in 1921, without recognising the essential differences in the situation. Only very gradually, after terrible tragedies and unnecessary loss of life, and after many failed or only partially successful initiatives, did people begin to appreciate the need for a comprehensive and radical settlement, negotiated in conditions of peace, that would draw the poison, not just of 30 years or even 80 years but of centuries, but also pick up on all the positive threads contained in previous initiatives.

It is not that history is over, or that any settlement from the Treaty of Limerick to the Belfast Agreement is final. But the difference is the acceptance that the future will be determined democratically, with agreement on what that means. Identity, now and in the future, will be protected, and full implementation of the Belfast Agreement should provide security, provided the paramilitaries can be persuaded to fade into the background along with certain ingrained reflexes. The future is open and is not predetermined. Whether the stronger economic attractions today of a united Ireland will carry weight with any part of the unionist community remains to be seen. But the Agreement at this point in time allows the two communities in Northern Ireland to try and combine the best of both worlds – the benefits of an Irish single market, and of UK membership. Unionists have every incentive to make the Belfast Agreement work, and nationalists likewise, because it alone offers everyone a prospect of transcending the conflict of the past, the insecurity, the fears for identity, and the loss of self-determination. Only this way can one be reasonably certain that each tradition will be winners and that there will not be, as there were in 1921, losers.

Notes

1 Emmeline W Hill, Mark A Jobling and Daniel J Bradley, 'Y-chromosome variations and Irish origins. A pre-neolithic gene graduation starts in the near East and culminates in Western Ireland, *Nature*, vol 404, 23 March 2000, p 351. (I am grateful to Professor David McConnell of Trinity College, Dublin, for drawing this to my attention.)
2 A Pearson, D Kyle, A Phillips and M Gresson, *The Annals of Kirkby Lonsdale and Lunesdale Today*, Kirkby Lonsdale, 1996, pp 7–9. (Information also derived from a family history.)
3 TW Rolleston (ed), *Prose writings of Thomas Davis*, London, 1889, pp 227, 280–1.
4 *Der Spiegel*, 52/2000, pp 112–6 (author's translation).
5 This motif was taken up by John Tenniel in a *Punch* cartoon of 19 March 1870 called 'The Irish Tempest', where Prime Minister Gladstone protects Hibernia/Miranda from 'Rory of the Hills'/Caliban, protesting "This island's mine, by Sycorax my mother." From exhibition on 'Images of Erin in the Age of Parnell', National Library of Ireland, Winter 2000–2001.
6 John Locke, *Two Treatises of Government*, ed by Peter Laslett, New York, Toronto and London, 1960, pp 433–42.
7 *Le Monde*, 4 January 2001 (author's translation).
8 *A Review and Analysis of Constructive Approaches to Group Accommodation and Minority Protection in Divided or Multicultural Societies*, Forum for Peace and Reconciliation, Dublin Castle, July 1996.
9 See article on this topic by Robert St-Cyr in the *Belfast Telegraph*, 12

November 1999.
10 Michael Davitt proposed that the Irish minority should have a guaranteed 25% representation in a Home Rule Parliament, with a list system to ensure some Protestant representation from Connaught and Munster, and he predicted that with the Home Rule Party breaking up into two or three parties they could hold the balance of power. Letter of 20 November 1887 from Land League Cottage, Ballybrack, Co Dublin, cited in Michael Davitt,'"Unionists" brought to book', London, 1888, pp 13–15.
11 Marianne Elliott, *The Catholics of Ulster*, Harmondsworth, 2000, pp 298–9. (See also evidence of Robin Glendinning to the New Ireland Forum, Dublin Castle, 5 October 1983: " . . . unfortunately the way the self-determination was given to the Unionists meant that half a million Nationalists lost the right of self-determination".)

Martin Mansergh is the son of the noted historian Nicholas Mansergh, author of *The Irish Question*. Having served as a civil servant and diplomat in the Irish Department of Foreign Affairs, he has been since 1981 the political adviser to three Taoisigh – Charles Haughey, Albert Reynolds and Bertie Ahern. In 1994 he was co-winner of the Tipperary Peace Prize (with Fr Alex Reid and Rev Roy Magee) for the part he played in brokering the first IRA ceasefire. Dr Mansergh was also part of the Irish delegation that negotiated the Belfast Agreement.

Orangeism and the Union: A Special Relationship?

Clifford Smyth

Background

The Loyal Orange Institution of Ireland[1] is the best known of a number of similar organisations in Ireland, also comprising the Apprentice Boys of Derry and the Imperial Grand Black Chapter of the British Commonwealth. All of these fraternal organisations uphold the principles of the Protestant Reformation and support the British constitution. In consequence, organisations like the Orange Order delineate the two great lines of cleavage on the island of Ireland: religion and ethnicity.[2]

The Orange Order was formed following a sectarian faction fight in Co Armagh known as the Battle of the Diamond. This firefight took place in September 1795 between members of a Roman Catholic secret society called the Defenders and local Protestants from the vicinity of Loughgall. Some of the Protestants were also Freemasons, while others had strong links with the forces of the British Crown.[3]

Those were turbulent times and within three years the widespread and complex rebellion of the United Irishmen would take place. The United Irishmen's rebellion was one of the factors setting in train those political events which issued in the Act of Union. The legislative Union between Britain and Ireland required the abolition of the Parliament in Dublin, a form of local administration dominated at that time by an unrepresentative minority termed the Protestant Ascendancy. Roman Catholics, who comprised the majority of Ireland's population, had yet to secure political emancipation.

The Orange Order therefore emerged at a time of political crisis when civil unrest and violence were features of life in Ireland. Not for the first time, the position of Protestants on the island was threatened.[4] There was a need for an organisation of self-defence for those who were determined to remain loyal to the Protestant throne of Britain.

It is possible to interpose the reactions of Orangemen to the Union with contemporary events, such as those involving the Orange protests over parade bans at Drumcree and the recent passage of the Police Bill through Parliament. If events both past and present are woven together, a remarkable continuity emerges over the years. Orangemen have consistently reacted to such events on the basis of the need to ensure the survival of Protestants on an island where patterns of ethnic cleansing[5] are well established.

Orangemen opposed Legislative Union

Many of the Orangemen of Ireland reacted with hostility to the prospect of a legislative Union between Great Britain and Ireland. The leaders of Orangeism quickly recognised that a movement which had succeeded in uniting Protestants throughout Ireland was in imminent danger of ripping itself apart on the issue of the proposed Union.

Believing that it was their duty to preserve the sense of brotherhood among the Protestant population which Orangeism encourages, the officers of the Grand Orange Lodge of Ireland issued an address towards the end of 1798 which advised the Orange brethren to:

> . . . strictly abstain from expressing any opinion pro or con upon the question of a legislative Union between this country and Great Britain, because that such expression of opinion, and such discussion in lodges could only lead to disunion.[6]

Nevertheless, Grand Lodge did allow for the expression of private opinion, from which it became apparent that many prominent Orangemen, including Mr John Claudius Beresford, one of the members of the City of Dublin, were deeply antagonistic to the intended legislation. Beresford spoke to a resolution opposing the proposed Act of Union at a meeting in the Session House, Dublin, on 10 January 1799. He explained: "I am convinced that no alteration in the Legislature, by which the Parliament of Ireland is to be incorporated with that of England, could be of service to us." Beresford predicted that such a proposed Union would "ultimately tend to the destruction of the Country, and the alienation of her affections from England".

Beresford was not alone. The Right Honourable G Ogle wrote a history of the events of the period and played a conspicuous part in opposing the United Irishmen in 1798. Now Ogle opposed the proposed Act of Union, as did another leading Orangeman called William Saurin. William Saurin was descended from an old French family driven out of France by the Revocation of the Edict of Nantes; and he regarded the Church of Rome as posing a threat to Protestant liberties. At a meeting of lawyers, this distinguished Orangeman argued vigorously against the Union.

Today the Loyal Orange Institution of Ireland is regarded as a bulwark of unionism in Northern Ireland. The Orange Order continues to send delegates in sufficient numbers to meetings of the Ulster Unionist Party, that the Order is not unreasonably viewed as exercising considerable influence over the outcome of crucial party votes and decisions. Yet 200 years ago feelings regarding the legislative Union within the Orange Institution were running so high that according to one historian, " . . . the conflict of opinion among the Orangemen was assuming serious aspects, and appeared to threaten the existence of the Society".

Charles Walpole, in his *Short History of the Kingdom of Ireland*, published in the late nineteenth century, commented on the whole episode as follows:

> The most violent of the anti-Unionists were the very people who had supported the government through the recent troubles [the 1798 rebellion], the Protestant nobility and gentry and the Orange lodges, among whom prevailed universal horror and disgust at the idea of a Union.

Dublin Orangemen were not the only Orangemen who opposed the Union. For example, the members of Orange Lodge 253, meeting in Charlemont, Co Armagh, the heartland of Orangeism to the present day, suggested that the Right Honourable George Ogle was the best person to fill the office of Grand Master for the incoming year, accompanied by John Beresford as Grand Secretary, "on account of their uniform support of the interests and independence of Ireland".

On Monday 3 February 1800, the Irish House of Commons met. Lord Castlereagh, a chief architect of the proposed Act of Union, was ill and unable to be present. However, William Saurin, using all his lawyer's eloquence, denounced the whole project, asserting that the Irish Parliament had not the power to give a new Constitution to Ireland. Saurin warned that the Union would "add to Irish divisions and distractions", which he predicted would last "in all human probability for another century with rancour and fury". He also prophesied that the legislation would create a new division between His Majesty George III's subjects in Ireland, some being unionists and others anti-unionists. Saurin, questioning the whole proposal for Union, passionately asked: "For what? to place the British connection in Ireland, which had stood immovable and unshaken, on a new, and, therefore, precarious foundation?"

The Orange spokesmen were not alone in opposing the legislative Union. Henry Grattan, who had been an earnest advocate of Roman Catholic claims, was overpowering in his address to the House:

> The Roman Catholic clergy are given to understand they shall receive salaries. Is it for the exercise of their holy functions? No! But it is for their political apostasy [sic]. I have been told that several of these clergymen were

rebels. Perhaps so. I know them not, but what follows? Let rebellion to their king be succeeded by treason to their country; and the union of both renders them the certain objects of Royal affection. Every former crime is done away and forgotten in their present infamy. I proposed a plan of tithes; they substituted for my plan an Imperial Parliament – a good substitution, perhaps, for tithes; but a bad one for honour.

Why were the Protestants of Ireland so set in their opposition to the legislative Union of the islands of Ireland and Great Britain under one Parliament? That question goes to the heart of Orangeism and why the movement came into existence after the Battle of the Diamond in 1795.

The Protestants believed that once Roman Catholics obtained complete emancipation in regard to their political rights, they would start to demand self-government. Protestants believed that if self-government was given to the Roman Catholics of Ireland, then the Protestant minority, loyal to the British throne, would be at the mercy of "a new and intolerable ascendancy".

Two centuries of Irish history separate the disquiet and alarm of Orange brethren at the prospect of an impending legislative Union, from the attitudes and disposition of Orangemen engaged in a stand-off and confrontation with the security forces and the British government on the low hills surrounding the Church of Ireland parish church at Drumcree. The security forces acted out their 'peace-keeping' role, having taken up position between Orangemen determined to march their traditional route from Drumcree church into Portadown, and nationalist 'residents' blocking the Garvaghy Road.[7]

Nationalist opposition to Orange parades has been a recurring feature of Irish history,[8] and the Orangemen at Drumcree found themselves caught up in a controversy with which their forefathers would have been all too familiar. For its part, the government showed partiality towards the nationalist protesters which only exacerbated the Orangemen's sense of insecurity.

Both the controversy over the legislative Union and the stand-off at Drumcree provide a valuable insight into the Orange Order, and into why it continues to enjoy the support of tens of thousands of Ulster Protestants, together with a minority of Protestants in the Republic of Ireland.

The 'Qualifications of an Orangeman' are a Core Text

It is the 'Qualifications of an Orangeman',[9] the core text of this fraternal society, which provide the answer and make the connection which binds the sentiments of Orange brethren in the past to those who continue to celebrate the 'glorious victory of the Boyne' at the beginning of the twenty-first century.

The 'Qualifications' begin by declaring that "an Orangeman should have a sincere love and veneration for his Heavenly Father; a humble and steadfast faith in Jesus Christ", and conclude with an exhortation that an Orangeman should be motivated by "the honour of his sovereign, and the good of his country".

The 'Qualifications' also contain an unambiguous rejection of the claims of the Roman Catholic Church, which puts the Orange Order at odds with the contemporary ecumenical movement.[10]

As it is the understanding of the nature and characteristics of Roman Catholicism, and especially Roman Catholicism as it is exhibited in Ireland, which unites the sentiments and beliefs of the Orangemen who opposed the Union in 1800 with those of their brethren at Drumcree in the late 1990s, it is necessary to look at the strictures on Roman Catholicism contained in the 'Qualifications' in greater detail. An Orangeman should:

> love, uphold and defend the Protestant religion, and sincerely desire and endeavour to propagate its doctrines and precepts; he should strenuously oppose the fatal errors and doctrines of the Church of Rome and scrupulously avoid countenancing (by his presence or otherwise) any act or ceremony of Popish worship; he should by all lawful means, resist the ascendancy of that Church, its encroachments and the extension of its power . . .

Other documents were circulating among Protestants and Orangemen at the time when the 'Qualifications' made their appearance. These enable the reader to analyse the motives that drove Protestants, divided by denominational rivalries, by class, and difference between town and country, to form the Loyal Orange Institution.

County Antrim brethren produced their own 'Rules and Regulations', the first proposition of which stated "that we associate for the defence of our persons, properties, and for preserving the peace and good order of our country".

An illustration of these concerns was provided in a testimony before the Select Committee set up to investigate the Orange Order in 1835. One witness, Hugh R Baker, provided the following anecdotal evidence:

> I heard it from a gentleman of great consideration in the county of Wexford that it was quite dangerous for a Protestant, even in the daytime, to ride along or travel the roads unarmed; they then formed Orange lodges and now,

I understand, they consider they can go about the county by day or night, from the mere moral effect of knowing that there is a body of men ready to support the police, with perfect safety.[11]

In this evidence it can be seen that the Orange lodges in Wexford fulfilled a paramilitary role in that the Orangemen provided "a body of men ready to support the police".

Orangemen were in no doubt that if Protestants were to survive in such a hostile environment, they needed to look to their own defence.

Furthermore, these 'Antrim Rules' plainly stated that:

we are exclusively a Protestant Association and that we will to the utmost of our power defend and support his present Majesty, King George the Third, the Laws and Constitutions of this kingdom and the succession to the throne.

These documents provided the basis for the Orange Order, and they expressed the deeply-felt concern of Protestants who believed themselves to be living in a hostile and violent environment in which their religious principles, their property and their lives were under threat.

As anyone who joins the Orange Order today is asked to give his free assent to the 'Qualifications of an Orangeman', and to adhere to them, it is not difficult to understand why the Orange Order has become a focus for controversy, and some of its marches the subject of vociferous and sometimes violent opposition from Roman Catholic and Irish republican 'residents' groups'.

The documents are essentially statements of cultural defence, propositions drawn up on behalf of a minority that foresees the dangers of expulsion or assimilation. Even a cursory glance at the press-releases and statements made by Orange spokesmen, in regard to the stand-off at Drumcree, demonstrate a remarkable continuity between the attitudes of Orangemen like William Saurin in 1800 and the contemporary feelings of Ulster's Orangemen.

Conflict Rejoined

The 1968–71 period was marked by escalating violence in Northern Ireland. The initial cause of the violence was a campaign for civil rights which mobilised nationalists in Northern Ireland and provoked counter-demonstrations from traditional unionists, led by the Rev Ian Paisley.[12] Although traditional unionists argued that the IRA was behind the Civil Rights movement, civil rights captured the attention of the media, and IRA involvement was downplayed or ignored.

By August 1969, events had escalated so much, and the danger of widespread inter-communal violence between Protestants and Roman Catholics had become so tangible, that British troops were sent into Northern Ireland in a 'peace-keeping role'.

Throughout all of these events the Orange Order, divided by internal party political divisions among the brethren themselves, played only a limited role. The Ulster Volunteer Force or UVF emerged in 1966, and within five years the Provisional IRA[13] and the Ulster Defence Association also came to prominence. This created a new situation. Many working class loyalists, particularly in Belfast, believed that the Orange Order had failed to act with sufficient vigour, and left the Orange Institution.

The Orange Order, despite being weakened by the departure of many rank and file members in Belfast, continued to play a limited role in the deteriorating situation. One writer, however, foresaw that the real challenge to Orangeism still lay in the future, and he came close to prophesying the kind of confrontations that would take place over 20 years later at Drumcree.

The author was a journalist and writer called Robert Moss, who allegedly wrote speeches for Margaret Thatcher and had highly-placed contacts, extending beyond the political establishment into the murky world of intelligence.

Andy Weir and Jonathan Bloch, correspondents for the People's News Service London, commenting on Robert Moss, wrote: "If one takes a straw poll of Robert Moss's best-known writings, it is plain to see that intelligence sources have provided him with the raw material on which he has based much of his reputation." Similarly, the *Spectator* magazine stated: "Much of Moss's information comes from government sources" and his articles read "as though they were based on security files".

Robert Moss's book was called *Urban Guerillas*[14] and was published in 1972. Obviously his information is of an even earlier date!

In Chapter 4, 'The Gun Speaks', Moss writes specifically about the growing violence and political crisis in Northern Ireland:

> When the crisis of 1971 erupted, the SDLP and other opposition deputies simply walked out of Stormont and left the government to fight a duel with the IRA. That action suggested the only genuine political forces in Ulster were the Orangemen and the terrorists.[15]

Moss had earlier predicted the fall of the Stormont Parliament. Unionists had thought their constitutional position was secure, but as a direct response to 'Bloody Sunday', the Heath government swept the devolved institution away overnight. As with the legislative Union of 1801, the British government imposed its own solution.

Orangeism and the Union

Later in the same chapter, Moss rightly identified the fact that the IRA and the Orangemen had the capacity to polarise Northern Ireland along the old fault lines of religion and ethnicity. He foresaw Drumcree a long way off.

There was another section in Moss's fourth chapter which has even more devastating implications. Moss also set out what he claimed was the IRA's master plan, the final objective of which was to be "the unresisting absorption of Northern Ireland into a United Ireland". Robert McCartney MP and the Rev Ian Paisley MP both assert that the Belfast Agreement will achieve this objective in the long term.

But how was the IRA plan to achieve this? The master plan as set out by Moss envisaged a "protracted campaign" lasting many years, producing the collapse of Stormont and direct rule from Westminster. Their long-term strategy, as Moss called it, involved the use of "world opinion".

On the Friday night before 12 July 1998, television viewers were astounded to learn that President Clinton, addressing a news conference in Hong Kong, took time off to talk about the Orange stand-off at Drumcree. In the same news broadcast, Gerard Rice, spokesman for the Lower Ormeau residents' group, opposed to Orange parades, called for the situation at Drumcree to be "internationalised". Gerard Rice was introducing delegates from South Africa and elsewhere to the media.

Most chilling, and most relevant to the Drumcree situation, was the IRA's intention to "divide" Northern Ireland "into Catholic and Protestant zones". In the years since Moss's book was published, terrorism and counter-terrorism have driven populations out. Villages that once were mixed, especially west of the Bann, have, as funeral followed funeral, became largely nationalist. These tactics had been applied with success on the Garvaghy Road.

Robert Moss's book can be written off as a curiosity. It is frightening to think that evil men could deliberately plan to set ordinary people at each other's throats. That would be devilish.

Moss, however, was not alone. Brendan Clifford also wrote about the years 1970 to 1971, stating: "The IRA was financed and supported in its initial phase by eminent people in all parties in the Republic." This was confirmed by WD Flackes in his *Political Directory*. Brendan Clifford went on: "I engaged in a number of debates with them in 1970–1971 . . . and became well acquainted with the elaborate strategy that had been worked out".[16]

Later in that same pamphlet, *Parliamentary Despotism*, written in

January 1986, Clifford gave us clues as to the nature of this "elaborate strategy":

> The respectable people (in the Irish Republic) who set up the Provisional IRA wanted it to create sufficient mayhem in the North to induce a British Government to adopt a policy designed to achieve peace by making an accommodation with the Republic which would overrule the will of the Ulster Unionists.[17]

The Significance of Drumcree

Contemporary Orange media releases and other documents are full of references to the ethnic cleansing of Protestants, to nationalist attacks on their British culture, and to the concessions offered by the British government to the SDLP and Provisional Sinn Féin in an attempt to ensure that the Provisional IRA does not resurrect its 30 year protracted campaign of terrorist violence. At Drumcree, the brethren of Portadown Orange District have attempted to assert their right to march or parade their traditional route from Drumcree parish church, following a service to mark the first day of the Battle of the Somme on 1 July 1916, back into Portadown town centre.

The continuing controversy over Drumcree, and other parading flashpoints like Belfast's Ormeau Road, at times endangered the current 'peace process', costing millions of pounds in the deployment of security forces, and widespread damage to property and the loss of innocent lives.

The Drumcree stand-off is seen as emblematic of the Northern Ireland problem: this is a deeply polarised society torn apart by mutually antagonistic aspirations. Northern Ireland's Roman Catholic nationalist and republican factions struggle to achieve Irish unification while varieties of unionists do not consent to such an outcome and seek to maintain the Union, and thereby the unity of the United Kingdom.

It is evident that the Orange Order has found the challenge presented by the agitation and opposition to the Order's culture of parading difficult to counter. Despite the violent confrontations at Drumcree and the lack of coherent leadership which the Order exhibits, the Orange Order's hold over the affections of so many supporters remains as solid as ever.

Betraying the Protestants

The answer to this conundrum is contained in the comment which Mr Stubber, a man of wealth and liberal principles, conveyed to a friend in a letter written around 1835: "If anyone had said to me five years ago, 'You will become an Orangeman', I should have looked upon that person as a very false prophet." Mr Stubber went on to explain how his opinion had changed over time. Clearly he had been educated by events: "Before Catholic Emancipation, I had looked upon the Roman Catholics as struggling for what they had a just right to demand." Then disillusionment set in. Mr Stubber complained: "I was humbugged by the professions of bishops, priests and laymen into the belief that they would rest satisfied with equal rights."[18]

The Orangemen noted that with the passing of the Relief Bill, the ulterior motives and objectives of the Roman Catholics had come more clearly into view. This, together with the violence and outrage in the countryside, helped to explain the increase of the 'Orange Societies', as Mr Stubber called them. He concluded:

> It is easy for Englishmen who are in total ignorance of the state of society in this country to condemn the Orange Institution. They have never lived among an ill-affected, hostile, lawless, and all but insurgent population . . . It is because I feel the necessity that exists for union among all Protestants in defence of life and property that I have joined the Orange Society.

There is a remarkable symmetry between the sentiments expressed by the liberal Mr Stubber and the contents of a speech by the unionist, Lord Rogan. Speaking in the House of Lords on 8 November 2000, on his amendment to the Police (Northern Ireland) Bill, Lord Rogan spoke from the heart. It was a speech which marked out the position of liberal unionists, those who support the Belfast Agreement, and see the 'peace process' as offering the only way forward for Northern Ireland.

Yet what came across was Lord Rogan's frustration and powerlessness to affect a situation in which he and his fellow 'Yes' unionists were attempting to work the Agreement, while Irish nationalists re-interpreted the Agreement in vexatious ways and used the threat of a return to violence to shackle the government of Tony Blair to the wheels of appeasement and more concessions to Irish republicanism.

Having granted so many experienced Irish republican terrorists early release from prison and having failed to secure any hand-over of weapons or explosives, the British government lives with the daily fear that any return to violence by the Provisional IRA could provoke a massive reaction by English public opinion against a government which had acted in such an ill-advised manner.

In his speech to the House of Lords, Lord Rogan stated:

> My Lords, in moving this amendment, please let us for a moment reflect on why we are discussing the RUC name at all. The future name of the police

service in Northern Ireland is being debated here today because some have mistakenly suggested that the current title 'The Royal Ulster Constabulary' is a substantial barrier to creating a police service in Northern Ireland which reflects the society that it polices . . .
I wish to address an important point of misinformation. Dropping the three words 'Royal', 'Ulster', and 'Constabulary' from the name of the police in Northern Ireland will not – I stress, will not – solve the problem of Catholic under-representation in the police service. Dropping those three words will serve only to increase unionist disaffection with the manner in which the Belfast agreement has been implemented so far.
The Government are ignoring the issue of intimidation . . . republicans intimidate young Catholic men and women not to join the police.[19]

David Trimble, the First Minister of the new Assembly, speaking in the House of Commons on 21 November 2000, was forthright in his opinion that:

The chief value of the agreement, from the point of view of the Unionist community, is that it settles the constitutional issue. If we find that the constitutional issue is reopened by constant challenges to the expressions of that legitimacy, support for the agreement will rapidly unwind.[20]

Both these speeches carry with them that whiff of betrayal, that awareness of being wilfully misunderstood which links contemporary circumstances with events 200 years ago. As both Lord Rogan and David Trimble are members of the Orange Order, their opinions reveal an attitude of mind which holds that the English do not understand Ireland, and have little conception or patience with the predicament in which Protestants and unionists find themselves.

Parallels from the Past, Challenges in the Future
Over the last 200 years, the Orange Order has responded to political developments in Ireland in a way which placed the interests of Ireland's beleaguered Protestant minority above all other considerations. A good example of this is found in the statement of Beresford that the legislative union "could be of no service to us". Trends within Orangeism which were identifiable at the beginning of the nineteenth century continue to characterise the Loyal Orange Institution down to the present time.

The need to unite Protestants, and to avoid internal rancour, were paramount considerations. Such a desire for unity has an important bearing on how the Grand Master and the Grand Orange Lodge of Ireland respond to the crisis over parading at Drumcree. In order to maintain unity, the brethren of Portadown District have considerable latitude in advancing their own policies and their own agenda. "They are the people on the ground. They know the situation best," is how the argument runs.

Such a determination to pursue unity has to be balanced against policies which may be at variance with the politics and policies of the Ulster Unionist Party.

The readiness with which Orangemen are willing to defend their position as Protestants can also create a climate which is favourable to paramilitarism; and there have been clear instances of this in the recent past.

Two hundred years ago, Orangemen and Protestants were incensed at the British government's decision to impose the Union upon them. The Orangemen were aware that the British government had not hesitated to use the strength of the Orange Order to assist the forces of the crown in suppressing the 1798 Rebellion. Once that danger was past, and there was no longer a threat from Irish rebels or their revolutionary French allies, the British government adopted another view. The government now promoted the Union. The Orangemen had become an embarrassment, and the government grew increasingly weary of their protestations.

A similarity can be observed in the cruel low-intensity conflict fought out between the British army and the Provisional IRA. It would appear that loyalist paramilitary elements were manipulated by the state and used as 'counter-gangs'[21] to wage war on the IRA when it suited the political agenda of the British government. Now that the 'peace process' is in place, people caught up in loyalist paramilitary activity have found out too late that they are expendable.

There is, therefore, an underlying consistency, or unity of belief and purpose, which links the Orange opponents of the legislative Union to their brethren marching into the twenty-first century.

Today, however, Orangemen and women face challenges hardly imagined in 1799 or 1801. The ecumenical movement which seeks to unite Protestants and Roman Catholics dominates the theological landscape, pushing the reformed beliefs to which Orangemen subscribe to the margins. Orangemen are perceived as extremists in an ecumenical age.

The rise of secular humanism also calls into question any religious belief system, or declares all religious belief systems to be of equal value. Again, Orangemen find themselves marching out of step with secular trends.[22]

These two developments have altered the whole political and cultural climate within which Orangeism seeks to articulate its beliefs and principles; but the most dramatic and threatening change of all has been

The Union

the rise of Sinn Féin and the Provisional IRA to a point at which Irish republican and Roman Catholic antagonism to the Orange Order and all it stands for presents the Loyal Orange Institution with the greatest and most exacting challenge in over 200 years of its history.

In recent years, the Orange Order has shown itself to be in all essentials a nineteenth century fraternal society, trying unsuccessfully to cope with violent revolutionary change. It remains to be seen whether the Orange Order can generate the quality of leadership necessary to cope with such challenges, or whether the Institution possesses the dynamism and flexibility required if the crisis is to be survived.

Notes

1 Ruth Dudley Edwards, *The Faithful Tribe*, Harper Collins, 1999.
2 MW Heslinga, *The Irish Border as a Cultural Divide*, Van Gorcum, 1979.
3 In a lecture to the Irish School of Ecumenics at Magee Campus, University of Ulster, the author reflected on the role of the British officers.
4 ATQ Stewart, *The Narrow Ground*, Faber & Faber, 1989.
5 Submission on ethnic cleansing from Ulster Community Action Network (Londonderry) to Amnesty International, 1986. Also submission by Edith Elliott and others to the European Commission on Human Rights, 1981.
6 RM Sibbett, *Orangeism in Ireland and Throughout the Empire*, Thynne & Co, nd.
7 Gordon Lucy, *Stand-Off*, Ulster Society (Publications) Ltd, 1996.
8 Controversy over parades features prominently in Orange balladry: see *The Orange Lark*, Ulster Society, 1987.
9 *Constitution, Laws and Ordinances of the Loyal Orange Institution of Ireland*, Belfast, 1967.
10 RC Sproul, *Getting the Gospel Right*, Baker Books, 1999.
11 Sibbett, op cit, p 337.
12 Clifford Smyth, *Ian Paisley: Voice of Protestant Ulster*, Scottish Academic Press, 1987.
13 Clifford Smyth, *The Enniskillen Massacre – Ireland's Physical Force Tradition Today*, Ulster Society, 1989 .
14 Robert Moss, *Urban Guerillas*, Temple Smith, 1972.
15 Ibid, p 102.
16 Brendan Clifford, *Parliamentary Despotism: John Hume's Aspiration*, Athol Books, 1986.
17 Ibid, p 13.
18 Sibbett, op cit, p 453.
19 House of Lords *Hansard*, 8 November 2000.
20 House of Commons *Hansard*, 21 November 2000.
21 Chris Moore, *The Kincora Scandal*, Marino, 1996. See also Frank Kitson, *Low Intensity Operations*, Faber & Faber, 1971; and Frank Kitson, *Gangs and Counter Gangs*, Barrie and Rockliff, 1960.

22 David Wells, *God in the Wasteland*, William B Eerdmanns, 1994.

Clifford Smyth is currently engaged in a cultural exploration of Ulster-Scots. Formerly an active member of the Orange Order, he commentates for BBC Northern Ireland on the annual Twelfth demonstration. Among his published works are *Ian Paisley: Voice of Protestant Ulster,* based on his doctoral thesis (QUB, 1983), *The Enniskillen Massacre – Ireland's Physical Force Tradition Today* and *Boycott.*

The Union

Ulster Protestants and the Union

Susan McKay

"I don't think Ulster was ever meant to be a place . . . it was just meant to be the Protestant people."

Young person in Desmond Bell's *Acts of Union*.

A travel feature in the British *Independent on Sunday* captured one of Northern Ireland's peculiar ironies. The author wrote of small town loyalist Ulster that "the patriotism which drives places such as these to paint their kerbstones red, white and blue, and to have Union Jacks fluttering from every lamppost, can be strangely unnerving".

The flags proliferate, and many now stay up all year round, rather than just during the marching season, as in the past. The political parties representing the vast majority of Protestants are, of course, unionist. They are divided over whether the Belfast Agreement means, as those who support it argue, that 'the Union is safe', or whether it means, as those opposed to it declare, that it is a prelude to 'Dublin rule'.

However, strangely, the nature of the Union with Great Britain did not emerge as a strong preoccupation of most of the people I interviewed in the course of research for my book, *Northern Protestants: An Unsettled People*. What did preoccupy was resistance to the menacing prospect of a united Ireland, the simplistic, passionate politics of 'No surrender'.

I had always sensed that it was the ground beneath our feet which mattered most, the sense that it was being taken away, the conviction that it had to be held. I chose in my book to look at northern Protestant people in six different places, focussing on issues which were in some way typical of each of them.

North Down, the so called 'Gold Coast', is a place where many people live comfortable, affluent lives, relatively untroubled by political strife. Overwhelmingly populated by Protestants, it is a heartland of 'middle unionism'.

North Belfast was once a heavily industrialised area, but has suffered acute economic decline. The Protestant population has fallen dramatically. Loyalist paramilitaries, those who claim they fight 'For God and Ulster' play a significant role in the community.

It would be impossible to try to understand Protestant thinking on the

Union without looking at Portadown, the 'Orange citadel', where the events known as Drumcree are played out each year now. The Co Armagh town is the focal point for those who see the Belfast Agreement as the final sell out, and Drumcree as a last stand for loyalist Ulster. "If we're bate at Portadown, we're bate," I was told.

Protestants from five of the north's six counties live along the border with the Irish Republic. Their experience of the Union is unique. This is a frontier, and it has a frontier's bloody history, with claims of IRA 'ethnic cleansing'.

Ballymoney is a small market town with a Protestant majority in the 'Bible belt' of Co Antrim. During the Troubles, it was quiet, but the parades issue brought violence. In 1997 loyalists kicked a policeman to death in the street. In 1998, they petrol bombed the home of a Catholic, burning to death three children.

Northern Protestants are inclined to be wary of art, of things not obviously useful. There is, however, an eloquent artistic and intellectual strand within the tradition, and those occupying the places of the mind have challenging things to say.

Derry, on the north-western edge of the north, and to the south of part of the Republic's most northerly county, Donegal, is famous for its siege in 1689. In the twentieth century it became infamous for the way unionist control of the city was manipulated, and as the place where the Troubles erupted in 1969. Protestants are in a minority. The place which gave loyalism its cry of 'no surrender' is becoming a place where political compromises may, tentatively, be reached.

This chapter is based on edited extracts from *Northern Protestants: An Unsettled People*.

North Down

Lesley, a hospital consultant, lives in Holywood, Co Down. Big house, golf, skiing, the Opera House: "a good life". She'd left the north to go to college in England: "I wanted to get away from parochialism." However, she had come back, married, and stayed. She wanted to "make the place better", joined the Alliance party. "The Unionists were still too entrenched." But Alliance had failed. They were too middle class, and, crucially, "They haven't made enough play of being for the Union with Great Britain."

North Down's MP, Bob McCartney, is a wealthy barrister who favoured integration with the UK. His argument against the Agreement was simple: "Why would 90% of nationalists be voting for the Agreement if it strengthens the Union?" he demanded. "The purpose of cross-border bodies is to bring about a united Ireland."

McCartney said this at a meeting in Bangor on the eve of the referendum on the Agreement. He was joined on the platform by Peter Robinson, deputy leader of the DUP, and Captain Austin Ardill. Ardill, now elderly, was a former UUP MP, and former deputy leader of the shadowy Vanguard movement. He called for Unionists to realign: "I would be proud to hold Paisley's hand," he said. The Agreement would "lead to the ruin of this little country that we have fought for".

At a meeting in the same hall the following night, former paramilitary David Ervine of the Progressive Unionist Party (PUP) insisted, "the Union is safe". He said that when the British had stated that they had no strategic interest in the north, it had "wounded the unionist community to its heart". However, the principle of consent, "the will of the people of Northern Ireland", was now enshrined in the Agreement. There would be no united Ireland. Two years later, with the agreement in place, his colleague Billy Hutchinson said, during a dispute about flags, that Sinn Féin would have to face up to the fact that they were administering British rule.

According to Irene Cree, a former mayor of North Down, "lesser unionists" like McCartney and Ervine were "breaking up the unionist family . . . doing the enemy's work for it". She said she was born in Northern Ireland and saw herself as "Irish, Ulster Irish", with an allegiance to the UK "while they want us, but I've a feeling they don't". She would opt for independence then, unless the south of Ireland became more pluralist. "If we got our share there, it could work."

The constituency of North Down is solidly and safely unionist, and people are not great voters. In 1994, a third of the north's GDP came from Westminster's financial subventions, and four out of ten workers were directly employed by the British state. Under direct rule, with no local parliament, the important links were with the 'mainland'. North Down's comfortable classes benefited greatly. There is even a local airport with multiple daily flights to London. The Union seems strong here – conversely, declarations of loyalty are low key, and many North Down citizens boast that they "don't bother with politics".

North Belfast

Billy Mitchell murdered for the Ulster Volunteer Force (UVF), went to prison and became one of the founders of the PUP. He is now a community worker: "The idea is to transform your idea of patriotism so that it can include things like rebuilding your community after years of war." The paramilitaries are denounced by most Protestants, but Mitchell blamed the officer class: "When you incite people to form armies and then walk away, you create a monster and the monster does what it wants."

The UVF had its origins in the force formed by Sir Edward Carson in 1912, the military muscle to back the Unionist rebellion against Home Rule. A crisis was averted when World War One broke out. More than 5,500 Ulster soldiers died at the Somme, proof, in Unionist eyes, of a loyalty to the Union which Britain must continue to reward.

Mitchell was influenced by the young Ian Paisley's early doomsday rhetoric. "We didn't have a coherent ideology. Our political analysis was that Ulster was being sold out. Our philosophy was not an inch. We knew what we were against, but we didn't know what we were for." Mitchell said middle unionism had been happy to see working class loyalists doing its dirty work. "They hate us because they can no longer use us as a threat . . . we've sheathed the sabre. They can't rattle it any more."

He insisted that unionism was still a valid philosophy which could embrace democratic socialism and pluralism.

The UVF took an integrationist approach to the Union; the other large paramilitary army, the UDA, had considered separatism. Its political wing, the Ulster Democratic Party, backed the Belfast Agreement, but latterly there has been a substantial retreat to the traditional certainties offered by Paisleyism and Orangeism, and to regarding anything 'lefty' as intrinsically republican.

John Gray, the librarian at the great Linenhall Library, had grown up in the 1950s in what he called Belfast's "legation quarter", a reference to imperial Peking. "It was an expatriate structure – the sun had never set on the Empire." At his prep school the headmaster encouraged the boys to make bombs out of weedkiller and sugar. "This was adventure play for children who would go on to maintain the frontiers of those bits of the map that were painted red." His English parents tried to stop him getting a Northern Irish accent. Gray had rebelled – he campaigned for civil rights and regarded his imagined and desired identity as Irish, "but I am very specifically Northern Irish".

Pearl, a working class woman who supported Trimble's leadership of the UUP, as well as the Women's Coalition, was proud to be Irish, and, as a unionist, proud to be British. "We are going into a more federal sort of United Kingdom anyway." Gwen, a young woman from a hardline loyalist estate and a harsh background, said politics should be directed away from the twin obsessions of the Union and a united Ireland, and towards poverty and social issues. "As far as I'm concerned, I'm Irish. My husband says we're British. Nobody cares about us anyway."

Portadown

"When the British people see British subjects being battered on the streets of Portadown, when they see British blood running down the faces of people that is only looking to walk the Queen's highway, they will think, hold on, these people has the right . . . " So said John, Drumcree stalwart, an Orangeman and a former UDA man. He was speaking as Drumcree 1998 loomed, and the Orange parade had been banned from the nationalist Garvaghy Road.

The Orange Order was set up in Co Armagh in 1795 to provide just the unity among Protestants that John craved two centuries later. There was ongoing sectarian strife over land and jobs, and the gentry feared the situation could get out of control. A local squire harnessed the energies of "stout Protestants of a character somewhat lawless". On the crucial issue of loyalty, they were not to be outdone.

In 1881, Michael Davitt told a Land League meeting in Co Armagh that the landlords of Ireland were "all of one religion – their god is mammon and rack rents, and eviction their only morality, while the toilers in the fields, whether Orangemen, Catholics, Presbyterians or Methodists, are the victims". The Grand Orange Lodge denounced the League as a conspiracy against "property rights, Protestantism, civil and religious liberty and the British constitution".

The Order became a central organisational link in the unionist political machine. It was Lord Craigavon who declared in the Northern Ireland House of Commons in 1934, "I am an Orangeman first and a politician and member of this parliament afterwards." David Trimble's hardline stance at Drumcree probably won him leadership of the UUP. The Order still has a bloc within the Ulster Unionist Council, which has the ability to bring down the Belfast Agreement.

Paisley said of Drumcree in 1995: "If we don't win this battle, all is lost. It is a matter of Ulster or the Irish Republic. It is a matter of freedom or slavery." The young DUP assembly man Paul Berry told me the Order was set up not just to protect the faith, but to protect the people. "If people hadn't got into militias in the past, where would we be?" If the legal means didn't work, illegal ones were justified. Otherwise: "our wee province is finished".

In 1998 Paisley preached on the site of the battle which led to the formation of the Order. The then Secretary of State for Northern Ireland Mo Mowlam was, he declared, a republican, Tony Blair was near enough a Catholic, and Trimble was a traitor. All would go: "But the Ulster people will not be going. We will still be there to fight the battle and fly the flag." He blamed ecumenism for Ulster's downfall.

When Queen Elizabeth prayed for the success of the Belfast Agreement, Paisley said she was "a parrot" of the British government. The idea that Ulster's constitutional status is under threat from the British as much as from the Irish, is widespread. Lorraine, a Portadown businesswoman, said the paramilitaries were "keeping the line". The secretary of state and "all the rest of them would be quite happy just to wash their hands of us".

She mentioned Billy Wright, the notorious 'King Rat', whose UVF gang had terrorised Catholics in mid-Ulster, and who had latterly broken with the pro-agreement PUP to form the Loyalist Volunteer Force, which vowed to ensure victory at Drumcree. "Some people say he was a psychopath, but he was intelligent, and at least he was OUR psychopath," she said. In July 2000, cavorting with the Orangemen was Johnny 'Mad Dog' Adair of the Ulster Freedom Fighters, killer of many Catholics, a stout Protestant of a character somewhat lawless.

The rage at Drumcree was fuelled by the idea that the Crown forces were protecting the disloyal Catholics while trampling on the 'God given rights' of loyal Protestants. The parade commemorates the Battle of the Somme, and among those camping on the hill at Drumcree in 1998, was a party of ex-servicemen. Bobby Todd had served Britain in England, Germany, Kenya, Swaziland, Uganda and Aden, as well as in Northern Ireland, where he had been in the UDR. "Tony Blair has bowed to Gerry [Adams]," he said. "The British have dealt with insurrection before, except in Aden where they gave up and withdrew."

Abey Rusk had a similar record of service. "We laid down our lives. We fought for freedom and liberty and we paid our rates. Now we can't walk down the road. It's a bloody disgrace." An English ex-soldier spoke up: "These men were more loyal to the crown than the English. It wasn't 'til I came here that I realised what these citizens of the Empire had to put up with. I'd love to give Mo Mowlam an enema with a six inch gun." One of the Portadown men smiled. "You're a Paddy. You're one of us," he said, affectionately.

The Border

Unionists are proud to celebrate their intransigence, to declare that they will not 'bend the knee' and that they will give 'not an inch'. This latter formula was Sir James Craig's election slogan in 1925, while the Boundary Commission was defining the border which would divide Northern Ireland from the Free State. The border winds a tortuous 300 mile route across Ireland at a point which, as the politically unaligned crow flies, measures just 50 miles.

The Special Constabulary of the 1920s could close long stretches of it, and some unionists take the view that intense border security would have thwarted the IRA during the recent Troubles. The border ensured a Protestant majority in the north, but the presence of many Catholics on the northern side was disquieting. Sir Basil Brooke infamously claimed that on his large border estate in Fermanagh he "had not a Roman Catholic about the place".

His grandson, the third Viscount Brookeborough and seventh baronet of Cole Brooke, Alan Henry Brooke, is a hereditary peer, a lord-in-waiting to the Queen, an Orangeman, and has served as a British army officer. However, he said that when he was growing up "the border meant nothing". He had hunted and entered showjumping contests north and south. "My opinion of Ireland is that it is your home," he said.

He had spent years in England before returning to the massive Colebrooke House and joining the UDR (later subsumed into the Royal Irish Regiment). Sir Basil had been one of the founders of its precursor, the Special Constabulary.

So many border Protestants joined the security forces that one woman described it as "virtually a type of farm diversification". It was dangerous – the killing rate along the border was three times higher than the north's average. Brooke said he joined the UDR because "while I'm not really political, I support Northern Ireland". Catholics, he said, could have moved over the border if they didn't like it.

John and Doreen live on a typical border farm, overlooking the big green hangars of disused British army checkpoints. Their children had been kidnapped during a botched IRA bomb attack on British soldiers. The couple felt bitter that the kidnappers had been able to escape into the Republic: "They just turn a blind eye." However, they said the British had not tried to defeat the IRA either.

They were emphatically British and not Irish, though as a border family, they had relatives in both jurisdictions. They felt Protestants in the south did not get fair play. By contrast, Eileen, a community worker in the area, felt that Northern Ireland had not worked and was finished as a political entity. "At this stage, I think the sooner a United Ireland the better. That, and a bit of dignity for the people. I think that might be the only way to stop the futile killings," she said.

Simon Bullock, a young border farmer, said he was Northern Irish first, British second. "We are part of the United Kingdom. We're going to have a United Europe, so a United Ireland wouldn't be so . . . " He paused, considering the import of what he was going to say and changed tack, slightly. "I have little respect for some of the politicians down south. They seem to be very ignorant of the north. It is alright for them in Dublin and

London to dictate to us, but unless they know what they are talking about . . ."

According to UUP MP and the party's security spokesman, Ken Maginnis, the border "never really existed" in south Armagh. It was, he said, "a lawless area". The Frazers of Markethill were a border security force family who had retreated back from the frontier. Margaret Frazer's husband was one of five members of the family who had been murdered. She was bitter: "They should never've let this boy Blair in. They should never've let the Free State in. They should never've done away with the B men."

Her son, Willie, was a staunch Orangeman. He said that "if the security forces had been allowed to do their job, there would never have been any need for the loyalist paramilitaries". He took me on a tour of places where IRA murders had been carried out. On an iron gate at Tullyvallen a poster hung: "The Union is safe – so was the Titanic."

Ballymoney

Alison, a young teacher from Ballymoney, but now living in the north of England, was shocked by the attitudes she encountered on her visits to her home town, particularly after the murders of Constable Greg Taylor and the three Quinn children. Ballymoney was in denial about sectarianism: "I am Irish. My family doesn't like me saying that. I have friends from Northern Ireland over in England and they feel the same as me. They have dissociated themselves from Northern Irish politics. I honestly don't think it would be such a bad thing if we were joined with the Republic. The economy seems a lot better than here.

"Britain is not what its made out to be – the part of England I live in has a lot of poverty and disadvantage. This clinging to the crown is ridiculous. Northern Irish Protestants deny their culture and heritage by dissociating themselves from their country. We look silly to other people." Schoolgirls Victoria and Donna did not feel strongly about the Union either. "I'm Irish," said Victoria. "I wouldn't care if we had an all Ireland. I'm neither nationalist nor unionist." "I'm Northern Irish," said Donna.

Many of those who attended the hearing in Ballymoney's town hall of the Independent Commission on Policing for Northern Ireland, would have shared the views of Willie Thompson on the commission's chairman. The UUP MP had said of Chris Patten, "Many unionists will remember Mr Patten as he stood lowering the Union Jack on Hong Kong and what we find in Northern Ireland is that the British government are slowly but surely lowering the Union Jack here."

A man describing himself as a "ratepayer from Ballymoney" said he had spent 25 years in the armed Special Constabulary, the UDR and the RIR. "We never defeated terrorism because we were shackled," he said. "If we'd taken the same stance against Hitler, we wouldn't be standing here." He was bitter about his sacrifice. "After 25 years of service I am crippled. Now they want to dump me on the street like a dustbin. That's the thanks I get."

Ballymoney had a 'liberal tradition'. Local historian, Alec Blair, said that during the 1798 rising, "the only people who were loyal were the Catholics". In 1913, local Presbyterian minister JB Armour had claimed that Home Rule was a Presbyterian principle, that the Stormont government was a "bastard parliament".

James Simpson was a disillusioned Ulster Unionist. "There is no radical centre party in which I could express the views I hold passionately. I'm a one nation Conservative, like Enoch Powell in 1950, or Edward Heath . . . I'm in the political wilderness. I would have been attracted by the UK unionists. They recognise that the Union can be broken by stealth," he said. He thought 'Union First', the breakaway UUP faction which opposed the Belfast Agreement, "could have potential".

Simpson described how the landlords, using the Orange Order as their machine, had led the movement against Home Rule. The Order had maintained a "strong class system" and a deferential attitude towards the upper classes. Nowadays, "Unionism is totally disorganised", but the deference, which he deplored, remained. He said the UUP "have to work out how to convince Catholics to vote for the Union, given that they may soon form a majority". Like many others, he felt that the smoothly running machine was now the pan-nationalist front of the SDLP, Sinn Féin, the Catholic Church and the GAA.

Local business consultant Gil Warnock felt unionism had not recovered from the break up of the old order. He saw advantages in cross-border trade and cooperation, but said change would have to be managed judiciously: "The unionist is like a child who has been slapped around the ears for 30 years. He may have deserved it, and he is going to have to grow up, but he needs help to get his confidence back."

The anti-Home Rule movement in Ballymoney was led by the Leslie family, whose large farm lies on the edge of town. Much to the annoyance of the likes of Simpson, the son of the big house, James Leslie, had returned from a career in international banking, to become a UUP politician, and had won an assembly seat. Leslie had, as a boy, gone to public school in England where he used to get "awfully angry" when people called him Paddy or Irish. "I am Northern Irish . . . I'd say, 'Look here, I'm sorry, I'm not Irish, I'm an Ulsterman.'"

He still believed the "big machine" was the UUP. Its anti-Agreement wing was he said, unwilling to face up to the sectarianism in its past, and extend a measure of trust to "the other side". He said they could not see "the macro political picture, which includes the Single European Act, the Maastricht Treaty and the Amsterdam Treaty, and the significance of these for "the sovereign integrity both of the Republic of Ireland and the UK". There was a lot of work to be done, he said, on "unionism's intellectual raison d'etre". Unionists didn't realise the benefits of the Agreement – like the dropping of the Republic's constitutional claim on the north.

Places of the Mind

Edna Longley, author and professor of English literature at Queens University, Belfast, was brought up in Dublin. She had written about the "Irish, Irisher, Irishest" approach to identity, which only referred approvingly to "patriot Prods" (Tone, Emmet, etc), and remarked bitterly that, "It sometimes seems as if Protestants have to die for Ireland to be allowed to live here."

She spoke about the "culture war", and the irony of the fact that it was the Protestant and aristocratic William Butler Yeats who had propagated the romantic "feminine mystique" of cultural nationalism. This was allied with the idea of woman as victim to male aggression – Britishness was male. Outsiders were more likely to sympathise with the desire of most Ulster Catholics for a united Ireland than with the desire of Protestants to remain part of the United Kingdom. "Irish nationalism is sexier than unionism, partly thanks to clearer self articulation and better propaganda, partly to less tangible assets."

The historian ATQ Stewart said the Northern Irish state had been set up to "provide a shelter for Protestants", and that what the British should have done was to "strengthen the majority position and then create a federal situation". Instead, since 1969, they had "created a *Konfessionskrieg* which the 1920s settlement had taken the heat out of". Stewart said there was no sense of state. "We are not in a United Ireland and we're not in the United Kingdom either." He said the government had taken sides. "Unfortunately not the Protestant one." The idea that the two sides had to come together was mistaken: "One side or the other has to surrender."

According to the Oxford-based poet and critic, Tom Paulin, the Northern Irish statelet had been "still-born". It had only ever been meant to be a holding operation. There had been no vision. "The root of it all is Calvinism. The sense of being persecuted and a member of an elect minority, feeding its persecution complex."

Paulin was passionate about the Belfast Agreement, praising its "classical, enlightened feel", fearing for it, given the the existence in Ulster of a "deep, permanent counter-enlightenment scepticism which mocks and derides any attempt to create political consensus". When the yes vote of 71% for the Agreement was announced, he wrote: "The new model Ulster is rising from the wreckage."

According to the painter Dermot Seymour, the Protestant people had been incapable of realising that 71% was a majority in a democracy, and that it didn't matter what percentage within that was Protestant. "If you wanted to save the Union, you might think of trying to make it more attractive to non-Protestants," he said. Like Paulin, he felt there was a destructive undercurrent. "Republicanism has stunted them even more than their own self-stunting mechanisms . . . There is no such thing as history. Everything is a retaliation for something else." Seymour, reared on the loyalist Shankill Road, had left the north for Mayo.

The late political historian, Frank Wright, divided unionists into two groups, those who want and believe it is possible to get Catholic support for the Union, and those who believe that Catholic unionism would be "undesirable, impossible or too conditional to depend on". Seymour believed that unionism, without the opposition of the Catholics, would collapse: "If 'them ones' became unionist overnight, what would be left? Your culture would be destroyed because it is based on war against 'them ones'. Protestants see sharing as losing. They are doomed, but it is almost as if they want to be doomed."

Derry

In his poem 'Derry Morning', Derek Mahon poses the question: "What of the change envisaged here,/The quantum leap from fear to fire?" Derry did seem to be changing, but in the 1960s Ivan Cooper had been a young Derry Protestant who wanted it to come and come quickly. He had seen working-class Protestants who were "near enough slaves" to the big farmers, the class from which the politicians were drawn.

His efforts to make the Civil Rights movement relevant to Protestants were thwarted. "The unionist establishment had so conditioned people into thinking that this was a republican communist plot, that Ulster was under threat, and in the middle of it all was this young Protestant man and he was a Lundy.

"They were conditioned into thinking that it wasn't about social issues, or about the fact that you lived in a dump. All it was, was about Ulster and Ulster's future." If loyalty is the highest Protestant virtue, Lundy, who wanted a "timely capitulation" to end the Siege of Derry in 1689, was its antithesis. Cooper gave up on trying to reform unionism after 'Bloody Sunday' in 1972, and became a nationalist. "I had decided we couldn't get the reforms in the British system."

It was the Apprentice Boys who had shut the gates of Derry against the forces of King James II in 1689, and the Orange Order continues to play a key role within loyalism. William Coulter, one of its senior members, had traditional views. He opposed the idea being floated by Trimble that the Orange link with the UUP might be broken. "The party was practically formed out of the Orange Order. If they lose the strength of the Order, they won't get far." However, after years of wrangling with the Bogside Residents Group over its right to march along the city walls, and violent clashes on the streets, compromises had been reached. The Apprentice Boys had begun to open up their celebrations of the Siege, too. There was blue-grass music on the walls.

Ulster Unionist Jack Allen claimed there had been no gerrymandering in Derry. He said change would have come naturally. "The border would go because we were entering Europe. It would have drifted away." He supported the Agreement, and said unionists had to stop looking to the past.

Mark Patterson, who, when I was writing the book, was director of the YMCA in Derry, had returned to the north after years in England, and was full of enthusiasm for the "new unionism". Old unionism, he said, was about "keeping the Catholics out". It was fundamentally wrong. "I am a unionist. But it was a journey of rage . . . I am an Ulsterman and a European. I have a regional identity and a Covenantal nationality. When it comes to war, like the 36th (Ulster) Division, we'll go with the Crown. We got the province. We give our loyalty for our statehood."

The idea that the IRA had succeeded in the twentieth century where James II had failed in the seventeenth, in uprooting the Protestants of Derry and driving them from the safety of their city, is a powerfully emotive one. But not everyone believed it. Ian Young was one of those whose business in the city had been blown up by the IRA in the 1970s, and he had relocated it across the River Foyle on the predominantly Protestant Waterside.

He was a unionist, though more orthodox unionists in the city muttered that he was SDLP in all but name. "I'm an unusual unionist," he admitted. "I believe totally in economics. You can't eat flags." Young, born across the border in Donegal, said he was "very Irish, though my heritage as a Protestant is very dear to me".

He believed that the economies of the north and south should have merged. "We could have got a good deal. We could have been part of the

'Celtic Tiger'." This view was shared by socialist and trade unionist Jim McCracken, from Derry's Low Pay Unit, though he criticised the 'Tiger' economy on social justice grounds. "Barricading themselves into the top corner of the country was a mistake," he said. "I'd say, if there hadn't been partition, Protestants would have been the dominant force in the country by now. We have been dragged back by the UK connection."

Young had for years held the view that "if a United Ireland or a new Ireland came about by agreement, I would have no trouble with it – it would be a great place to do business". He said there was a need to stop dividing people up into unionists and nationalists: "There is only one sort of democracy, and it is about the will of the people."

In his masterly *A History of Ulster*, Jonathan Bardon notes of the Act of Union in 1801: " . . . it was greeted neither by enthusiastic support nor by strong hostility – most people in Ulster were simply thankful they had survived". Two centuries later, northern Protestants do not celebrate the Union which is at the core of their political identity, though many are fearful that it is being broken and dismantled, and that they will be left exposed and abandoned. The Union, then, for those who cannot adapt to political change, is a source not of pride, but of humiliation.

For those interested in further exploring the book from which the above edited extracts are taken, *Northern Protestants: An Unsettled People* is published by the Blackstaff Press (2000, ISBN 0-85640-666-X) and retails at £12.99.

Susan McKay, formerly a community worker in Belfast, Sligo and Co Fermanagh, is a staff journalist with the *Sunday Tribune*. She won the Print Journalist of the Year award in the National Media Awards (Republic of Ireland) in 2000 for her writing on Northern Ireland and about social affairs. In addition to *Northern Protestants: An Unsettled People,* she is also the author of the best selling *Sophia's Story* (Gill and Macmillan, 1998), a biography of a child abuse survivor.

The Union

Shaping the New Political Landscape: An Engagement Strategy for Thinking Unionism

Dave Christopher

> Ulster stands at the crossroads . . . What kind of Ulster do you want? A happy respected province . . . or a place continually torn apart by riots and demonstrations, and regarded by the rest of Britain as a political outcast?
>
> Terence O'Neill, Prime Minister of Northern Ireland, 1968

It is a daunting thing to be asked to comment on the future of anything, let alone on something so complex as the future of the Union. We have the privilege of living in a period of rapid change, a time when the pace of change itself seems to be increasing. Accurate prediction of specifics is impossible in such circumstances. In setting forth this argument therefore, my aim is neither to add more fuel to the Agreement debate nor to dwell much on the short-term specific problems facing unionism at present. Rather, I wish to concentrate on the wider picture – in the first instance by sketching a general overview of the vastly changed political landscape in which unionism now finds itself; secondly, by highlighting the kind of opportunities and threats facing unionism in this new landscape; and, finally, by talking in broad terms about the sort of strategy unionism needs if it is to deal effectively with these challenges and secure the long-term future of the Union as the cornerstone of Northern Ireland's cultural, economic and political life.

In this sense, the focus of my argument is primarily aimed at the people whom Eoghan Harris calls "Thinking Unionists". Once one actually begins to look in detail at the situation facing unionism at present, and at the kind of strategy best suited to that situation, the more one becomes convinced that the pro-Agreement unionists have got it right. This is not to say that pro-Agreement unionism hasn't made mistakes over recent years, but the consequences of a collapse of the Agreement would be disastrous for unionism and is perhaps the only thing that could imperil the future of the Union itself. But let us put further discussion of this topic aside for now, and first look back at how the new political landscape emerged.

The Emergence of a New Political Landscape

Many within unionism have been taken aback by the speed at which the political, cultural and economic landscape of these islands has been transformed in the past decade. Others have been angered by these changes and have lent their voice to those seeking conservation of the way things were. A few, emboldened by the prospect of change, have cast their eyes to broader horizons and, excited by the benefits to unionism they see there, have set out on the tortuous path of shaping the process of change, and changing the future of unionism.

The 1990s saw a transformation of the political landscape of the British Isles. Whilst Northern Ireland politicians were still getting to grips with the bones of the Belfast Agreement, devolution speedily took on practical shape in Scotland and Wales. The Irish Republic, for her part, experienced in the 1990s both an economic boom and an entrenchment of a neo-liberal consensus between her major political parties. Both of these factors have done much to change attitudes towards both the British in general and unionism in particular.

For the sake of simplicity I propose to look separately at change in Great Britain, change in Northern Ireland and change in the Irish Republic, before seeking to draw these three strands together to paint a more coherent picture of the new political landscape of these Isles.

Change in Great Britain

Many of the political changes seen in Great Britain can be traced to the general election victory of 'New' Labour and the rise to power of Tony Blair. This change of government resulted in an immediate raft of constitutional initiatives, radically transforming the shape of the Union. Constitutional affairs afforded the Blair government the kind of opportunity for radicalism that other issues, such as health and education, could not.

Although it is still early days, the system of devolution appears to be bedding down rather well. The very fact that there have been significant upheavals in the early life of both the Scottish and Welsh administrations signifies the robustness of the devolution system. The accession of the populist Labour dissidents Rhodri Morgan and Ken Livingstone to lead Wales and London have lent an air of democratic legitimacy to the new institutions, with every sign that devolution has, in the short term at least, taken some of the steam out of those advocating outright separation.

This opens up some really intriguing opportunities for unionism. The idea of devolution as a balancing of centre and periphery, the manner in which the Union has proved adaptable to shifting patterns of identity, the obsolete nature of anti-English separatism – all these are solid grounds for a new unionist project across the 'Celtic fringe'. Such a project could work for close cooperation between the Celtic assemblies, but *for* the Union and without the dated nationalistic antagonism towards the English implied in outright separatism.

Many unionists regret the passing of the old Union, and the certainty a unitary state provided. However, there is little doubt that most of the changes outlined above enjoyed the support of a majority of our 60 million British fellow-citizens in Great Britain. There is, at any rate, little point in trying to turn back the clock. The challenge for unionism is to adapt to past change and thus position itself to shape future change.

Change in Northern Ireland

Progress in the Northern Ireland peace process can often seem to occur agonisingly slowly, particularly to those watching from the sidelines in Great Britain or the Republic of Ireland. Gazing back over the past ten years however, there can be little doubting the significance and extent of the changes we have seen. Central to this change was the Belfast Agreement, and all that has flowed from it. Not only did the Agreement change the very way in which people conduct politics right across Northern Ireland, it also rendered in sharp focus divisions that had been under the surface of unionism for decades.

For all that the Agreement has reshaped the political landscape of Northern Ireland as a whole, the most immediate effect of its implementation was a discernible falling away of Trimble's support base within the UUP. It is always easy to criticise with the benefit of hindsight, but one key defect of the Belfast Agreement was the manner in which most of the gains for nationalism contained therein (prisoner releases, policing reform, cross-border bodies) were concrete, highly visible and to be implemented in the short-term. The gains for unionism, on the other hand, whilst no less significant, revolve largely around the long-term resolution of complicated issues of constitutional politics and are thus far more difficult to explain to the man on the street. 'Bread tomorrow' was always going to be thin gruel indeed on which to succour the critical middle ground of the Ulster Unionist Council.

A more sensitive implementation of the Agreement may have mitigated this effect somewhat. However, rather than giving Trimble the space to highlight the benefits of the Agreement to unionism, the governments pursued a much more erratic course, consistently creating the impression in 'Middle Ulster' that they were biased in favour of nationalism. Many unionists who initially voted for the Agreement have grown disillusioned with it.

Not only has this allowed the Paisley–McCartney–Robinson wing of unionism to cobble together a more coherent anti-Agreement strategy, but also, more worryingly, it has enabled the sceptics within David Trimble's party to grow in number, leading to the series of cliffhanger votes within the Ulster Unionist Council.

Voices which, three years ago, were stridently calling for 'unionist unity' have either grown silent or been forced to come down on one side or the other of an increasingly polarised Agreement divide. It now requires not just a leap of the imagination, but almost a transcendence of political realities to envisage David Trimble and Ian Paisley engaging in even the kind of issue-based tactical alliance at which nationalists excel. Divisions are now so deep that, whilst 'unionist unity' makes a good soundbyte, those politicians genuinely seeking unity across the gamut of the unionist political spectrum are engaged in a pointless quest. Those unionists committed to shaping, rather than destroying, the new dispensation are clearly convinced of the justness of their cause and are to be commended for, among other things, getting unionism thinking again.

Change in the Irish Republic

One of the most significant features of the new political landscape has been the increasing secularisation of the Irish Republic, associated, to some extent at least, with unprecedented levels of economic growth. The passing of the referendum on divorce, the legalisation of homosexuality and the election of Mary Robinson as President all signified fundamental shifts in Irish attitudes.

Particularly noticeable has been a rise in positive sentiment towards the British. This has been helped along by a number of factors – the election of the Labour government; the close cooperation of the Dublin and London governments as 'co-sponsors' of the peace process; the reign of Mo Mowlam as Secretary of State for Northern Ireland; and the growth in circulation of the British print media. In particular, the advent of devolution for Scotland and Wales reinforced a far more positive image of the UK in the minds of southerners than had previously been the case.

Southern attitudes towards unionism in particular have, however, taken somewhat longer to begin melting. There is a tendency in the Republic of Ireland to see the peace process as a framework within which a string of concessions to nationalism could be won from the recalcitrant grasp of a declining unionism. That northern nationalists will eventually outnumber northern unionists remains a truism in the Republic of Ireland, and this contributes to a widespread perception of a unionism in decline, with no future except eventual assimilation as a 'valued tradition' within a united Ireland.

Times have changed, however, and there is undeniably a new willingness in the Republic of Ireland to listen to the point of view of unionism. President McAleese, herself a northern nationalist, expressed this openness in a recent speech on the topic of cross-border cooperation at Queen's University:

> We are at a pivotal point in our history, when it is truly possible to move forward, without suspicion, without threat, towards a new partnership on this island, a partnership which respects borders but which is also confident enough to widen the focus, to alter the perspective, to see the bigger picture.

Senior Unionist Party members have become household names across the Republic. Unionists comfortable with 'Irishness', such as Ken Maginnis and Chris McGimpsey, have been the most effective at undermining the old caricatures of unionism. Steven King's contributions to the *Irish Times*, on the other hand, are worthy of note for giving southerners an unprecedented insight into the new thinking of those close to Trimble. Again, this has helped produce a more sophisticated understanding of the challenges facing the unionist leadership.

One indication of the extent of these changes was the comment of the then leader of the Irish opposition, John Bruton, who envisaged, in a recent debate at Trinity College, the development in the British Isles of what he called "a multi-polar variable geometry federalism". Whilst cumbersome, this phrase accurately delineates the new political environment, and is particularly notable for what one might playfully term the neo-Redmondite notion that the Irish Republic could somehow be encompassed by such a federalism.

The age-old cultural divisions between Britishness and Irishness, which once fanned the flames of sectarian conflict, thus now seem to be breaking down. Investment by leading British shopping chains, for example, has ensured that Dublin now increasingly resembles a major provincial capital of the UK. While it would be ridiculous to claim that many in the south seriously entertain the possibility of reunification with the UK, it is important all the same to acknowledge that cultural differences between 'Catholic Ireland' and the rest of the British Isles, which at the beginning of the century were used as a justification for nationalism, are finally beginning to break down. Perhaps, in the future, Britishness and Irishness will come to be seen as complementary, rather than mutually exclusive identities. The cultural differences that remain are, in this sense, perhaps most appropriately viewed within the context of a diversely multi-ethnic British Isles.

Another concomitant of change has been the desire to look afresh at key tenets of republican ideology. The republican 'story of history' is no longer going unchallenged. Some commentators, most notably Kevin Myers and Eoghan Harris, have courageously taken it upon themselves to act in the forum of southern debate as a sort of 'devil's advocate' on behalf of unionism. Such commentators have stopped short of actually crossing the dividing line itself – of becoming unionist, rather than merely explaining or defending unionist beliefs. There have been notable exceptions to this – the defection of intellectual heavyweight Dr Conor Cruise O'Brien to the unionist camp, when he accepted an invitation to become president of the United Kingdom Unionist Party, is a case in point.

The late 1990s also saw a revival in both cultural and political forms of unionism south of the border. Groups such as the 109 Group, the Irish Unionist Alliance, the Reform Movement and Young Unionists at Trinity College, UCD and the DIT took the opportunity provided by the Belfast Agreement to lend voice to a range of new and broadly unionist perspectives. Southern Orangeism has also experienced a revival in Dublin and the border counties of Ulster, most notably resulting in the 1999 invitation from President McAleese to an Eleventh Night bonfire at Áras an Uachtarainn.

The British embassy in Dublin receives 60,000 passport renewal applications each year from residents of the Irish Republic. Given that passports need to be renewed every ten years, this points to a staggering 600,000 residents who are British citizens. Reform, a non-unionist minority rights movement in the Republic, have been vigorously campaigning for all southern residents to have an automatic right to British as well as Irish citizenship, corresponding to the right enshrined in the Belfast Agreement for Northern Ireland nationalists to hold Irish citizenship. Apart from the benefits accruing once the campaign succeeds, it also provides an excellent pointer to the kind of 'imaginative politics' at which unionism can excel.

The Emergence of the New Political Landscape

In conclusion, we can see that Northern Ireland, Great Britain and the Republic of Ireland have each, in their own way, undergone great change in the past decade or so. When viewed as a coherent whole, however, these changes hold manifestly profound significance for the future direction and unity of the peoples of these Isles. Processes of change have transformed the previously sterile environment in which unionism operated into a new political landscape, with a whole raft of intriguing challenges and fascinating opportunities for "Thinking Unionism".

It is to a closer examination of these challenges and opportunities that I now turn.

Unionism in the New Political Landscape
– Strengths, Weaknesses, Opportunities, Threats

Strengths
(a) Demographic Change and the Principal of Consent

Any critique of strategy post-Agreement needs to be prefaced with a repudiation of the truism that the perceived differential between Catholic and Protestant birth rates will lead inevitably to a united Ireland. This idea, rooted in age-old sectarian myth and propounded most famously by Tim Pat Coogan, is plainly false. For many years the differential between the birth rates has been decreasing, to the extent that the rate is now broadly even across the communities.

Nor does the 'Count the Catholics' approach take any account of the wide disparity between pro-Union sentiment in the Catholic community, and pro-united Ireland sentiment in the Protestant community. Consistently 20–35% of Catholics inform pollsters that they would vote for the Union, rather than a united Ireland, in a referendum. The figure for united Ireland support among Protestants has, by contrast, been consistently beneath 5%. Taking even a 'worst case' scenario, where 80% of Catholics and 5% of Protestants vote for a united Ireland, there would need to be a Catholic majority of 60% for the united Ireland vote to prevail. This clearly bats the whole question of a united Ireland well into the closing decades of this century and into a Northern Ireland likely to be very different from that which we know today.

It may sound sectarian, but it is important to run through these demographic fundamentals. Unionism is permeated at every level with the notion that a united Ireland is somehow inevitable. A united Ireland is nothing of the sort. Copperfastening the consent principle was a major gain for the unionist strategists who negotiated the Belfast Agreement.

(b) Support outside Northern Ireland

One of the major factors sapping the confidence of the unionist community is the perception of isolation. The real problem for unionism in this respect is not lack of support, but rather failure to capitalise adequately on the support that is out there. This is not in any way to denigrate what has been achieved; it is rather that the admirable extent that initiatives such as Anne Smith's work in the UUP office in Washington have justified themselves, given even limited investment, points to yet greater returns for unionism from an increased investment. My experience with the Unionist Network, a worldwide support community for unionism on the Internet, suggests that support for unionism across the world is far stronger than most unionists give themselves credit for. The challenge lies in channelling such support so that it produces positive benefits for the position of unionists in Northern Ireland. North America has long been a source of financial support for Sinn Féin for example; why not for unionism as well?

Weaknesses
(a) Unionist Division

The politically active segment of the unionist community is utterly at odds with itself over its response to the Belfast Agreement. Most of the political energy generated within the unionist community gets expended attacking other unionists. While there have been significant divisions within unionism since the beginning of the Troubles, and indeed since the formation of Northern Ireland, it took the Agreement to set these divisions in their starkest light. Since the Agreement, it is clear for the first time that not only do the UUP and DUP represent *different shades* of unionist opinion, but also that these parties hold radically divergent and *conflicting* visions of the future of Northern Ireland.

Nationalists, on the other hand, have demonstrated a consistent ability to ally with each other, particularly around specific issues, and have gained enormously by drawing support from outside the immediate political arena – for instance from the US Congress.

(b) Low Self-Confidence

It has always struck me as almost tragic that so few unionists seem to have confidence in their own future. Unionism simply does not recognise its own strength – almost half of unionists in a poll two years ago said that they didn't believe the Union would exist in 2020. Compounding this problem, many liberal Protestants are also labouring under a form of, if I may borrow the term from Ruth Dudley Edwards, a "Most Oppressive People Ever" guilt syndrome, which precludes them from playing an active role in unionist politics.

I am proud to call myself a unionist. I believe in the Union as an idea – as something vibrant and dynamic, rather than merely as a stagnant 'tradition'. My unionism believes that the Union of these Isles is a union of cultures – a Union which by its very nature is not the exclusive

Shaping the New Political Landscape

property of any one tradition, but rather something which transcends and accommodates all traditions here – Protestant and Catholic, Orange and Green – and in a Union which can also accommodate our new immigrant communities in Belfast and Dublin. It is a unionism drawing on the best from the past, a unionism confident in the future.

I am a unionist, but I am not a defeatist. I resent the fact that defeatism seems to permeate right through unionism – crippling the ability to think and act imaginatively. Unionists are not a besieged people, but rather part of a wider British family of peoples and a still wider global community in the Commonwealth. Why must unionism condemn itself to the sterile politics of inevitability, when to do so is simply to betray the struggles of the past and people's hopes for the future.

The negative consequences of this lack of self-confidence are all too clear. Belief in the inevitability of defeat permeates the thinking of far too many unionists. Not enough unionists get involved in unionist politics, or even bother to vote for a unionist candidate, largely because they have lost faith in the ability of unionist politics to deliver them from a united Ireland.

Unionism will never be able to engage nationalism effectively until some measure of self-confidence has been restored to the unionist people. Raising morale is largely the job of the generals in the unionist leadership, but groups at community level must play their role too.

If the Union is to survive we must get rid of this 'backs to the wall' mentality that has so bedevilled unionist political thinking in the past. Unionists should become, in a sense, political guerrillas, operating in a political landscape that is often hostile, but unafraid to advocate their ideas to the wider world and unafraid to press on with boldly *shaping* the peace process so that it benefits and enhances the Union. Unionism has certainly got the ability to do this; what it needs most is the self-confidence to grasp the nettle and get on with the job.

(c) Image and Unionist Isolationism

Perhaps the greatest weakness of modern-day unionism is its inability to effectively project a positive image of what it stands for. This is partly due to the wider divide within unionism. However, there is also a hardy, individualist streak among northern unionists which, whilst useful when building empires and admirable as a personal characteristic, does unionism's cause little good when it manifests itself in the political arena as isolationism. 'Go it alone' unionism, as best practised by the DUP, is always recognisable by its failure to balance, or even to see any need to balance, the sectional interests of Northern Ireland unionists with the

The Union

common interests of the British people as a whole.

A unionism which, whilst pursuing its own objectives, was also perceived as being mindful of the common interests of all British people and sensitive to the needs of the nationalist minority, would be a unionism capable of redressing its poor image on the mainland; a unionism listened to with respect around the world.

Opportunities
(a) Broadening Unionism's Support Base

The emergence of the new political landscape offers a wealth of opportunity to "Thinking Unionists". "Thinking Unionism" recognises that sectarianism is both wrong in principle and, in particular, is poison for unionism. Sectarianism obscures the extent to which both traditions have things in common and, crucially, it obscures the fact that most of what we have in common with each other we also have in common with Great Britain.

"Thinking Unionism" has also seen that power sharing, and embracing the concept of multilateral partnership with the minority community, is the best way to begin the long process of eradicating sectarianism.

Once the obscuring mists of sectarianism begin to lift from over Northern Ireland, a number of groups who would be open to a reasoned appeal from unionism come to mind. There are the 40% of the unionist people who don't even bother to vote, let alone get active in protecting the Union. There are the 20–35% of Catholics who tell pollsters that they are pro-Union, but who vote SDLP and Alliance. There is the support base of the Alliance party itself, which, from the evidence of recent elections, David Trimble's UUP have already begun to eat into. There are many young unionists with progressive opinions who are not joining unionism because every young unionist group north of the border is opposed to the Agreement.

Encouragingly, many within unionism do appear to have recognised the imperative of broadening unionism's support base. For instance, moves have been taken to improve the 'tea-lady' image of women in unionism, and more encouraging still has been the formation of the Re-Union Group, with the specific aim of broadening unionism's appeal.

(b) The debate about European Integration in the Irish Republic

This may seem a curious thing to bring up under the heading of opportunities for unionism, but the European question in the Irish Republic has profound consequences, both for Northern Ireland and for the whole future pattern of relationships in the British Isles. Furthermore,

Shaping the New Political Landscape

Europe is not an issue around which the usual three-way alliance of Sinn Féin, SDLP and Irish government can unite. Sinn Féin is instinctively 'Eurosceptic', as is a sizeable chunk of the support base of Fianna Fáil in rural Ireland.

Since joining the European Economic Community 30 years ago, the percentage of trade the Republic does with Europe, as opposed to with the UK, has increased markedly. Statistics demonstrating this trend of a decreasing UK share of Irish exports are regularly bandied by Irish Europhiles as evidence of, to use the greenspeak, "Ireland's decreasing reliance on Britain".

These statistics, however, do not tell the whole story, and it is this that is the nub of the Republic's European question. Raw export figures mask the fact that foreign-owned multinationals have been responsible for much of the increase in Irish trade with Europe. Multinational firms have brought unprecedented prosperity to the Republic of Ireland. However, many of these multinationals will, when the time is right, 'up and leave' Ireland's increasingly expensive labour market in search of greener and cheaper pastures in eastern Europe and beyond. The rapid expansion of the EU to include the more advanced of these eastern European economies will accelerate this process.

Irish-owned industry still exports primarily to the UK, and thus it is Irish-owned industry that would suffer most if a scenario develops whereby the Republic is inside Euroland whilst the UK has voted to stay outside. It is difficult to see how a situation where the Irish–UK exchange rate is based on the economic fundamentals of continental Europe could be allowed to continue by the Republic indefinitely. One fascinating possibility is that upon a firm UK rejection of the Euro, the Irish Republic would, in its own self-interest, leave the Euro in order to have a punt/pound exchange rate reflecting more accurately the fundamentals of the British Isles economy.

Given the consistent rise of Eurosceptic sentiment in the UK, and the rejection of the Euro by Denmark, this sequence of events is hardly inconceivable. To date, however, the thinking of the political élite in Dublin on the Euro has been characterised for the most part by wishful thinking about early UK entry to the Euro. Little attempt has been made to get to grips with the problem of what happens if the UK either votes against joining, or indeed never votes at all. Can the Irish Republic really afford to be in a different lane from Britain in a two-speed Europe?

Northern unionists would find themselves unusually in a win-win situation should the UK reject the Euro. Should the Republic remain inside the Euro zone in such circumstances, the cultural/economic threat to the Union, flowing from the neofunctionalist dynamic between Northern Ireland and the Republic of Ireland, would be seriously blunted. On the other hand, if the Republic were to leave the Euro zone this would reinforce the closeness between the peoples of these Isles – something that any unionist would welcome.

Threats to the Union
(a) Potential collapse of the Agreement

Much of the whole concept of a 'new political landscape' in Northern Ireland depends upon the Belfast Agreement. Should the Agreement collapse, there would be little scope for creative thinking within a unionism once again stuck in the rut of a laager mentality. Whilst unionists have been justly irritated by the imbalanced implementation of the Agreement, the fact remains that the post-Agreement landscape is far more conducive to being shaped in unionism's favour than the pre-Agreement landscape was.

Given that a collapse of the Agreement would almost certainly be blamed on unionists, such a collapse would isolate unionism both here at home and on the world stage. Most seriously, unionism would alienate an increasingly sympathetic population on the British mainland. Given no prospect of local control over local affairs, young Protestants would be likely to take little interest in the affairs of unionism. The 'brain drain' effect of young Protestant migration to the mainland, which was reversed by the Agreement, would restart. Economically, the inward investment we have seen since the start of the peace process would dry up once again.

(b) The Real Threat to the Union

The Belfast Agreement has overwhelming support within the minority community. Undoubtedly some nationalists in Northern Ireland genuinely see it as an 'honourable compromise' with the majority tradition, and aren't unduly concerned about its long-term constitutional implications. Other nationalists, particularly those driving the wider nationalist agenda, have a different interpretation. Sinn Féin have made little secret of the fact that they view the Agreement essentially as a 'stepping stone' towards joint authority or a united Ireland. There are many different shades of nationalism, with differing priorities and conflicting objectives. But, without implying the existence of a 'pan-nationalist front', the three-pronged alliance of Sinn Féin, SDLP and Irish government has amply proven its ability to unite around key short-term goals at critical times.

Unfortunately, at present it is Sinn Féin's views that are driving what Austen Morgan terms "the pan-nationalist consensus". Whether as a result of nationalist sentiment, or merely a hard-headed desire to keep Sinn Féin at the talks table, the Dublin government, throughout the peace process, has proved itself more than willing to accommodate Sinn Féin's position on the crunch issues.

As for the SDLP, it is impossible to predict its long-term future with any degree of accuracy. In the immediate future, however, it seems a safe bet that we will see further Sinn Féin gains at the expense of the SDLP. Many nationalists, north and south, perceive Sinn Féin as having opted for the political rather than the terrorist path, and one concomitant of this is a growth in support for Sinn Féin among the greener elements of the SDLP and Fianna Fáil support bases.

But, worrying as growth in Sinn Féin support is, the real threat to the Union from nationalism is not, as was the case in the past, political, but is rather a threat striking along the cultural and economic axis – a threat aimed at little less than the hollowing out of the Union.

Responding to the New Political Landscape: An Engagement Strategy for Unionism

> To shed our parochialism is not to deny our inheritance. To broaden our outlook means no weakening of our faith. Toleration is not a sign of weakness, but proof of strength. This will require considered words instead of clichés, reasoned arguments instead of slogans.
>
> Sir Clarence Graham, Unionist Party Chairman, 1959

Part of what lies behind the tendency of many unionists to adopt inflexible hard-line positions is the combination of the belief that the position of unionism has been in decline for many years (correct), with the conviction that the Belfast Agreement sets the seal on this decline and is unduly weighted towards nationalism (incorrect). The thinking behind the latter belief fails to appreciate the complexity of the Agreement and the multiplicity of institutions, processes and ideas flowing from it. The reality is that the Union enjoys a far stronger foundation than most unionists believe – a foundation based not solely on political aspects of Britishness, but more particularly on the vast web of cultural and economic interactions between the peoples of the British Isles. The Union exists in the invisible net of shared cultural values, common language and shared economic exchanges from Limerick to Liverpool, Dungannon to Dundee. In effect there are cultural and economic unions underpinning the political Union.

Without the cultural and economic union of these isles, the political

Union would wither away and die. This is what republican and nationalist strategists mean when they talk of 'hollowing out' the unionist community. This is also why a growth in DUP support at the expense of 'thinking unionism' would be bad for the Union as a whole. Throughout the post-Agreement debates, the DUP have concentrated excessively on symbolic issues. Whilst one cannot for a moment doubt that symbolism is a substantive issue in the context of Northern Ireland, it is but one of many substantive issues. The DUP predilection for defending symbolism over these other issues thus plays right into the hands of those who would hollow out the Union by undermining the cultural and economic base on which it rests.

This is not to say that unionists should not be concerned with the political Union. Protecting the political Union of Northern Ireland with Great Britain was the primary goal of unionism throughout the twentieth century. But now, at the dawn of the twenty-first century, universal recognition of the 'principle of consent' means that the political Union is secure until well into the foreseeable future. The real threat to the Union now is that the north–south dynamic flowing from the Agreement will gradually create a Northern Ireland 'pink on the map but green on the ground'. This threat is based around an economic and cultural axis rather than an explicitly political one. To deal effectively with this threat unionism needs first to free itself from the straitjacket of rigid past strategy. Unionism needs a new departure – a strategy of engagement.

So what should such a strategy consist of? Firstly, let us lay to rest the notion that 'engagement' equates to merely rolling over and giving way on every issue. Engagement implies, above all, *flexibility*. This was hardly a noticeable characteristic of unionist strategy in the past, but until a few years ago this didn't matter because it wasn't a characteristic of nationalist strategy either. Then we had the Hume–Adams initiative, and since then unionism has found itself increasingly on the defensive, outflanked by an Irish nationalism capable of portraying itself as flexible on issues it knew it couldn't win (ie the constitution) in order to win significant concessions on others.

Any general will tell you that a flexible strategy of offence and defence is preferable to an inflexible strategy based solely around defence alone. Part of the aim in any war is to force one's opponent into a situation where all he can do is defend. His actions are then predictable and easily responded to.

The parallel with unionism's position in recent times is all too clear. The tragedy, however, is that unionism is most emphatically not in a position where all it can do is defend. The problem is rather that its leaders, particularly those in the DUP, so often act as though it is. A less dogmatic, more flexible approach is not only possible, but is in fact of critical importance if unionism is effectively to respond to and reverse the 'hollowing out' of the Union. Sensible, constructive engagement with the Irish Republic, for instance, does not imply any weakening of the Union and, indeed, such engagement can be used to strengthen the Union. But if grassroots unionists are to be persuaded out of the straitjacket of inflexibility, the unionist leadership must elucidate its strategy clearly and explain that the aim is to expose the weakness of nationalism by engaging with nationalism. Once that point is understood, necessary departures from traditionalist positions can be advocated in the context of a broader coherent strategy aimed at securing the long-term future of the Union. Otherwise, such departures will continue to be perceived as elements of a seemingly endless list of concessions to nationalism.

Indeed, unionism already holds a significant advantage over nationalism on the cultural and economic battlefields – the logic of existing cultural and economic interactions being clearly tilted in favour of 'ever closer union' between the British Isles, and not in favour of cutting Northern Ireland away from the Union into a separate all-Ireland state – 'drawing the border in a different place'.

So long as unionism can keep politically motivated intervention in the north–south and east–west cross-border bodies to a minimum, the decisions they make are therefore more likely to flow along the more logical line of cooperation within a British Isles context, rather than along lines overly tilted towards all-Ireland imperatives. The chief adviser to the Taoiseach, Dr Martin Mansergh, acknowledged this recently when he predicted:

North–South co-operation along with the other institutions of the Agreement help to underpin peace and stability in Northern Ireland after 30 years of tragic conflict and will also contribute to employment and prosperity. Left to itself it will develop, I suspect, along the lines of a compromise between two schools of thought to be found particularly both in the business and the more middle-of-the-road sections of political opinion.
On one side are those enthused by the potential of an all-Ireland domestic market and for example the Dublin–Belfast economic corridor, without prejudice to existing constitutional arrangements. On the other side Northern Ireland, given the chance, will develop a dynamic economy of its own, as a regional economy within the UK and the EU, parallel to and to a degree in competition with the Republic's economy, with North–South co-operation playing an auxiliary rather than a determining role.[1]

In Conclusion

Unionism stands once again "at the crossroads", in a time of bewildering change. Decisions made over the coming years will shape her destiny for generations to come. We have witnessed a new political landscape come into being, with profound implications for the way in which unionism should act on the political stage. Encouragingly, at least some unionists have recognised these implications and have been working to change the way unionism does business and, indeed, the way unionism engages with the world.

In essence, the challenge for such unionists is to ensure that most of the processes flowing from the Agreement take place in the context of a pluralist, multi-polar British Isles, rather than in the more restrictive all-Ireland context. For the most part this implies letting time and the natural logic of unionism take its course, all the time maintaining a protective eye over institutions which, if left alone, should prove little threat to the Union.

This challenge clearly necessitates a strategy of engagement rather than one of isolation. No strategy of isolation could stop, let alone reverse, the integrative processes released by the Agreement. Such a strategy would merely lose unionism control over those processes. As things stand, however, a wise unionism, securely anchored in her demographic majority, would adopt the role of watchful guardian over Northern Ireland's new democratic institutions – protecting them both from those nationalists seeking to work them to a separatist agenda and from those unionists who would rather destroy local Stormont democracy than engage constructively across the sectarian divide.

Unionism is setting out on a new road. She has already begun to dismantle many of the barriers that have in the past prevented Irish nationalists from wanting to engage with the peoples of the rest of these Isles. There is a sound basis for confidence in her future. David Trimble has achieved much for someone who only came to power just over five years ago. Most of the people around him have a far clearer idea of where they are going than they are often given credit for. The idea of a pluralist, inclusive Union, capable of embracing all identities in Northern Ireland, is nothing new, but it remains unionism's best defence against tribal separatism.

Notes

1 'Mansergh doubts the GFA will lead to unity', *Sunday Tribune*, 1 October 2000.

Dave Christopher, a native of Co Galway, is a freelance web designer based in Dublin. An honours graduate, in history and politics, of Trinity College Dublin, he has been active in southern unionist politics for a number of years. He is a co-founder of the College Unionist Association at TCD and of the Unionist Network, and is a member of both the 109 Group and the Irish Unionist Alliance.

The Union

Down the Aisle or Down the Isles? Norman Davies' Prophecy of the Break-up of the United Kingdom

Esmond Birnie

Introduction

The 1801 Act of Union, along with the earlier Scottish–English Union of 1707 and the subsequent partition of Ireland in 1921, established the basis of the modern UK state. It is therefore appropriate for this book to include a critical review of a work which attempts to be an obituary for that state.

Professor Norman Davies' *The Isles: A History* (1999)[1] is both significant and long. For many readers it will provide a useful quarry of facts and observations which can be mined to provide a better understanding of these islands over the preceding millennia. Davies can be commended for bucking the trend in historiography towards specialisation. Such specialisation can lead to a narrowness of detail which becomes deadening. His is a work of synthesis which is accessible to the general and lay reader.

Davies is not shy of big ideas. This too is unfashionable and commendable. One of his big ideas, that English and British history are not one and the same thing is a valid point, though not one which is likely to come as a surprise to the readers of this publication. Another of his big ideas, that the UK is about to decompose, is probably just plain wrong.

In short, Davies reverses the old Whig triumphalism and optimism about the UK state and doubts if that state will endure. It is also the case that whereas earlier British historians tended to be pro-Protestant and, in modern parlance, Euro-sceptical, Davies has simply gone to the other extreme and provides a history coloured by pro-Catholic and pro-EU views.

Summary of *The Isles*

His book represents a brave attempt to write the history of England, Scotland, Wales and Ireland in the 6,000 or so years before 2000. It may well be the case that previous historians too often presented the formation of 'modern Britain' as the inevitable outcome of a relatively unproblematic process.[2] Davies rightly notes that the route to the present was a jagged one and contingency was often of critical importance. In this he reflects the views of an earlier and great historian, HAL Fisher:

> Men wiser and more learned than I have discerned in history a plot, a rhythm, a predetermined pattern . . . I can see only one emergency following upon another as wave, follows wave . . . the play of the contingent and the unforeseen.[3]

There is a refreshing novelty in the time periods into which Davies slices up our history and how he characterises these.[4]

English History does not equal British History

Davies amuses himself by noting how British history has often been collapsed into English history (eg in the classification of Oxford's OLIS Library service).[5] However, that which Davies implies is a great innovation in history writing is nothing more or less than that which Irish, Scottish and Welsh residents within the British state have known for several hundred years; that they had multiple identities. In other words, that it was possible to be 'British and . . . '. Davies does quote John Buchan, who was an early exponent of multiple identities, when he said, "Britain cannot afford . . . a denationalised Scotland. In Sir Walter Scott's famous words, 'If you un-Scotch us, you will make us damn mischievous Englishmen.'"[6]

Davies seems to imply, and here he closely follows another didactic historian of the 1990s, Professor Linda Colley,[7] that 'Britishness' only came into being as a result of high-powered cultivation during the high noon of nineteenth century imperialism. Such a fragile flower, so their argument goes, will hardly survive in the very different climate of the early twenty-first century. A contrary view has recently been suggested by Professor JCD Clark who illustrates how nineteenth century Britishness was a heterogeneous and relaxed affair which was not much reliant on the central institutions of the British state.[8] Clark makes a number of detailed refutations of Colley's thesis that Britishness was a comparatively late manufacture in England and Scotland, forged from common imperial interests and joint Protestant wars against continental Catholic powers. In particular: there was, he argues, a strong national sense of Englishness long before 1700; opposition to the outsider and the 'other' presupposes an already strong identification of the self; wars did not always act to cement the UK (sometimes they had a centrifugal effect); and religion did not always promote common Britishness. It could be added that Colley's book ignores Ireland completely. Interestingly, Clark chides some academics for adopting a false consciousness view of Britishness. Similarly, nationalists often dismissed unionism in terms of false consciousness (" . . . they are part of the Irish nation and one day they'll realise it").

Davies writes that the UK is neither a federal nor a unitary state. This is correct. The UK has in fact been characterised as a 'union state'. That is, it combines some centralisation of political decision making in London (though this is now subject to devolution) whilst preserving a remarkable degree of variety in other regards, such as separate systems of law, schooling and national churches. Contrary to Davies' suggestion, this approach is a source of strength and not weakness. Davies claims to identify an anti-Celtic bias in English historiography. He, for example, chides an old history by Fletcher[9] which pronounced, regarding the failure of the Romans to get to Ireland: "So Ireland never went to school and has been a spoilt child ever since." However, Davies himself is not beneath submitting to the dictates of political correctness. He, for example, refuses to use the term British Isles even though its origin lies with the ancient Greeks. Similarly, it might seem a bit discordant that Davies quotes, apparently uncritically, GM Trevelyan's probably rather anachronistic characterisation of William Wallace as a Scottish democratic patriot.

The UK's Obituary?

Drawing on his earlier historical 'blockbuster', *Europe: A History* (1997),[10] Davies points out just how transient some European states have been. If 1707 or even 1801 is taken as the start date of the UK, then by comparison with most of the contemporary political units lying between the Atlantic and the Urals the UK is now a relatively old timer. And Davies more than hints that its time may well be up.

His justification for his diagnosis of terminal illness is partly that he sees (wrongly, in my view – see above) the British identity as a fleeting spirit. Over and above this, he has two other explanations for the collapse of the UK. The first is the perceived relative decline of the UK economy. In this case his analysis now seems dated. His presentation of data on national output (GDP), trade and industrial production does not allow for the now considerable body of evidence which suggests that since 1979 the relative decline of the UK economy as compared to those of, say, Germany, France, the USA or Japan has, at the very least, been halted and may even have been reversed. One judgment is that from the 1950s to the 1970s there were "mistaken economic policies and institutional deficiencies" which had to be corrected if Britain's relative economic decline was to end. The 1979–97 governments "left long term growth prospects in Britain better than would have seemed possible eighteen years ago . . . Microeconomic radicalism paid off handsomely", though macroeconomic management was less successful.[11] It is ironic that his book was published at the time when the UK economy was overtaking both the French and Italian ones in terms of the total value of its output.[12]

Incidently, through his exaggeration of the extent of decline of the national UK economy Davies leads himself to some rather florid judgments on Northern Ireland's economic and political future: "Northern Ireland was an artificial creation from the start . . . It pays a heavy fine every day for keeping its distance from a prospering Republic . . . In the long run, its destiny can only lie in a united Ireland". Davies' grasp of economic history has sometimes been shown to be awry. He neglects the fact that the Republic of Ireland 'Celtic Tiger phenomenon' followed on from over 60 years of relatively low growth rates. Davies ignores the comparatively poor performance of the Republic of Ireland economy during 1921–86 and simply asserts, "It performed much better outside the UK than it ever did inside it."[13] Northern Ireland's market penetration into the southern Irish market is already relatively high, but Northern Ireland firms sell four times as much to Great Britain as to their southern neighbour. To sever Northern Ireland from the rest of the UK single market and currency area would be a commercial folly as much as a political one.[14] Ironically, given Davies' doom-laden pronouncement, several years before his book was published unemployment rates in Northern Ireland actually fell below the EU average.

Rather like the Scottish National Party and sections of Irish nationalism, Davies seems too ready to assume that development of the European Community/Union (EC/EU) will inevitably lead to the break-up of the UK. This is another case of disputable historical prophecy. Will the EU in fact continue down a federalist road? (Very possibly, though the December 2000 Nice inter-government conference illustrated some of the cracks in the European project.) Even if it does, will the UK remain within any vanguard of integrationist countries? (This is now becoming increasingly unlikely.) More powers may be ceded from London to Brussels, but this does not necessarily imply that Belfast, Edinburgh and Cardiff will find it advantageous to strike out on their own. It is, however, likely that the web of interconnections within the British Isles will become more complex. Instead of simple centre–periphery links between London and each of the UK 'national capitals', there may well be multilateralism between all these centres of government and also including Dublin. One of the vehicles for such multilateralism is likely to be the British–Irish Council. Davies has himself recognised this in a recent article[15] in which he comments: "It is interesting that the Council of the Isles emerged from the tangled affairs of Northern Ireland, and even more so that apparently it was the brainchild of the Ulster Unionists. This is extremely encouraging." Compliments are always welcome, but one rather gets the impression that

The Union

Davies thought the UUP incapable of any form of political enlightenment!

Davies the Anti-Whig

Davies implies that the traditional Whig historians made a cardinal error in writing history through reading the present backwards. Maybe this is a fault in historians. If so, it is a common one and perhaps it is unavoidable. Davies himself has a very strong teleology and his view of the past is coloured by the constitutional developments of the 1990s and what he sees (and would welcome?) as the unpicking of the UK.

It is probably true that before 1900 most British historians wrote with a pro-Protestant bias whereby the Reformation, the Civil Wars and the Glorious Revolution were seen as, on balance, good things.[16] This may well have been a bias, but nevertheless this need not mean their judgment was wrong.

Davies for his part strongly hints that Reformation and the consequent centuries of partial isolation from the continental mainstream were bad and disrupted "natural" historical development.[17] However, what is natural? We simply have Davies' own bias on that. Would we have had the Elizabethan and Jacobean flowering of culture, let alone the acceleration of historical development after 1603, if England and Scotland had remained within the orbit of continental Catholicism, or if England had become part (as it very nearly did) of the Spanish and Hapsburg Empires?

At least in terms of timing, the great economic and political success of England, Britain and the UK followed the rupture with Europe which Davies seems to mourn. During 1500–1900 Britain/the UK increasingly used seapower to its advantage. Could it have done this if it had been tethered to a continental power?

Davies on Ireland

By his own admission, Davies came to the history of the constituent parts of the British Isles as a non-specialist in these fields.[18] This need not invalidate his writing. At the same time it is worrying how many gross mistakes he makes when dealing with Ireland.[19] It not just a quibble to point out that, contrary to Davies's assertion, Ian Paisley's Free Presbyterian Church has never been one of the largest Protestant churches in numerical terms. Neither could there have been Free Presbyterians of Ulster origin in nineteenth century Scotland since Dr Paisley's Church is a post-1945 phenomenon. The emancipator of the Catholics was in fact Daniel O'Connell, not O'Connor (at least Professor Davies did not credit emancipation to Daniel O'Donnell!). De Valera was not the victor in the

Irish Civil War. What is truly alarming is Davies' account of the 'Bloody Sunday' incident at Croke Park, Dublin, in 1921: " . . . a British armoured car drove onto the pitch of a Gaelic football match and opened fire on the players" – there is no reliable evidence that this happened. Are we to assume that Davies has been watching the *Michael Collins* film? In the history according to Davies, the "West Lothian Question" unfortunately becomes the "Midlothian Question". Many Irish historians would also disagree with Davies' characterisation of Patrick Pearse as an apostle of religious tolerance.

Such errors of fact would be forgivable but one has more than a feel that Davies has surrendered uncritically to a fairly romantic and, by implication, 'green' interpretation of Irish and Ulster history. His characterisations of Ulster Protestantism and unionism are generally as unfair as they are hard. In contrast, the SDLP is described as "a brave, moderate, anti-terrorist and *non*-sectarian party" (emphasis added). Much more so than any of the countless other invasions and population shifts which Davies recounts in the book, the 1600s Plantation is given a moral evaluation. He glosses it as a "fatal harvest".[20] Davies' judgment is as follows: " . . . it is difficult to make an assessment of the Ulster Plantation. In Protestant eyes, it had been a grand success: in Catholic eyes, the incarnation of failure. To anyone of objective disposition, it was clearly the tragic source of endless, irresolvable conflict".

He then implies that there was some inexorable road from the Londonderry of 1607 to the Derry of 1968. He also seems to have swallowed, in undigested form, the nationalist nightmare interpretation of the working of the old Stormont Parliament (1921–72).[21] Lastly, his interpretation of the delay in devolution during 1998–99 lays the blame at the door of the UUP rather than the refusal of the IRA to begin decommissioning.[22]

Conclusion

The Greeks referred to "big book, great evil". Davies' book is large but it would be going too far to term it as evil. It will provide a useful summary of British history in the widest sense. At the same time, and notwithstanding his criticisms of earlier historians, Davies has not managed to avoid writing history backwards. Readers need to be forewarned about the consequent bias in this work. His historical judgment has been too much coloured by the contemporary pessimism as to the survival of the British state. In truth, the reality of multiple identities amongst the peoples of the UK does provide a sound basis for the continuation of that state. Moreover, there is no pressing reason in terms of the likely development of either the British economy or the European Union to make it necessary for the UK to disintegrate. The continued pragmatic evolution of the British constitution – and devolution to Belfast, Cardiff and Edinburgh provides a very good example of this – strengthens rather than weakens the UK's blend of variety and centralisation.

To be fair to Davies, he himself records what is a useful cautionary note for all historians in the form of the gloss provided by the ancient Irish chronicler on the dispute between Medb's army and Cú Chulainn: "I, who copied this history down, or rather this fantasy, do not believe in all the details. Several things in it are devilish lies. Others are the invention of poets. And others again have been thought up for the entertainment of idiots." Davies' book is marred by its many factual errors relating to Ireland and Ulster. The ultimate irony is that this implies that he has not avoided writing a rather Anglo-centric history.

Notes

1 N Davies, *The Isles: A History*, Macmillan, 1999.
2 Davies notes that in the fifth century AD a future where the two islands would be dominated by people coming from Ireland was quite conceivable. Davies is also particularly good in illustrating how James VI and I set out to achieve "one kingdom, entirely governed" in Great Britain and how he was frustrated in this objective.
3 HAL Fisher, *A History of Europe*, Fontana, 1960.
4 First there is the 'The Midnight Isles' period pre-BC 600. The succeeding periods are 'The Painted Isles' of c 600 BC–AD 43, 'The Frontier Isles' of 43–c 410, 'The Germanico-Celtic Isles' of 410–800, 'The Isles in the West' of 795–1154, 'The Isles of the Outremer' of 1154–1326, 'The English Isles' of 1326–1603, 'The Three Kingdoms' of 1603–1707, 'The British Imperial Isles' of c 1700–1918 and 'The Post Imperial Isles' of c 1900 onwards.
5 Davies produces a characteristically acerbic quotation from AJP Taylor in defence of English (British) history: "But what have the Scots ever contributed to History?"
6 J Buchan in House of Commons, 24 November 1932, *Hansard*, vol 272.
7 L Colley, *Britons Forging the Nation 1707–1837*, Pimlico, 1992.
8 JCD Clark, 'Protestantism, nationalism and national identity, 1660–1832', *Historical Journal*, vol 43, no 1, pp 249–76.
9 CRL Fletcher, *History of England*, Clarendon Press, 1911.
10 N Davies, *Europe: A History*, Pimlico, 1997.
11 See NFR Crafts, 'The Conservative Government's economic record: An end of term report', *Occasional Paper*, no 104, Institute of Economic Affairs, 1999.
12 Admittedly such headline comparisons of GDP in common currency terms are distorted by short-term fluctuations in the Pound Sterling relative to the Euro exchange rate. That said, we can now be fairly confident that average living

standards, as accurately compared in so-called purchasing power parity terms, in the UK are similar to the average for the fifteen EU members.

13 On the explanation of the Celtic Tiger phenomenon see F Barry, *Understanding Ireland's Economic Growth*, Macmillan Press, 1999.

14 For a critical evaluation of the likely gains from increased north–south trade see JE Birnie, 'Trading partners: Northern Ireland's external economic links', in D Kennedy (ed), *Living with the European Union*, Macmillan Press, 1999, pp 94–114; and JE Birnie, 'The economics of unionism and nationalism', in PJ Roche and B Barton (eds), *The Northern Ireland Question: Nationalism, Unionism and Partition*, Ashgate, pp 139–60.

15 'Isle seat on the flight from conflict', *The Times*, 18 December 1999.

16 Davies may well be right that the extent of European-connectedness of the medieval English church has hitherto been downplayed.

17 He quotes J Lingard, W Cobbett and the Catholic Truth Society.

18 He admitted this in his interview with John Tusa on BBC Radio Three, 1 October 2000.

19 D Kennedy, 'Acclaimed history gets Ireland alarmingly wrong', *Irish Times*, 2 October 2000, provides a useful summary. He notes with particular concern that there is little evidence that the "fully revised paperback" edition of 2000 has corrected the many errors contained in the original edition of 1999.

20 This is a quotation from the earlier historian JR Green, *A Short History of the English People*, Newnes, 1892–94.

21 Davies dismisses the post-1921 Northern Ireland as a protestant reservation [and a] retarded time capsule", and loosely asserts that every attempt since 1972 to re-establish devolved government has been undermined by loyalist strikes.

22 Some unionists will, however, be cheered by Davies' account of the development of the Scots language which, he notes, was the native tongue of King James VI and I.

Dr Esmond Birnie is an MLA (Ulster Unionist Party) for South Belfast. He is Chairman of the Assembly Committee for Higher and Further Education, Training and Employment. He is also a Senior Lecturer in Economics (on leave of absence) at the Queen's University of Belfast. He has published extensively on economics, education and environmental policy in Northern Ireland, the Republic of Ireland, Great Britain, Germany and eastern Europe.

Index

36th (Ulster) Division 149
109 Group 156
1641 Rebellion 114
1798 Rebellion 9, 16, 23–4, 34, 39, 45–6, 126, 135, 146

Acheson, Dean 100
Act of Union (1801) 7, 9–19, 21–2, 24–30, 36, 40, 118, 124–28, 130,135, 150, 168
Acton, Lord 62–4
Adair, Johnny ('Mad Dog') 83, 143
Adams, Gerry 143, 164
Addington, Henry 19, 36, 38
Aden 143
Adrian IV, Pope 21
Ahern, Bertie 106, 109
A History of Ulster 150
Aland Islands 98
Alexander, Viscount and Baron of Caledon see Caledon, Earl of
Alien Office 13, 15
Allen, Jack 149
Alliance party 79–80, 83, 139, 160
American War of Independence 117
Amsterdam Treaty (1997) 100, 147
Ancient Order of Hibernians (AOH) 50
Andersonstown 86, 88–9
Anglo-Irish Agreement/accord (1985) 76, 78, 106
Anglo-Irish Treaty (1921) 55
Anglo-Irish war 55–6
Antrim, Co 36, 53, 112, 128, 139
Antrim, Presbytery of 35
'Antrim Rules' 129
Apprentice Boys of Derry 124, 149

Aragon 98
Áras an Uachtarainn 156
Ardill, Capt Austin 140
Armagh, Co 49, 57, 124, 126, 139, 142, 145
Armour, Rev JB 45, 49, 146
Asquith, HH 50–2
Atlantic Ocean 170
Austria 98, 101
Austro-Hungarian Empire 63
'Auxiliaries' 55

Baker, Hugh R 128
Ballymena 40
Ballymoney 45, 49, 139, 145–46
Bandon, Earl of 22
Bandon, Viscount see Bandon, Earl of
Bangor 140
Bank of England 100
Bann, River 131
Banner of Ulster 42–3
Bardon, Jonathan 150
Barker, Ernest 62–4, 70
Barnavi, Elie 115
Barr, Glenn 74–5, 77–8, 81
Barrington, Jonah 12
Basque country 98–9, 111
'Battle of the Bogside' 91
Battle of the Boyne 114–15, 128
Battle of the Diamond 124, 127
Bavaria 98
Beattie, Jack 87
Belfast 36–7, 40–1, 43, 50–1, 53–7, 72, 78–83, 86–7, 119, 130, 132, 138, 140–41, 147, 159, 165, 171, 174
Belfast Academical Institution 37–8

Index

Belfast Agreement 60–2, 66–70, 74, 78, 81, 84, 95, 111, 106, 116, 122, 131, 133–34, 138–43, 146–49, 151–54, 156–58, 160, 162–66
Belfast City Council 77
Belfast Lough 90
Belfast News Letter 40
Belgium 53, 98
Beresford, John Claudius 125–26, 134
Berry, Paul 142
Beyond the Religious Divide 75–6
Bill of Rights (1689) 24–5
Birmingham, George A 50
Black, Rev Robert 34, 36–40
'Black and Tans' 55
Blair, Alec 146
Blair, Tony 61, 64, 99–100, 104, 106, 133, 142, 143, 145, 152
Bloch, Jonathan 130
'Bloody Sunday' (1921) 172–3
'Bloody Sunday' (1972) 130, 149
Bogdanor, Vernon 60
Bogside Residents Group 149
Bonaparte, Napoleon 36
Bonar Law, Andrew 51, 53
Bordeaux Declaration 98
Boru, Brian 112
Boundary Commission 57, 121, 143
Bradford, Rev Robert 78
Britain 9, 19, 29, 23–6, 34, 39, 43–5, 48, 50, 52, 55, 60–4, 70, 72, 75, 86, 92, 94, 98–109, 111, 114, 117–19, 124–25, 138–39, 141, 143, 145, 151–53, 156, 160–61, 164, 168–72
British army 53, 88, 92–3, 130, 135, 144
British Commonwealth see Commonwealth
British embassy (Dublin) 156
British Empire 26, 28, 65, 93
British government 17, 52, 58, 66, 70, 83, 92, 101, 105, 107–08, 118, 121, 127, 130, 132–33, 135, 143, 145
British–Irish Association 69
British–Irish Council 120, 171
British Isles 152, 155–56, 161, 163, 165–66, 170–72
Britons 64
Brittany 98
Broadway (Belfast) 88
Broadway Presbyterian Church 89
Brooke, Alan Henry 144
Brooke, Sir Basil 144
Brookeborough, Third Viscount see Brooke, Alan Henry
Brown, Archie 61
Bruce, Rev William 36
Bruces of Scotland 112
Brussels 105, 171
Bruton, John 155
'B' Specials see Ulster Special Constabulary
Buchan, John 169
Buckingham Palace Peace Conference 52
Bullock, Simon 144
Bunting, Major 90
Butt, Isaac 48

Caledon, Earl of 22
Camden, Earl 9–10
Campbell, William 35
Cardiff 70, 171, 174
Carlile, Rev James 38
Carrickfergus Borough Council 77
Carson, Edward 51–5, 93–4, 105, 141
Castile 98
Castledawson 51
Castlereagh, Lady 14
Castlereagh, Lord 9–19, 36–9, 126
Catalonia 98
Catholic emancipation 10–12, 15, 17–18,

177

24–5, 29, 39–40, 44, 117, 120, 124, 127, 133, 172
Cavan, Co 49, 56, 94
Charlemont 126
Charter of Rights 100–01
China 84, 116
Churchill, Winston 52, 55–7
Church of England 21, 25, 29
Church of Ireland 25, 29, 40–1, 43, 48, 127
Church of Scotland 41–2
City of Derry Grand Orange Lodge 54
Civil Rights movement (NI) 74, 88, 90–1, 121, 129, 148
Civil Rights movement (USA) 89
Clark, JCD 169
Clifford, Brendan 131–32
Clinton, Bill 106, 131
Clontarf 112
Coal and Steel Community 105
Coalisland 53
Cold War 114
Colebrooke House 144
College Green (Dublin) 51
Colley, Linda 43, 64, 169
Collins, Michael 57
Combat 73
Committee of Ministers (EU) 99
Committee of the Regions (EU) 98
Common Agricultural Policy 105
Common Market 99
Commons, House of (British) 9, 17, 22, 27, 48, 56, 99, 101, 134
Commons, House of (Irish) 10, 12–13, 15, 22–3, 26–7, 126
Commons, House of (Northern Ireland) 142
Commonwealth 76, 103, 159
Common Sense 76, 78

Connolly, Bernard 101
Connolly, James 53
Conservative party 43, 48–9, 51, 58, 119
Coogan, Tim Pat 157
Cooke, Edward 10–11, 16
Cooke, Rev Henry 38–42
Cooper, Ivan 148–49
Corby Way (Belfast) 86
Cork 15
Cornwallis, Lord 10–12, 17–19, 25
Coronation Street 88
Corsica 99
Cosgrave, WT 57
Coulter, William 149
Council of Europe (EU) 97–9
Council of Ireland (1920) 56–7, 121
Council of Ministers (EU) 100–01
Council of the Isles 171
Cowen, Brian 69, 109
Craig, Capt Charles 56
Craig, Capt James 51, 55–8, 142–43
Craig, William 74
Craigavon, Lord see Craig, Capt James
Cree, Irene 140
Crumlin Road Prison 87
Cú Chulainn 174
Cullen, Cardinal 44
Cumbria 112
'Curragh Incident' 52
Curtin, Nancy 44
Cyprus 99, 116
Czechoslovakia 97

Dail Eireann 55–7, 106
Dave Allen Show 91
Davies, Norman 168–74
Davies, Ron 67
Davis, Thomas 113
Davitt, Michael 123, 142

De Fellenberg Montgomery, Hugh 49
Defenders 124
Delors, Jacques 100
De Valera, Eamon 54–5, 172
Democracy in Europe 104
Democratic party (USA)
Democratic Unionist Party (DUP) 72–3, 77, 79–80, 82, 84, 140, 142, 158–59, 164–65
Dempster, Geordie 86
Denmark 161
Derry (see also Londonderry) 34, 57, 74, 76, 78–9, 90–1, 93, 139, 148–50, 173
Derry, Siege of 115, 148
'Derry Morning' 148
Devlin, Joe 50–1, 53–6
Devlin, Paddy 75, 93
Donaldson, Jeffrey 108
Donaldson, Willie 78
Donegal, Co 56, 94, 139, 149
Donegall Road (Belfast) 89
Down, Co 9–10, 36, 50, 57, 86, 138–39
Downey, Hugh 87
Downing Street Declaration (1993) 66
Downshire, Marquis of 36
Dowse, Richard 43
Drennan, William 37–9, 43
Drogheda 114
Dromore (Co Down) 86–7
Drumcree 83, 124, 127–32, 134, 139, 142–43
Dublin 9–11, 21, 28, 38, 41–2, 44, 49, 51, 53–4, 56, 66, 84, 87–8, 93–4, 108–09, 112, 118–19, 124–26, 138, 144, 147, 154–56, 159, 161, 163, 165, 171, 173
Dublin Castle
Duke Street (Londonderry) 89
Dunally, Lord see Kilboy, Baron
Dundas, Henry 18, 26

Dundee 163
Dungannon 163

East Antrim (constituency) 78
East Belfast (constituency) 74, 78–9
East Belfast UDA 74
Easter Rising 53
East Tyrone (constituency) 54
Edict of Nantes (1685) 120, 125
Edinburgh 70, 171, 174
Edward I 21
Edwards, Ruth Dudley 158
Eide, Asbjorn 116
Elizabeth I 114
Elizabeth II 143
Emmet, Robert 147
England 12, 17, 23–5, 61, 70, 75, 86, 88, 94, 102, 104, 112, 114–15, 125, 139, 143–46, 149, 168–69, 172
Ervine, David 73, 78–9, 82–3, 140
Essex County (Massachusetts) 90
Euro 99, 105, 161–62,
Europe 12, 19, 34, 53, 80, 90, 97–100, 102–06, 111–12, 144, 149, 161, 172
Europe: A History 170
European Community (EC) 97–8, 100, 104–05, 171
European Convention of Human Rights 100–01
European Court of Justice 101
European Economic Community (EEC) 76, 161
European Parliament 79, 101
European Union (EU) 97–101, 105, 108, 161, 165, 168, 171, 173–74
Evangelical Society of Ulster 39
Exeter Cathedral 24

Falls Library 90

The Union

Falls Road (Belfast) 50, 55, 88–9, 91
Faulkner, Brian 93
Feetham, Judge Richard 57
Fermanagh, Co 23, 52, 57, 144
Finaghy Road (Belfast) 86
Finland 98
Fisher, HAL 169
Fitt, Gerry 90, 93
Fivemiletown 49
Flackes, WD 131
'Flight of the Earls' 113
Forum for Peace and Reconciliation 116
Foster, John 15
Foyle, River 149
Frameworks Documents (1995) 106, 109
France 23–4, 34, 44, 62, 98, 100–01, 104–05, 114–15, 125, 170
Frazer, Margaret 145
Frazer, Willie 145
Freedom party 101
Free Presbyterian Church 172
French Revolution 23, 39, 62

Gaelic Athletic Association (GAA) 88, 146
Gaelic League 50, 53, 113
Gaiety Theatre (Dublin) 88
Galicia 98
Gardai 87–8
Garvaghy Road 127, 131, 142
General Assembly (Presbyterian) 41–2, 44
General Post Office (GPO), Dublin 88
Gerry, Elbridge 90
George III 17–18, 22–4, 28–9, 117, 126, 129
George VI 28
Germany 98, 104–05, 114, 116, 143, 170
Gibson, Ken 77, 80
Gladstone, WE 44–5, 48, 60, 67
Glen Road (Belfast) 86

Glorious Revolution 115, 172
Good Friday Agreement see Belfast Agreement
Gorbachev, Mikhail 119
Goudy, Rev AP 42
Government of Ireland Act (1920) 21, 28–9, 56, 121
Graham, Sir Clarence 163
Grand Orange Lodge of Ireland 125, 134, 142
Grattan, Henry 14–16, 23, 27, 117–19, 126
Grattan, Henry Jnr 14, 16
Gray, John 141
Great Britain see Britain
Great War (see also World War One) 52
Greyabbey 35, 42
Griffith, Arthur 50, 57, 63
Grosvenor Road (Belfast) 86

Hague, William 103
Hamill Street (Belfast) 50
Hannay, Rev James 50
Hansard 87
Hapsburg Empire 63, 172
Harris, Eoghan *151, 156*
Harrowgate 19
Heath, Edward (Ted) 92, 99, 130, 146
Henry II 21, 112–13
Henry VII 112
Henry, Denis 49
Herron, Tommy 74, 77
Hiberno-Norse settlement 111
Hillsborough 40
Hitler, Adolf 97, 104, 146
Hobart, Emily 10
Hobhouse, Henry 19
Hobson, Bulmer 50
Holland 75

180

Holywood 139
Home Government Association 48
Home Office 13
Home Rule 45, 48–58, 60–1, 65, 92, 94, 119–20, 141, 146
Home Rule Bill, First (1886) 44, 48, 119
Home Rule Bill, Third (1912) 51–2
Hong Kong 131, 145
Hope, Jemmy 43
Hopkin, Mary 90
Human Rights Commission 69
Hume, John 79, 164
Hutchinson, Billy 73, 78–9, 83–4, 140

Imperial Grand Black Chapter of the British Commonwealth 124
Independent Commission on Policing for Northern Ireland 145
Independent on Sunday 138
Industrial Revolution 119
International Hotel 90
Ireland 9–10, 12, 16–19, 21–30, 34, 36, 39–41, 43–5, 48–52, 54–8, 64–7, 70, 75, 80, 88, 91–6, 106, 108–09, 111–22, 124–28, 131, 134, 138, 140–45, 147, 150, 155, 157, 159, 161–62, 165–66, 168–72, 174
Irish Citizen Army 53
Irish Civil List Act 13
Irish Civil War 172
Irish Constitution (1937) 106
Irish Convention (1918) 54
Irish Free State 57, 91, 143, 145
Irish government 17, 25, 45, 66, 106–08, 121, 161
Irish News 87, 90
Irish Parliamentary Party 50, 119
Irish Republic see Republic of Ireland
Irish Republican Army (IRA) 55–6, 69, 72, 74, 81, 84, 87–9, 92–3, 129–32, 135, 139, 144–45, 149, 173
Irish Republican Brotherhood (IRB) 50, 52–3
Irish Sea 111
Irish Times 155
Irish Unionist Alliance 156
Irish Volunteers 52, 53, 55
Islanderry 86
Italy 43, 98
Iveagh 88

James I 114
James II 24, 114–15, 120, 149
James III 25
Jamieson, John 38
Jamieson, Richard 83
Japan 170
Joy, Henry 40–1

Kenya 143
Kerr, Ken 76, 78–9, 81
Kerry, Co 87
Kilboy, Baron 22
Kilfedder, James 89
Killeen 88
King, Steven 155
Knox, Alexander 36–7
Konfessionskrieg 147
Küng, Hans 113

Labour government 88–9, 154
Lake, General 34
Land Act (1903) 49
Land League 142
Lavery, Seamy 87
Lecky, WEH 34–5
Leeson Street (Belfast) 91

Leinster House 87
Lenaghan, Paddy 91
Leslie, James 146
Liberal party 43, 45, 48–50, 55, 63, 65, 119
Libya 114
Limerick 163
Linenhall Library 141
Lisburn 76, 78–9
Lisburn Defence Association 75
Liverpool 163
Livingstone, Ken 104, 152
Lloyd, John 67
Lloyd George, David 52, 54–6
Locke, John 115–16
Loftus, Baron 23
Loftus, Lord see Loftus, Baron
Logue, Cardinal 55
Lombardy 98
London 17, 24, 27, 29, 57, 70, 84, 104, 108, 114, 140, 145, 152, 154, 170–71
London Hibernian Society 39
London Missionary Society 39
Londonderry (see also Derry) 43, 74, 173
Londonderry, Lord 17
Long Bar (Belfast) 91
Long Kesh (see also Maze Prison) 73
Longley, Edna 147
Lords, House of (British) 17, 21–2, 28–9, 48, 50–1, 100, 133
Lords, House of (Irish) 22
Loughgall 124
Louis XIV 120
Lower Ormeau residents' group 131
Low Pay Unit (Londonderry) 150
Loyalist Association of Workers 81
Loyalist Volunteer Force (LVF) 82–3, 143
Loyal Orange Institution of Ireland (see also Orange Order) 124–25, 128, 134, 136
Lynch, Jack 94
Lynd, Robert 50
Lyttle, Tommy 77

Maastricht Treaty (1992) 98, 100, 147
MacDermott, Sean 53
MacNeill, Eoin 53
McAleese, Mary 91
McAliskey, Bernadette 81
McAughtry, Sam 87
McBride, Dr Ian 35
McBride, Sean 87
McCartney, Robert 79, 131, 139–40, 154
McClure, Thomas 43
McCormick, Neil 61
McCracken, Henry Joy 40
McCracken, Jim 150
McCracken, Mary Ann 41
McCullough, Denis 50
McDonald, Flora 117
McGimpsey, Chris 155
McKey, James 36
McKnight, James 42
McMichael, Gary 76, 78, 81
McMichael, John 75–6, 78, 81
McTier, Martha 39
Magee College 46
Maginnis, Ken 145, 155
Mahon, Derek 148
Major, John 100
Maidstone, HMS 90
Mandelson, Peter 109
Mannheim, Karl 65, 67
Mansergh, Martin 165
Markethill 145
Marshall, RL 46
Mary (joint sovereign with William III) 25
Mary I 114

Index

Massachusetts 90
Mayo, Co 148
Maze Prison (see also Long Kesh) 82
Medb 174
Michael Collins (film) 173
Middle East 115
Midleton, Lord 54
Millar, Sammy 77
Miller, DW 51
Miller, WL 61
Mitchell, Billy 82, 140–41
Molyneaux, Lord 68
Monaghan, Co 56, 94
Montgomery, Henry 39
Moore, Baron 22
Moore, Lord see Moore, Baron
Morgan, Austen 162
Morgan, Rhodri 152
Moss, Robert 130–31
Mountpottinger 36
Mount Stewart 10
Mowlam, Mo 142–43, 154
Munster 114
Myers, Kevin 156

Nairn, Tom 62
Naples 98
Nation 113
National Character and the Factors in its Formation 63
National League 49
Nelson, Rosemary 83
'New' Labour 60, 67, 103, 152
Ne Temere decree (1908) 120
Newtownabbey 79
Newtownards Road (Belfast) 86
New Ulster Political Research Group (NUPRG) 74

Nicholson, Jim 79
Nixon, Richard 84
North Belfast (constituency) 79
North Down (borough) 140
North Down (constituency) 139–40
Northern Ireland 28–9, 49, 55, 57–8, 61, 65–70, 72, 75–8, 83, 92, 94, 99–100, 105–06, 108–09, 111, 114, 116, 120–22, 125, 129–34, 138, 140, 142–45, 151–54, 156–60, 162, 164–66, 171
Northern Ireland Assembly (1973) 74, 77
Northern Ireland Assembly (1988) 68, 77, 79, 106, 134
Northern Ireland Labour Party 80
Northern Ireland Negotiated Independence Association 75
Northern Ireland Parliament (see also Stormont Parliament) 57
Northern Protestants: An Unsettled People 138–39
Northern Whig 41
Northern Whig Club 15

O'Brien, Conor Cruise 156
O'Connell, Daniel 12, 40, 43, 172
O'Doherty, HC 57
O'Donnell, Daniel 172
Ogle, George 125–26
O'Higgins, Kevin 120
Oldpark Defence Association 74
OLIS Library service 169
Omagh 57
O'Neill, Terence 90, 151
Orange Order (see also Loyal Orange Institution of Ireland) 25–6, 49, 94, 124–25, 127–30, 132, 134–36, 142, 146, 149
Ormeau Road (Belfast) 132

Ostpolitik 116
Oxford 69, 147, 169

Paisley, Eileen 74
Paisley, Rev Ian 72–3, 79, 82, 89–91, 129, 131, 140–43, 154, 172
Pale 112
Paris 105
Paris Peace Conference (Versailles) 55
Patten, Chris 108, 145
Patten Report 69, 108
Patterson, Mark 149
Parekh Report 70
Parliament (British) 10, 21–9, 52, 55, 100–01, 124, 127
Parliament (Irish) 10–12, 14–16, 19, 21, 23–9, 114–15, 117–18, 124–26
Parliament Act (1911)
Parliamentary Despotism 131
Parnell, Charles Stewart 48
Paulin, Tom 147–48
Pearse, Patrick 53, 173
Peel, Robert 37–8, 41–2
Penal Laws 117
People's Democracy 90
People's News Service London 130
Petrograd 61
Pitt, William 10, 12–13, 18–19, 24–6, 28
Philip II 114
Place Act 11
Plunket, William 14, 16
Poland 97
Police (Northern Ireland) Bill 124, 133
Political Directory 131
Ponsonby, George 11, 14
Portadown 82–3, 127, 132, 139, 142–43
Portadown Orange District 132, 134
Portaferry 10
Porter, Rev James 35, 42

Portlaoise Prison 87
Portland, Duke of 11, 18–19
Poynings' law 23
Prince's Case 22
Progressive Unionist Party (PUP) 73–4, 77–85, 140, 143
Protestant Ascendancy 25, 42–3, 117, 124
Provisional IRA (PIRA) 107, 130, 132–33, 135–36
Provisional Sinn Féin (see also Sinn Féin) 107, 132

'Qualifications of an Orangeman' 127–29
Quebec 25
Queen's University of Belfast 90, 155
Quinn children 145

Radio Eireann 88
Radio Free Belfast 91
Radio Telefis Eireann (RTE) 88–9
Radio Ulster 91
Rankeillour, Lord 58
Redmond, John 50–4, 120, 155
Reform Act, Third (1884) 48
Reformation (Protestant) 112–13, 124, 172
Reform Movement 156
Relief Bill 133
Remembrance Day 102
Republican News 92
Republican party (USA) 84
Republic of Ireland 127, 147, 153–56, 161–62, 171
Re-Union Group 160
Rice, Gerard 131
Robinson, Mary 154
Robinson, Peter 140, 154
Roden Street (Belfast) 78
Rogan, Lord 133–34

Roman Catholic clergy 15, 91, 126
— Church 25, 94, 125, 128, 146
— hierarchy 12, 35
Roman Empire 112
— Republic 102
Rome 25, 50, 89, 94
Royal Irish Constabulary (RIC) 52, 55
Royal Irish Regiment (RIR) 144, 146
Royal School Armagh 10
Royal Ulster Constabulary (RUC) 78, 86–7, 89, 91–2, 95, 108, 133–34
Runnymede Trust 103
Rusk, Abey 143

St Andrew (cross of) 29
St Mary's Hall (Belfast) 54
St Patrick (cross of) 29
Sands, Bobby 77
Sandy Row (Belfast) 78
Saunderson, Col Edward 49
Saurin, William 125–26, 129
Savoy 98
Scotland 61, 64, 67, 70, 98, 100, 111–12, 114, 152, 154, 168–69, 172
Scott, Sir Walter 169
Scottish National Party 171
Secession Synod 41
Session House (Dublin) 125
Seymour, Dermot 148
Shaftesbury Square (Belfast) 90
Shakespeare, William 114
Shankill Road (Belfast) 72–3, 91, 148
Sharing Responsibility 74, 80
Shaw, JJ 44
Short History of the Kingdom of Ireland 126
Siedentop, Larry 104–05
Sidmouth, Lord see Addington, Henry
Simpson, James 146

Sinclair, Thomas 45, 65
Single European Act (1986) 100, 147
Sinn Féin (see also Provisional Sinn Féin) 50, 54–5, 57, 69, 72, 74, 77, 79–82, 84, 89, 107, 136, 140, 146, 158, 161–63
Smallwoods, Ray 81
Smith, Anne 158
Smith, John 67
Smyth, Hughie 73, 77, 81
Smyth, Rev Martin 78
Social Democratic and Labour Party (SDLP) 74–5, 77, 79–80, 93, 130, 132, 146, 149, 160–63, 173
South Africa 115, 131
South Antrim (constituency) 78
South Armagh (constituency) 54
South Belfast (constituency) 78
Soviet Union 84, 97, 114
Spain 43, 98, 111, 113–14
Spanish Empire 172
Special Constabulary see Ulster Special Constabulary
Spectator 130
Spence, Augustus 'Gusty' 72–4, 82
Statute of Winchester 21
Statutes of Kilkenny 112
Stewart, ATQ 146
Stewart, Robert see Castlereagh, Lord
Stormont Parliament (see also Northern Ireland Parliament) 58, 72, 75, 80, 87, 91–4, 105, 121, 130, 131, 146, 166, 173
Streseman, Gustav 68
Strongbow 112
Stubber, Mr 132–33
Sturrock, Rev William 10
Sunday Press 89
Sunningdale Agreement 93
Swaziland 143

Switzerland 98
Syllabus of Errors 44
Synod of Ulster 35–41

Tate, Nicholas 102
Taylor, Constable Greg 145
Taylor, Martin 90
Thatcher, Margaret 100, 130
The Future of Multi-Ethnic Britain 103
The Great Escape 88
The Isles: A History 168
The Rotten Heart of Europe 101
The Tempest 114
The Witness 51
'Third Force' 82
Thompson, Willie 145
Tiger's Bay (Belfast) 91
Todd, Bobby 143
Toler, John 11
Tone, Wolfe 147
Tory government 42
Trade Boards Act (1909) 50
Trafalgar Square 104
Tralee 112
Treaty of Limerick 115, 122
Trevelyan, GM 170
Trimble, David 60, 68–9, 78, 82, 106, 134, 141–42, 149, 153–55, 160, 166
Trinity College, Dublin 55, 155–56
Troubles 30, 72, 80–1, 91, 106, 139, 144, 158
'Twelfth' 86
Tyrie, Andy 76
Tyrol 99
Tyrone, Co 49, 52, 54, 57

Uganda 102, 143
Ulster 23, 34–6, 39–45, 48, 50–2, 54–7, 60, 62, 64–6, 74–5, 80, 82, 90, 108–09, 112–14, 117, 120, 127, 129–30, 134, 138–43, 146–51, 153, 156, 172–74
Ulster Clubs 78
Ulster Defence Association (UDA) 72, 74–84, 130, 141–42
Ulster Defence Regiment (UDR) 143–44, 146
Ulster Democratic Party (UDP) (see also Ulster Loyalist Democratic Party) 76, 78–9, 81–5, 141
Ulster Freedom Fighters 143
Ulster Herald 57
Ulster Loyalist Democratic Party (ULDP) (see also Ulster Democratic Party) 75–6, 78
Ulster Loyalist Front 73
Ulster Plantation 173
Ulster Special Constabulary (USC) 56
Ulster Unionist Council (UUC) 49, 51, 93–4, 142, 153–54
Ulster Unionist Party (UUP) 49, 51, 55, 60, 72–3, 78–80, 84, 89–90, 106, 108, 119, 125, 132, 135, 140–42, 145–47, 149, 153, 158, 160, 171–73
Ulster Volunteer Force (UVF) 51–3, 56, 72–4, 77, 79–84, 130, 140–41, 143
Ulster Workers' Council (UWC) 73–4, 93
Ultramontanism 43
'Union First' 146
Union Jack 18, 86, 138, 145
Unionist Network 158
United Irish League (UIL) 50
United Irishmen 23–4, 34–7, 40–1, 43–6, 92, 119, 124–25
United Kingdom (UK) 18, 21–2, 27–9, 44, 48, 60, 64–7, 69–70, 76, 99, 106, 109, 120–22, 132, 139–41, 144, 147, 150, 154–55, 161, 165, 168–74
United Kingdom Unionist Party (UKUP)

146, 156
United Loyalist Front 77
United States of America (USA) 75, 89, 106–07, 158. 170
University College, Dublin (UCD) 44, 156
Upper Bann (constituency) 78
Urals 170
Urban Guerillas 130

Vanguard 74, 77, 81, 140
Venice 98
Vietnam War 90
Village area (Belfast) 78
Volunteers (of c1782) 34, 41, 117
Volunteer Political Party (VPP) 73, 77
Von Buitenen, Paul 105

Wales 61, 64, 67, 70, 98, 100, 112, 152, 154, 168
Wall, Maureen 44
Wallace, William 170
Walpole, Charles 126
Warnock, Gil 146
Wars of the Roses 112
Washington (DC) 158
Waterside (Londonderry) 149
Waugh, Evelyn 62
Weir, Andy 130
West Belfast (constituency) 56, 89
Westminster 9, 21, 49, 52, 54–6, 58, 76–8, 94, 105–06, 109, 119, 131, 140
Westminster Abbey 19
Westminster Confession of Faith 39
Westport 50
Wexford, Co 34, 50, 114, 117, 128–29
Whig government 40–1
Whig historians 172
White, John 81
Whitehall 10, 12–13, 17

Wicklow, Co 52
William III 24–5
Wilson, Harold 89
Women's Coalition 141
Woodenbridge 52
Woodvale Defence Association 74
Woodvale Road (Belfast) 91
Worker's Republic 53
World War One (see also Great War) 51, 141
World War Two 87, 97, 102, 104, 106, 116–17
Wright, Billy ('King Rat') 82–3, 143
Wright, Frank 148
Wyndham, George 49

Yeats, William Butler 147
YMCA 149
York dynasty 112
Young, Ian 149–50
Young Unionists 156